Pelican Books
Towards One Europe

Stuart de la Mahotière was born in London and
educated in France, Spain, and Italy. He spent much
of his youth working and travelling in Western
Europe, and after observing the progress of
Mussolini's Fascism and the decline of the Third
Republic in France considered emigrating to America.
In the 1930s he started a career in journalism, and he
is currently The Deputy City Editor with the Agence
France Presse in London. He has been an intelligence
officer with the Eighth Army in the Middle East,
North Africa, and Italy, a lobby correspondent in the
House of Commons, and a diplomatic correspondent
for the *Birmingham Post*. In 1964 he contested
Croydon North-East as a Liberal in the general
election. He has broadcast on international affairs
and finance, and his first two books were *The Common
Market* and *The Hard Sell*. An early member of the
Sail Training Association, he crossed the Atlantic in
the 1964 Tall Ships Race. He now lives in Hampstead
and is married, with two daughters.

D1305091

Towards
One
Europe

Stuart de la Mahotière

Penguin Books

Penguin Books Ltd, Harmondsworth,
Middlesex, England
Penguin Books Inc., 7110 Ambassador Road,
Baltimore, Maryland 21207, U.S.A.
Penguin Books Australia Ltd, Ringwood,
Victoria, Australia

Published in Pelican Books 1970
Copyright © Stuart de la Mahotière, 1970

Made and printed in Great Britain by
C. Nicholls & Company Ltd
Set in Monotype Times

Contents

HC
241
.D38

330.94 (crossed out)
D37 (crossed out)

We need not waste our time in disputes about who originated this idea of United Europe. There are many famous names associated with the revival and presentation of this idea, but we may all, I think, yield our pretensions to Henry of Navarre, King of France, who, with his great Minister Sully, between the years of 1600 and 1607, laboured to set up a permanent committee representing the fifteen – now we are sixteen – leading Christian States of Europe. This body was to act as an arbitrator on all questions concerning religious conflict, national frontiers, internal disturbance, and common action against any danger from the East, which in those days meant the Turks. This he called 'The Grand Design'. After this long passage of time we are the servants of the Grand Design.

WINSTON CHURCHILL, *the Hague Congress, May 1948*

Preface

After years of semi-stagnation, the European Communities are on the move again. The long winter of Gaullist obstruction ended dramatically at The Hague in December 1969. At the historic summit meeting of the Six, the new French President made the first clean break with Gaullist foreign policies by removing the automatic veto on the admission of new members.

For over seven years, Britain and the other three candidates – Norway, Denmark, and Eire – had been kept waiting on the doorstep. Little wonder that some of them got cold feet. The idea of European unity began to lose its attraction. In Britain, in particular, all sectors of the public had second thoughts on the wisdom of joining. The anti-Marketeers gathered new strength. The genuine doubters saw their doubts confirmed. The pro-Marketeers were under increasing pressure to justify their arguments.

Those who favoured participation on political grounds were as convinced as ever. But those who saw the economic argument as paramount were less convinced. At the time of the 1967 application to join, the Confederation of British Industry had no doubt whatsoever that the long-term economic advantages were compelling. But that was before the Kennedy Round negotiations for the lowering of world tariffs within the framework of G A T T had been brought to a successful conclusion. By the end of 1969 the need to join in order to clear the E E C tariff hurdle was less obvious. The equally powerful Institute of Directors was of much the same opinion. It was generally assumed in industrial and financial circles that if the cost of joining were too high, then even the political argument might look less attractive. This could happen if the Common Market's agricultural policy and requirements on the unrestricted movement of capital meant a burden which the British balance of payments could only carry if deflationary policies at home were pursued on a more or less permanent basis – obviously a condition which no government could tolerate.

Preface

The political aspects of membership are therefore far-reaching. In the author's view they are overriding and are dealt with at some length in the following chapters for, in the final analysis, the building of European unity must be a political act of faith, which is what the founding fathers of the Common Market saw with great clarity.

Landmarks: Chronology of Main Events

1946

16 September Winston Churchill, in Zurich, urges Franco–German reconciliation within 'a kind of United States of Europe'.

1947

5 June General Marshall proposes American aid to stimulate recovery in Europe.

29 October Creation of Benelux – economic union of Belgium, Luxembourg and the Netherlands.

1948

17 March Western European Union – signed by the Six plus Great Britain.

16 April Convention for the Organization for European Economic Co-operation (OEEC) signed.
(OEEC later becomes OECD – Organization for Economic Co-operation and Development.)

1949

4 April North Atlantic Treaty Organization (NATO) signed by the Six (except Germany), Canada, Denmark, Iceland, Norway, Portugal, the United Kingdom, and the United States (Greece and Turkey acceded in February 1952 and Germany in May 1955, making fifteen signatories in all).

5 May Statute of the Council of Europe (specifically excludes defence matters) signed by fifteen member countries (the same as for NATO but excluding US, Canada, and Portugal and including Eire, Austria, and Sweden).

Towards One Europe

1950

9 May — Schuman Declaration: Robert Schuman's historic proposal to place French and German coal and steel under a common authority.

1951

18 April — Treaty setting up the European Coal and Steel Community (ECSC) is signed in Paris.

1952

27 May — European Defence Community (EDC) treaty signed in Paris.

10 August — ECSC High Authority starts work in Luxembourg under its first president, Jean Monnet.

10 September — ECSC Common Assembly holds its first session in Strasbourg, and elects Paul-Henri Spaak as its first President.

1953

10 February — ECSC common market for coal, iron ore, and scrap is opened.

1 May — ECSC common market for steel is opened.

30 August — EDC Treaty rejected by the French Parliament.

1954

21 December — An *association* agreement between the United Kingdom and ECSC is signed.

1955

1–3 June — Messina Conference: the foreign ministers of the Community's member-states propose further steps towards full integration.

1956

26 June — Negotiations on Rome Treaties start in Brussels.

1957

25 March — *Signature of Rome Treaties.*

Landmarks: Chronology of Main Events

1958

1 January	*The Rome Treaties come into force setting up the Common Market and Euratom.*
9 February	E C S C transition period ends – full operation of common market for coal and steel.
19–21 March	First session of the European Parliament – Robert Schuman elected president.
1 June	Government of de Gaulle accepted by French Assembly.
28 September	Constitution of Fifth Republic accepted by referendum.
21 December	De Gaulle elected President.

1959

1 January	First tariff reductions and quota enlargements in the Common Market. Establishment of common market for nuclear materials.
20 November	European Free Trade Association convention (EFTA) signed between Austria, Denmark, Norway, Portugal, Sweden, Switzerland, and United Kingdom.

1960

3 May	EFTA convention in force.
10–12 May	Community decides to speed up its timetable for implementing the Common Market and first steps towards a Common External Tariff are taken (a year early).

1961

1 July	Finland becomes an Associate of EFTA.
9 July	Greece signs association agreement with EEC (entry to come into force 1 November 1962).
18 July	The six Community countries issue Bonn Declaration aiming at political union.
1 August	The Republic of Ireland applies for membership of the Common Market.

10 August	*Great Britain and Denmark request negotiations aiming at membership of the Common Market.*
8 November	Negotiations with Great Britain open in Brussels.
15 December	The three neutrals, Austria, Sweden, and Switzerland, apply for association with the Common Market.

1962

14 January	Community fixes basic features of common agricultural policy, and regulations for grains, pigmeat, eggs and poultry, fruit and vegetables, and wine are issued.
9 February	Spain applies for association with the Common Market.
2 March	*Great Britain applies for membership of the ECSC and Euratom.*
30 April	Norway requests negotiations for membership of the Common Market.
15 May	Community decides on second speeding-up of Common Market timetable.
16 July	Conclusion of 1960–62 negotiations (Dillon Round) for worldwide tariff cuts in GATT; Community substantially reduces common external tariff.
30 July	First regulations implementing the common agricultural policy come into effect.

1963

14 January	*President de Gaulle declares that Britain is not ready for Community membership.*
22 January	Franco–German Treaty of Co-operation signed in Paris.
29 January	British negotiations with Six broken off.
1 July	Signature of Yaoundé Convention, associating eighteen independent states in Africa and Madagascar with the Community for five years from 1 June 1964.

| 12 September | Turkey signs association agreement with Community (entry into force 1 December 1964). |
| 23 December | Common farm policy regulations for rice, beef, and dairy products agreed. |

1964

| 4 May | Kennedy Round negotiations open in Geneva. |
| 31 December | Equal pay applies throughout E E C. |

1965

8 April	Treaty establishing a single Council and a single Commission for the three Communities signed in Brussels.
30 June	French delegates walk out of Council meeting because of opposition to majority voting.
5 July	French boycott of all E E C institutions for next seven months.
December	Commission proposes complete removal of customs duties and completion of common agricultural market from 1 July 1967.

1966

1 January	French return to E E C. Third and last stage of E E C begins.
12 May	Common agricultural policy agreed.
12 July	Nigeria signs association agreement with E E C.

1967

16 January	Harold Wilson and George Brown begin tour of Community to sound out chances of second British application.
11 May	*Britain, Denmark, Norway, and Ireland make second application to join E E C.*
June	Commemoration of tenth anniversary of Treaty of Rome. De Gaulle's hidden veto sensed in his pronouncement that the Six must present a common front among themselves before enlarging E E C.

1 July	Single Council and single Commission under Jean Rey take over from the EEC and Euratom Commissions and the ECSC High Authority.
October	Opinion of Commission on British, Danish, Irish, and Norwegian applications considered.
19 December	*Council deadlock on enlargement owing to de Gaulle veto – applications left on table.*

1968

	Euratom enters on sandwich year owing to failure to agree new programme.
May–June	Riots in France.
1 June	Beef and dairy policy (postponed from 1 April) agreed.
1 July	EEC customs union complete. Common agricultural price levels agreed. First stage of Kennedy Round (negotiated 1963–7) comes into effect.
20 August	Czechoslovakia invaded by Russians.

1969

January	President Nixon takes office.
28 April	Resignation of de Gaulle.
1–15 May	D-mark crisis – speculators move into D-marks on hopes of revaluation.
22 June	Pompidou elected President of France.
August	French devalue: to avoid consequent bonus to farmers, French agriculture isolated from Common Market for two years.
September	German elections – Brandt becomes Chancellor.
October	Germans revalue D-mark; to avoid consequent loss to farmers, dispute breaks out on compensation by subsidy.
October	Euratom in state of collapse: no agreement on a bridging budget.
15 November	Hague summit to discuss development of EEC and enlargement – postponed to 1 December.

31 December   End of transition period – new finance regulations for common agricultural policy agreed at marathon session.

1970

1 January   Second stage of Kennedy Round should take effect.

1 Economic Revival in Europe

Victory over Germany in 1945 left Europe in ruins. Her economy was shattered and her resources were all but exhausted. The damage could only be repaired with American help. To their eternal credit, the American people did not repeat the mistake they made after the First World War when they reverted to isolationism and indifference to the affairs of Europe. After the Second World War they came to the immediate aid of the old continent. They had every encouragement to do so.

Their only rivals – the USSR – were firmly entrenched on the borders of the free world, threatening to sweep across Europe from East Germany to the Atlantic, setting up puppet Communist governments in their wake. Only American atomic power prevented the Russians from rushing the Western defences. President Roosevelt in his declining years had thought that coexistence with Stalin was possible. His successors thought otherwise. The Atlantic Alliance preserved the military fruits of victory. But the peace could be lost if the economies of Western Europe were allowed to collapse beyond repair. Political chaos would have ensued. Marshall Aid was the immediate answer. Between 1948 and 1952 the USA poured $13,812m. into Western Europe – $3,421m. to Britain, $2,753m. to France, $1,511m. to Italy, $1,389m. to Germany and the rest to the smaller countries. In fact very much more was injected into the European economy by way of capital outflows including military purchases, 'offshore' procurement, etc., which between 1945 and 1955 amounted to nearly $26,000m., quite apart from the technical 'know-how' that went with much of the aid.

Marshall Aid (named after General George C. Marshall, wartime US Chief of Staff and later Secretary of State under President Truman) was distributed very successfully through the

19

Organization for European Economic Co-operation, later to become, with the addition of the USA, Canada, and Japan, the Organization for Economic Co-operation and Development.

In 1961 the OEEC considered its task completed and handed over to the OECD. Its achievements had been remarkable. In thirteen years most of the eighteen member-countries – Austria, Belgium, Denmark, West Germany, France, Greece, Eire, Iceland, Italy, Luxembourg, Netherlands, Norway, Portugal, Sweden, Switzerland, Spain, Turkey, and the United Kingdom – had achieved a degree of prosperity hitherto unknown. The major ones had more than doubled their industrial production since the war. The OEEC had presided over a vast liberalization of trade and had operated a parallel European Payments Union as a clearing house for settling debts in strong currencies. By 1958 currencies whose convertibility had been tightly controlled like those of the pound and the franc were made freely convertible and this was the measure of its success.

The OECD's task was to carry on where OEEC had left off, i.e. to achieve 'the highest possible sustainable economic growth and employment and a rising standard of living in member-countries while maintaining financial stability', thus contributing to an ordered development of the world economy. A further aim was to contribute to sound economic expansion in countries which were not members and to contribute to the expansion of world trade on a multilateral, non-discriminatory basis in accordance with international obligations. Still today it provides a regular meeting ground for ministers and high-ranking officials of the Western World, who appoint working groups to study particular problems. Thus, Dr Otmar Emminger, Director of the German Bundesbank, in charge of international monetary affairs, was asked in July 1969 to head a study group on monetary reform.

But it fell to the OEEC to be not only the main architect of Europe's astonishing economic recovery in a mere decade, but also to show that collective aid (as opposed to bilateral aid) was a first step towards economic integration. The path to integration had already been mapped out by the French economist M. Jean Monnet, the founding father of the European Economic Community. He received great encouragement from the Americans for his idea of a United States of Europe, for which he is still actively working despite his eighty-one-odd years.

One of the turning-points – and divides – in history took place in the European Coal and Steel Community, the first of the supranational organizations to be set up in post-war Europe. From Britain's refusal to join stems the economic division of Europe today, which most nations and governments deplore and which for twenty years was the main obstacle to further economic and political progress in Europe.

Had Britain taken part in this first historic effort at integration in the limited field of iron, coal, and steel, she might have found it easier to take the other, logical step forward and become a founding member of the European Economic Community as did the Six who had set up the ECSC.

But this was not to be. The reasons for not joining provide the key to Britain's hostility towards economic integration, hostility which lasted up to the time of the first application to join in 1961.

The first post-war Labour Government was in office at the time and it was no part of socialist doctrine that a Labour Government, whose party had not held power since the days of Ramsay Macdonald, should suddenly surrender to a supranational institution the mandate it had just acquired from the electorate to nationalize Britain's own iron, coal, and steel industries. Nationalization was one thing: internationalization was another. The Labour movement had long been internationally minded, particularly when it was in opposition between the wars. But in 1950 it was in no mood to engage in an international exercise of the magnitude of the Iron, Coal, and Steel Pool, as it was originally called. This was an imaginative, indeed revolutionary and highly controversial project for which the Labour movement as a whole was not politically prepared. Only a handful of Socialists were in favour of co-operation on this scale and they were mostly advocates of world government.

And it must be said that at the time very few Conservatives were in favour of M. Schuman's proposals. Churchill himself, who had led the European movement and made resounding speeches on unity at Zurich and The Hague, was categorically opposed to any surrender of sovereignty by Government or Parliament. Indeed, in this particular case, the Conservatives' ambition was to denationalize iron and steel as soon as they got back to power – which they did. They therefore supported the Labour Government on this issue despite some tactical skirmishing in Parliament when they were in opposition. Furthermore, the French approach to Britain at the time was somewhat clumsily framed. M. Robert Schuman, the French Foreign Minister, was of an Aristotelian frame of mind, and presented the case for supranational institutions in a rigid, dogmatic fashion, leaving little room for negotiation. It was calculated to frighten off even the most internationally minded of Englishmen, let alone hardened pragmatists like Clement Attlee and Ernest Bevin.

The position remained the same when Eden succeeded Churchill. There was still time to steer a course towards Europe as the Six were only beginning to work out the next steps – at Messina in June 1955 and Venice in May 1956. But Eden's aims for Europe were no more ambitious than Labour's. He declined an invitation to take part in the Messina conference and later withdrew the British representative attending committee meetings, at which proposals for an Economic Community were drawn up – under the chairmanship of the Belgian Foreign Minister, M. Paul-Henri Spaak. Ten years after the war relations had reached a low ebb between Britain and the Continent, the more so as Eden had persuaded Churchill not to take part in the proposed European Defence Community concluded in 1952, although two years earlier Sir Winston himself had succeeded in persuading the Consultative Assembly of the Council of Europe to set up a 'European Army under the authority of a European Minister of Defence, subject to European democratic control'. It is arguable that if Churchill had lent his great prestige to the European Defence Community project when he was in office, the French Parliament might not have rejected it – which it did in August 1954 by 319 votes to 264.

Be that as it may, the process of economic integration went forward with great vigour on the Continent. It was bitterly rejected by the Conservative Government in Britain. Opposition was fundamental. It was based on one central theme. The British

Government were prepared, indeed eager, to co-operate with any and all Governments in the pursuit of economic prosperity and political stability. But co-operation must be at governmental level. There could be no question of any British government surrendering its sovereignty, and by implication, that of the British Parliament, to a supranational organization. Later, when the outline project revealed that executive power was to shift progressively to an unelected body (the European Commission) at the expense of a governmental body (the Council of Ministers) with no effective democratic parliamentary control whatsoever, opposition hardened even further.

The British Government argued, very forcefully at times, that integration of this sort would divide the members of the OEEC between themselves and create two rival trading blocs, the one discriminatory and inward-looking, the other – the rump of the OEEC – expansionist and multilateral. Such a division of Europe would be bad economically and dangerous politically since innumerable tensions would result from the deliberate distortion of traditional trade patterns.

Mr Reginald Maudling, Paymaster General at the time, fought long and hard to prevent these two blocs forming. Matters were brought to a head soon after de Gaulle came to power when Mr Maudling was chairman of the Intergovernmental Committee of OEEC handling the negotiations for a free trade area.

The French argued strongly that the Free Trade Area and the European Economic Community were incompatible and that there was no point in pursuing the discussions on an association. Negotiations were formally broken off in December 1958 and the two groups went their separate ways.

EUROPEAN FREE TRADE AREA – EFTA

Seven of the remaining eleven members of OEEC – the UK, Norway, Sweden, Denmark, Austria, Switzerland and Portugal – started immediate negotiations for the formation of a European Free Trade Association and the seven signed a convention to this effect at Stockholm on 20 November 1950; Finland later became an associate member. Free trade in agricultural goods and certain marine products was excluded but the Seven agreed to facilitate trade in agriculture by bilateral agreements.

It was to be a purely economic and temporary arrangement, aimed at progressive elimination of tariffs and customs between the member-states; there were never any political or social objectives, no common defence plan or policy – not even a common external tariff. In fact such ambitions were hardly feasible. All tariffs between member-states on goods of EFTA origin were eliminated by the end of 1966, when the Free Trade Area was finally established, though concessions were made to Norway and Finland on certain products – these concessions to end by 1 January 1970, and to Portugal to end on 1 January 1980.

The organization of EFTA has a Nordic simplicity compared with the complicated bureaucracy of Brussels, but it is, of course, only a makeshift organization dealing with trade and tariffs and does not have to oversee the multifarious activities engendered by the Rome Treaty. The EEC does not recognize EFTA as a negotiating body and negotiates separately with each member as and when necessary. The entire administrative staff of EFTA numbers a little over one hundred; its offices are in Geneva where the Council of seven permanent representatives (holding ambassadorial rank) meets weekly to deal with routine matters; and from time to time the seven ministers of commerce or trade convene in Geneva or one of the other EFTA capitals to confer on future policy. Decisions are taken by a simple majority vote, though formal recommendations dealing with more important matters usually need a unanimous vote. The chairmanship of the Council passes in rotation every six months; the Secretariat consists of four departments – Trade Policy, General and Legal, Economic, and Press and Information. There are six departmental standing committees to deal with the work of Customs, Trade Experts (who interpret the rules and regulations), Consultation (small representative delegations of three to five members from each member-state representing employer, trade union, industrial, commercial, and professional interests), Economic Development, Agricultural Review, and Budget.

EFTA suffers from being very lop-sided; of its total population of 97 million, the UK accounts for more than half – 54 million, and she plays by far the dominant role; at times the other members have felt that they were mere pawns in Britain's game with de Gaulle and the Common Market. Norway, in particular, became progressively disillusioned with Britain's import duties, then with her export rebates, and finally with her establishment of an aluminium smelting industry in direct competition with the Norwegian industry, with what Norway considered barely concealed subsidies. Half of EFTA's trade in the world is the UK's trade; the other half is a German preserve. All the other members do more trade with West Germany than they do with the UK; in the early 1960s all of them bought more from West Germany than they sold to her. West Germany was thus gradually cornering the markets of central and northern Europe.

Small wonder that the EFTA countries, and Denmark in particular, have been enthusiastic supporters of the bids to join the EEC. Between the veto on the first application and the decision to apply a second time, much water had flowed under the bridge in Britain. All three political parties had become reconciled to the fact that Britain was part of Europe, and that being so, should play a significant part in shaping its future. The second application was made after exhaustive studies by Whitehall and the Confederation of British Industry had shown that there was a certain and continuing advantage on balance for British industry in joining a wider trading community in Europe. After the Prime Minister, Mr Harold Wilson, and the Foreign Secretary, at the time Mr George Brown, had sounded out the various European capitals, the second application was filed in May 1967 and received even shorter shrift than the first. Negotiations did not even begin, although the European Commission had produced an analysis in depth of Britain's application, under the direction of a French member, M. Raymond Barre. This was a factual report and fairly set out the dangers of accepting an ailing applicant with an extremely precarious economy, a shaky pound, and a balance of payments in constant deficit at the time. But it concluded that none of these factors was necessarily an obstacle to the opening of negotiations which should begin at the earliest opportunity. But again the General said no, and roughly for the same reasons: the time was not ripe for British membership, which was as good an excuse as any for again barring the 'Anglo-Saxons'. The truth of the matter, of course, was that he had no intention of sharing the leadership of Europe with the British. He would still deal with the Germans single-handed.

Severe as the blow was to Britain and the EFTA partners, they were soon casting about for useful temporary alternatives. In 1968 and 1969 the Nordic Council, an assembly of members of parliament from the Scandinavian members of EFTA, worked on a plan for a Nordic customs union. Scandinavia already had a common labour market, reciprocal social security benefits for workers migrating between Scandinavian countries, and co-operated in education, science, technology, transport, and taxation. But the Danes and Norwegians especially wished to prepare a common position, reasoning that a common tariff wall and common industrial and agricultural policies would strengthen their hand when the day came to negotiate entry into the EEC.

Danish industry was at first a stumbling block because the Danish manufacturers did not want import tariffs imposed on their raw materials. Danish farmers, on the other hand, were feeling the pinch, particularly in West Germany, owing to the EEC's restrictive farm policy, and they were agitating for a Nordic agricultural fund to stabilize farm prices and facilitate structural reforms. A great deal of useful spadework was being put in against the day when Europe might be truly united and the other members of EFTA were secure in the knowledge that any tariffs imposed while matters were being sorted out would not apply among themselves.

ECONOMIC CO-OPERATION WITHIN THE EEC

Meanwhile, on 1 July 1968 the EEC Customs Union was complete – all tariffs between the Six themselves had been eliminated – in general this had involved a raising of tariffs by Benelux and Germany and a lowering of tariffs by France and Italy.

The basic rate of the common external tariff (CET) was intended to be the average of the tariff rates for each product levied in the four tariff areas before the Rome Treaty came into effect, but for some products special rates were negotiated between the Six.

The rates were also affected by the Dillon Round (1960–62) which secured cuts averaging 20 per cent on tariffs on many manufactured articles and the Kennedy Round (1963–7) which introduced larger and more widely spread cuts – two fifths of which were incorporated in the CET which was applied from 1 July 1968. The final Kennedy Round tariff cut takes place on 1 January 1972.

The average EEC tariffs after this final cut have been calculated at 7·6 to 7·7 per cent; the UK average as 10·2 to 12·1 per cent (but this ignores all Commonwealth preferences) and the US average as 11·2 to 11·8 per cent (but it is difficult to compare US rates with those of the EEC and the UK because the US does not use the Brussels customs classification).

Comparison of Tariffs on Certain Manufactured Goods

Product	EEC (common external tariff) (% ad-valorem import duty)			UK	USA
	Basic Rate	1 July 1968	1 January 1972	1 January 1972	1 January 1972
Synthetic fibre yarns	12	10·8	9	13	10·5 – 25*
Woollen fabrics	13	13	13	17·5	3·2 – 30*
Domestic glassware	24	20·6	15·5	15·5	10 – 30
Earth-moving vehicles	12	11·6	11	7·5	5
Rotary printing presses	9	7·2	4·5	7·5	6
Machine lathes	8	8	8	9	6 – 7·5
Passenger cars	22	17·6	11	11	3 – 5·5
Goods vehicles:					
over 2·5 litres	22	22	22	22	0 – 3
others	22	17·6	11	11	0 – 3
Watches	11	8·6†	7·5†	17	8·5 – 16*
TV and radio sets	22	18·8	14	15	5
Dolls	20	18·4	16	12·5	17·5
Electric shavers	13	10·4	6·5	7·5	6·5
Typewriters	13	10·4	6·5	7·5	0 – 5·5

* plus specific duty
† subject to minimum specific duty

There remained only the less obvious but most tiresome invisible tariffs to hinder trade between the Six. Different standards of safety in cars and electrical consumer goods seriously interfere with intra-Community trade, and disparities in definition of pure wool and of additives in food and beverages hamper the free flow of trade. In March 1968, acting under Article 100 'for the approximation of such statutory and administrative provisions as have a direct incidence on the establishment or functioning of the Common Market', the Council tackled this problem. By 31 December 1970 it will have eliminated by a five-phase programme technical obstacles to trade in foodstuffs, taking in its stride anti-oxidants, emulsifying and stabilizing agents, wrappings and tins, labelling, etc. And on industrial products the Council hopes to have decided on appropriate action by 31 December 1970, scheduling the work into a three-phase timetable – the first phase dealing with motor vehicles, crystal glassware, oil pipelines, and textiles among other things; the second chiefly with motor vehicles, measuring instruments, and precious metals; and the third with an enormous range of manufactured goods and miscellaneous items. Common standards are expected to ease problems of production and so contribute to the greater integration of European industry.

Quite as bad as the disparity in standards were border taxes which had the same effect as tariffs. In its annual report for 1968 the Commission stated that it had been able to identify 380 different types of tax which fell into this category. One of its difficulties is that governments within the Six have exercised great ingenuity in thinking up new taxes just as fast as they agreed to eliminate the old ones at the request of the Commission. They include quite subtle variations on stamp duties, licence fees, 'statistical' duties, fees for veterinary control of animals, sanitary controls of food including plant-control, landing and embarkation fees, etc. If governments were more co-operative, the Commission would not have to waste so much time and energy discovering whether it is entitled to take legal action for the suppression of these taxes under Articles 12, 13, and 16 of the Treaty.

The classic case of stretching customs and excise duties to ludicrous lengths happened when the Commission was asked to investigate the case of a gift of twenty-four bottles of wine costing £7 10s. sent from France to Belgium. Duty paid amounted to £3 19s. – over 52 per cent. The Commission discovered that the sender had filled in the wrong form. But if he had filled in the right form, a different set of taxes, including excise, a 'transmission' tax and various other charges would have amounted to £3 10s. – over 46 per cent.

BRITAIN AND THE EEC

In June 1969 the Commission, encouraged by the election of M. Georges Pompidou as President, decided to overhaul their 1967 opinion on British membership and especially to up-date the section on the UK economy and see how this might affect the Commission's Barre Plan for strengthening monetary and economic co-operation among the Six. Although there was much talk of a Community of seven, i.e. just including Britain for the time being (the supporters of this view feeling that Britain would be more than enough for the EEC to digest at one meal), the consensus of opinion was that there should be an enlargement by four – the UK, Denmark, Norway, and Ireland. Tough times lay ahead. France would insist on cast-iron guarantees on the financing of the common agricultural policy (CAP) before committing herself to the opening of negotiations; Germany was still unwilling to go on underwriting French agriculture; and a feeling was growing throughout the Six that the only way was to go ahead with the negotiations and hope that everything would come right in the end.

Most political observers and economists – at least those who now favour European unification – agree that Britain's obstinate refusal, both under a Labour and a Conservative government, to take part in the early tentative moves towards unity was a grave error of judgement at a time when the political omens and economic currents were beginning to point strongly towards the creation of a united Europe capable of holding its own against the two giants – the USA and the USSR.

The error gained in magnitude because for two decades it delayed what is now considered indispensable and inevitable by a large majority of people in Britain. If we had taken the plunge while there was a chance of success, we would not have found ourselves in the humiliating position of being kept waiting by de

Gaulle while he fought his battles with the EEC, ourselves, and the Americans.

Not that any UK approaches to the problem of Britain's relations with the Continental powers have revealed great skill in preparation and presentation. This was because no political party, and least of all the British people, had any clear idea of what these relations should be beyond those already existing in the shape of treaties and traditional trade patterns.

The phrase most commonly used in the 1960s, during the debate which followed the first application to join the Common Market, was that Britain was 'going into Europe', which implied that up till then Britain had not in fact been in Europe at all. Hence the shock of discovering that in joining the Common Market we were being asked suddenly to become European. The first application came like a bolt out of the blue. It was sprung on an ill-prepared public which knew little or nothing about the institutions which we were seeking to join. It divided the country from top to bottom and cut across the political parties.

Mercifully for the anti-Marketeers de Gaulle's veto solved the problem – at least temporarily. But the mistrust of British motives for wanting to join in the first place has never wholly been dispelled on the Continent. The strongest suspicion of all is that Britain would attempt to break up the EEC from within, having failed to do so from without. This would presumably be done by forcing a radical change of course, which would amount to the same thing.

It is based on the argument that Britain has never in history tolerated for long a combination of forces on the Continent which might threaten her position as a leading commercial and financial power. The circumstances have of course changed but the suspicion remains. The legend of 'perfidious Albion' and the tricks she will get up to, pitting one Continental country against another while she herself retains the balance of power, dies hard. It was reinforced between the wars by the ambivalence of British policy towards both Germany and France when we supported first one, then the other, and at times both together.

The argument that Britain was going in to take over the effective leadership of Europe received further support at the time of the first application when Mr Harold Macmillan said we could 'lead better from within' and the *Sunday Times*, in its pre-Thompson era when it was taken to reflect the outer workings of the Conservative mind, said Britain's purpose would be to prevent the Common Market from taking sides either for or against the USA or Russia. Neither motive commended itself to the Continental nations. The second application evoked much the same response. Many responsible quarters and political leaders on the Continent refused to take it seriously – or at least as representing a genuine change of heart in Britain as a whole. Specifically, they saw it as a political gimmick by a shrewd Prime Minister, who could not resist making political capital out of it one way or the other. If it failed, then the Conservatives in any future election could not use the Common Market as a weapon against Labour, or if they did they would have to produce some very convincing arguments to show that the application failed because of a faulty approach or faulty negotiation by the Labour Government. If it succeeded, then Labour got all the glory. The application, furthermore, could be made the more confidently because at the time, with the General in power, there was little chance of its being successful.

When the General resigned and the chances of joining suddenly became less remote, anti-Marketeers in both the Labour and Conservative parties became more vociferous. Mr Harold Wilson and his supporters were persistently pressed to reveal their intentions. This the Prime Minister equally persistently refused to do, no doubt feeling that he had been hoist with his own petard by the General's unexpected and dramatic removal from power. The stock answer was that the Government accepted the Treaty of Rome – no more no less – exactly as the members of the Community themselves had done. The rest would be played by ear but with no great emphasis on acceptance of integration beyond what was called for in the Treaty. This gave little encouragement either to the federalists or to the Commission in Brussels where supranationalism is accepted doctrine, the more so as it is to be applied by the Commission itself. It did, however, give support to those favouring co-operation at governmental level, which, it was assumed, would be the policy of the French Government under

M. Pompidou, and which on the whole corresponded to the views of the majority of the British people and possibly of the peoples of the Six.

Co-operation at governmental level had in fact been accepted policy by both the major political parties in Britain and by the Foreign Office. Where there had been divergencies, they concerned methods of approach, particularly when de Gaulle was in command in France. At one stage Foreign Office policy was to 'smoke the General out' and for this it enlisted the support of his opponents in the Common Market, mainly the Dutch and the Belgians, who had most to gain from maintaining the supremacy of the Common Market institutions, and from the Italians, traditionally in favour of Britain's active participation in European affairs. Also, since there was no love lost between the Commission and de Gaulle, the Commission's support was sought by maintaining the pretence of full British support for the Treaty of Rome as it stood, with all options open on the subject of political unity in Europe, the construction of which might well need new institutions.

In an effort to lend credence to the second application, the cost of joining was deliberately played down by the Government on the argument, no doubt sound at the time, that until we knew what the precise terms were and how they would affect British agriculture and the balance of payments, it was a fruitless exercise to try to count the cost. In any case, one could not judge the merits of joining merely on the cost of tomatoes or butter, although clearly in its own mind the Government knew that the cost, based on the most conservative interpretation of the new Mansholt Plan for E E C agriculture, would in theory mean a burden on the balance of payments of anything between £500m. and £1,000m., with many noted economists favouring the upper end of the bracket if the French insisted on maintaining the chief features of the C A P even after devaluation, which temporarily isolated their own farming community.

Clearly, the sudden realization that membership might become a distinct possibility, following the Common Market summit meeting in December 1969 on the subject, *inter alia*, of enlargement, caught many people unawares and forced a careful reassessment on those who up till the spring of 1969 had thought the whole subject academic. Marketeers and anti-Marketeers marshalled their forces and their arguments. The debate became fierce but after the speeches of the leaders of the three main political parties at a Guildhall banquet, one hardened continental diplomat, well-versed in the affairs of Britain, repeated apropos of the Labour application Roy Jenkins's taunt against the Macmillan Government in 1961 that if it entered the Common Market at all, it would be like a man 'standing backwards on an upward-moving escalator and occasionally taking a few steps down'. The metaphor was reinforced by Mr Enoch Powell during a speech at Smethwick in September 1969. Mr Powell had previously supported the Labour Government's application to join, but, quick to sense a shift in public opinion, he began to cast doubts on the wisdom of joining on anything like the terms which might be insisted upon by the Six.

Very wisely, from a tactical point of view, in the run-up before the general election, the Common Market issue was neatly played down by both Labour and Conservatives at Brighton in October 1969. To have given it another thorough airing would have been embarrassing all round, particularly before the Six's summit conference at The Hague.

There are roughly three schools of thought on what Britain's approach to eventual negotiations should be: the first has been dubbed by anti-Marketeers the 'sign-at-any-price' school, which has some sympathizers in the Foreign Office, including one of its former members, Lord Gladwyn, and is favoured by some devoted 'Europeans' in all parties. The tag, however, is unfair for no one in his right mind would want to sign on the dotted line without knowing exactly what he was letting himself in for. The 'sign-at-any-price' school could be more accurately defined as those who wish to sign with the minimum of pre-conditions which might put insurmountable obstacles in the way and arouse further suspicions on the Continent concerning British motives. Much of the bargaining, they argue, could be done once we were inside the EEC; this has been the practice of the Six themselves. Negotiating points should be kept to a minimum.

The second school wants to drive as hard a bargain as possible on agriculture, which is the great stumbling block. It also wants clear agreement on the balance-of-payments issue, which is not only affected by the impact of agricultural levies but also by the need for Britain to continue for some unspecified time to restrict capital movements out of Britain in order to keep the balance of payments in equilibrium. They argue that unless a satisfactory solution can be reached on these two subjects, Britain should not join.

The third school recognizes the force of the arguments produced by the other two but feels that all these problems can best be solved by a package deal within the framework of a wider political agreement on the future of Europe. It argues that all negotiating in the last resort is political since economics and politics are interdependent, particularly in the modern technical age, and that it is unrealistic to think of European unity in terms merely of the economics of the Treaty of Rome; negotiations are far more likely to succeed if all the implications of unity and future integration are considered *en bloc*. Nuclear and technological co-operation in Europe, both civil and military, with their repercussions on foreign policy, are clearly subjects which cannot be treated in isolation. And it is in these fields that Britain has much to offer. They constitute good bargaining assets.

No school was in the ascendant at the end of 1969, although much preliminary plotting of courses had taken place in Whitehall. All options, however, were left open in true Wilsonian fashion. So that no department of state should have the exclusive duty – particularly not the Foreign Office – of presenting the overall balanced picture of the conditions of entry, various watchdog assessors were appointed by 10 Downing Street, to keep an eye on all the facets of negotiations and to keep the politicians informed of what was going on, stage by stage. At the Foreign Office Mr George Thomson was made Minister in charge of 'Europe' and Sir Con O'Neill was appointed chief negotiator at Brussels. Sir Con is a career diplomat, who crossed swords with George Brown when the latter was Foreign Secretary, over the Bonn ambassadorial appointment. He resigned from the Foreign Service only to be recalled when the Common Market suddenly became a live issue.

At Cabinet level and supervising both was Sir William Nield, who spent most of his post-war career at the Ministry of Agriculture, working closely with Mr Christopher Soames, Britain's Ambassador in Paris, when the latter was the Conservative Minister of Agriculture. After that he became permanent head of the defunct Department of Economic Affairs, and in October 1969 was made an 'additional permanent secretary' to the Cabinet. Sir William is a committed Common Marketeer but is not a member of the 'sign-at-any-price' group, and is known to hold some forthright views on politics and politicians on the Continent. He was a member of Mr Edward Heath's negotiating team at Brussels in 1961–3.

What is certain is that the subjects for negotiation will be kept to a reasonable minimum. There will be no repetition of the irrelevancies which bogged down the first negotiations such as the fate of Pakistani kips and coir mats, or duties on ferrochrome, or whether Singhalese sailors should be able to obtain a special type of rice duty-free in Antwerp.

At the Hague summit conference in December 1969 it was agreed that the Community should adopt a common negotiating position. Even before the conference permanent representatives of the Six had been working on a preliminary list of subjects which could form an agenda when the time came for negotiations with the applicant countries.

There were six main headings: (1) agricultural finance, i.e. fixing the level of financial contributions to the European Agricultural Guidance and Guarantee Fund (FEOGA) by each applicant; (2) the transitional period required by agriculture and industry to enable them to adapt themselves; (3) major Commonwealth problems (foremost among them Commonwealth preferences, Caribbean sugar and the position of New Zealand as a large supplier of foodstuffs to Britain); (4) adaptation of the Community's institutions (the most important alterations being to the voting procedure in the Council of Ministers; the number of additional members of the Commission; increased representation in the European Parliament, and the appointment of extra judges to the Court of Justice, etc.); (5) negotiating procedures, i.e. how negotiations should get under way; who will negotiate for whom (presumably the Commission under Articles 228 and 237 of the Treaty of Rome?), and whether the four applications should be considered *en bloc* or separately; (6) economic and financial issues, and problems arising from Britain's entry to Euratom and the Coal and Steel Community.

There could clearly be some overlapping between subjects but these are roughly the topics which must come up for discussion both between the Six themselves and between the Six and the candidate countries. It may well be that where agreement had been reached on certain subjects during the previous negotiations in 1961–3, the same ground will not be gone over again; but, as much time has elapsed, both sides may feel that it is better to start from scratch and merely refer to the previous negotiations where convenient.

ECONOMIC GROWTH IN THE EEC

When Britain joins the Common Market – and it is highly unlikely that if negotiations get under way they will be allowed to fail – she will be joining a Community which, for all its shortcomings, has achieved unparalleled economic growth. How much of this growth is due to the Customs Union brought about by the Treaty of Rome and how much to the expansion of world trade in general is difficult to assess. But whatever the percentage, the growth has been remarkable by any standards and it has been achieved despite widely differing political and economic systems within the Six.

In Germany, for instance, very considerable success has been achieved through the operation of a social market economy based on a free-wheeling liberalism, subject to minimum guidance from the central and Länder governments. The government in Bonn acts as a watchdog and referee as between one industry and another, but is nevertheless prepared to give selective financial help to certain sectors of industry such as iron, coal and steel, oil, and electronics.

In France, on the other hand, detailed market planning has been the order of the day since the end of The Second World War, with progressively greater governmental intervention in all sectors.

This pattern, *mutatis mutandis*, has been adopted by Italy and the Benelux countries, with less emphasis, however, on state planning in Holland. Demand management, as a method of regulating the economy, has been increasingly resorted to in all countries since prosperity has brought in its wake the inevitable bouts of inflation and severe overheating.

The economies of the Six individually are still far from coordinated as various financial and economic crises have shown, and a long path lies ahead to a full economic union, which it is the aim of the Treaty of Rome to provide. As will be seen in a later chapter currencies are still seen by the governments of the Six as symbols of national sovereignty, and the use of the monetary mechanism in guiding the economy as very much the prerogative of governments and not of organs of the Community. The clash of ultimate authority between responsibly elected governments and the Commission on economic and monetary problems has already led to major political battles and more are no doubt to come.

Even so the Community is the fastest growing economic grouping in the world. Intra-Community trade quadrupled between 1958 and 1968 and trade with the rest of the world expanded vigorously, exports rising by 118 per cent and imports by 108 per cent.

In 1968 exports of manufactured goods by Community countries to themselves represented about 71 per cent of their global exports. But this was not achieved at the expense of trade with countries outside the Community, since exports rose by 10 per cent in 1968 and imports by 9·5 per cent. Both percentages were considerably higher than the expansion of world trade generally – which testifies to the competitiveness of EEC industry on world markets.

This high degree of competitiveness, achieved in recent years mainly by the Germans and the Italians, has enabled the Community to run a trade surplus with the rest of the world since 1966. And this in turn contributes to the Community's maintaining a more or less permanent surplus in its balance of payments, despite the fact that both Germany and Italy in 1967 and part of 1968 encouraged the export of capital to counterbalance the effects of embarrassingly high surpluses on commercial account.

The Community's strong external-trading position arises from its rapid internal growth. Except for the mini-slump year of 1967 (when the rise was only 2·9 per cent), GNP in the EEC as a whole has risen on average by 5 per cent per annum since 1958. The 1968 figure of just over 5 per cent was achieved despite the fact that the May–June riots in France in 1968 caused a loss of production equivalent to a drop in GNP of about 2·5 per cent. This expansion has not taken place at the expense of the UK's trade with the Community. When the Common Market was formed, Britain's trade with the Six constituted about 14 per cent of her total trade. Today, it is around 20 per cent both for imports and exports.

Nor, contrary to popular belief in Britain, is the Community any more inward-looking commercially than any other comparable industrial country or grouping. By the time the Kennedy Round tariff cuts are completed on 1 January 1972, the average incidence of the EEC's external tariff on manufactures will be around 7 per cent, whereas the United Kingdom's average industrial tariff will be just over 10 per cent – assuming she has not joined the EEC by then. In the USA the equivalent tariff is around 11 per cent.

Quite apart from official American aid under the Marshall Plan, much of Europe's post-war economic growth is directly attributable to a vast increase in American investment. Up-to-date statistics of private international capital movements are not readily obtainable, but according to figures released by the US Department of Commerce in September 1968 direct American investment in the EEC at the end of 1966 amounted to $7,586m. West Germany got the lion's share with $3,077m. as against France's $1,758m., Italy's $1,148m., Holland's $858m., and Belgium–Luxembourg's $745m. United States investment in Britain at the same date amounted to $5,652m. Since then there have been many American take-overs of firms in Britain, not least the Chrysler take-over of the Rootes Motors group and Leasco's of Pergamon Press.

The extent of American investment in Europe displeased de Gaulle, although at the time it was no higher than European portfolio investment in America. But it was the selective nature of the American investment, in key industries such as automobiles, chemicals, and computers, which the Gaullists disliked. This led the General in his heyday to attack what he called 'dollar colonization' in Europe. The aim was to undermine confidence in the US currency, and this he did by intensive selling of French currency reserves for gold in an attempt to force the Americans to raise their selling price of $35 per ounce, a price they had artificially kept down since 1934. The campaign against the dollar was timed to coincide with increasing American balance-of-payments deficits caused by the Vietnam war and the enormous size of American financial aid all over the world. These deficits provided the world with vast amounts of liquidity (monetary reserves) but they were the wrong type of liquidity – the type that perpetuated America's grip on world economic and monetary affairs because the dollar was the world's primary reserve currency and, so long as confidence in it was not undermined, few countries wanted to convert their dollars into gold.

France found some support for this policy among orthodox economists in various countries, particularly among those who were arguing in favour of an upward revaluation of gold as a means of increasing world liquidity (despite its inflationary tendencies) instead of the special-drawing-rights scheme, now in operation, of the International Monetary Fund. But support faded out very quickly when France herself ran into severe balance-of-payments troubles after the May–June riots in 1968.

Even before that date economic growth in the EEC was beginning to lessen and France's external finances were looking far less healthy as the trade balance began to deteriorate through a lack of industrial competitiveness.

THE FRENCH MAY–JUNE RIOTS AND THE AFTERMATH

This was the position at the time of the riots in Paris and elsewhere. The riots, started by the students, quickly spread to two thirds of France's 15-million labour force involving a loss of some two to three weeks' production and a loss of reserves of $1,300m. during the two months of May and June alone.

The riots cut far deeper into the heart of France than the Government were prepared to admit. What was on trial was not merely the inadequacies of the Government of the day but the whole of French society, French institutions, indeed the French way of life.

The students were not concerned with wages and working conditions. But in the general strike of May–June 1968, they found themselves on the same side of the barricades as the workers – and for the same reasons. Both felt they were victims of 'the system'. In the universities it was the *système magistral* with its emphasis on dogma and not debate; where lectures were one-man orations and teaching hopelessly inadequate in a modern society. Both students and workers felt they were being crushed by the weight of a bureaucratic hierarchy which dated back to Napoleonic times.

Respect for this hierarchy had become the supreme virtue of French life. It ran through the services of the state and through commerce, banking, and industry. The higher echelons of the 'cadres' harboured men who had often been to the same *grandes écoles* and operated as a self-enclosed élite far removed from the bench or the factory floor, or indeed from the everyday workings of the business and industrial world. The mandarins seldom communicated with the lower orders. Decisions were arbitrary and passed down the line in military fashion. Secretiveness was the rule at all levels of management. Workers and office personnel were kept in ignorance of the affairs of their own organizations. At times this devotion to secrecy achieved conspiratorial dimensions. De Gaulle was fond of keeping his ministers and close collaborators in complete ignorance of what was going on in his own Government. One of his finance ministers, M. Antoine Pinay, a much-respected elder statesman of France, used to complain bitterly that cabinet ministers learned quite by chance, and more often than not through the press, of decisions the General had taken days or even weeks before.

On one famous occasion, when the General decided to pull the French Mediterranean fleet out of the military organization of the North Atlantic Alliance – a subject of vital importance to the future of France – the first his ministers heard of it was when they saw the text of a speech he had delivered weeks earlier to the École Militaire, the French general staff college.

Similarly, the General did not tell his ministers of his intention to give Algeria independence. The list of vital decisions taken by de Gaulle without consulting or even informing any of his Ministers is a long one. But high-handed action of this sort was not peculiar to de Gaulle. It pervaded the whole of French life. The Vichy régime, which on paper ruled unoccupied France during The Second World War, behaved in exactly the same way. Marshal Pétain used to tell those of his ministers who were bold enough to offer advice that he alone was the maker of policy and his alone the responsibility.

Extraordinary circumstances in both cases? Perhaps. But arrogance was not the prerogative of governments. Chairmen and boards of directors in industry claimed the right to keep the staff and shareholders in the maximum amount of ignorance allowed by law. The shareholders of Pergamon Press, in the run-up to the take-over by Leasco, were bombarded with accurate information compared with the treatment meted out to shareholders in the abortive take-over battle between Boussois-Souchon-Neuvesel and Saint-Gobain.

When the French Government decided to give the workers at the nationalized Renault factory shares in the firm, the Director-General, M. Pierre Dreyfus, was not even told of the decision.

Years ago even de Gaulle, whose own methods of government were autocratic in the extreme, sensed this lack of contact between managements and workers. Managements consisted largely of the *haute bourgeoisie*, whom de Gaulle held responsible for the downfalls of the Third and Fourth Republics, and who opposed him through most of the Fifth, particularly after Algeria, where they felt he had betrayed them. He in turn accused them of clinging to outmoded techniques of management which led to a depersonalized society in which the workers had no sense of belonging. Both sides became permanently estranged, locked in a conservative, rigidly hierarchical organization which was no match for the flexible management techniques of France's major competitors and particularly of the 'Anglo-Saxons'.

The factory floor and the street thus became the only places where the workers could give vent to what they considered legitimate grievances, which went far beyond the problem of mere wage claims.

Under the Gaullist régime lobbying one's deputy was a waste of time because Parliament was a rubber-stamp. Access to radio and TV was denied because they too were in Gaullist hands. This sense of frustration was the immediate spur to revolt in what was one of France's most tragic periods of civil disorder.

In the teeth of opposition from the *Patronat* (the French equivalent of the Confederation of British Industry) and, ironically, in some cases from the workers themselves, de Gaulle introduced his worker-participation scheme. Opposition from the workers was based on the argument that in the board room they would be hopelessly out-classed and out-manoeuvred by their better-educated bosses. Their immediate concern was that French workers were the second lowest paid in the Common Market, just ahead of Italy, but humiliatingly behind the Luxemburgers, the Germans, the Belgians, and the Dutch.

The scheme had an inglorious birth and was applied with little enthusiasm on either side. By July 1969 only 252 *accords de participation* between workers and managements had been concluded, covering 206,642 wage-earners, or 1·4 per cent of the working population.

But it was a modest beginning of an attempt to change the face of French society. More human relationships between all classes and between the state and the people became the central theme of the 'new society' introduced by President Pompidou and his Prime Minister, M. Jacques Chaban-Delmas, at the opening of the Pompidou régime. The indictment of the old order was absolute. Pre-Gaullist administrators had sapped the moral foundations of the state by their inefficiency, short-sightedness, and lack of courage; they were the mirror of the nation itself. The egotism of the individual had spread to all strata of society and led inevitably to dissension and revolt.

What M. Chaban-Delmas could not say was that the Gaullist régime itself had been guilty with the rest, except that the General had never lacked courage, whatever else could be said of his policies. But other Frenchmen were saying it. They accused the General of turning the energies of the nation away from urgently needed social and educational reforms towards a costly *politique de grandeur*, which eventually took France to the verge of collapse.

The May–June riots, which were the immediate result of deep-seated social unrest, triggered off the slow decline of French power and influence. According to figures published by the US Federal Reserve Board, during the fourteen-month period May 1968 to August 1969, the Banque de France lost between $4,000m. and $5,000m. in reserves. When President Pompidou defended the devaluation of the franc (by 12·5 per cent in relation to the US dollar), he admitted that France's reserves would have been exhausted by the end of the year had the franc not been devalued. During the one week alone before the parity was altered, the reserves had fallen by as much as $300m.

He implied that if devaluation had taken place a year earlier, in July 1968, when he had recommended it, the decline in France's fortunes might have been arrested. In a sense, therefore, General de Gaulle's decision to appeal to the people for approval of his proposal to alter the Senate and strengthen regional administration was a blessing in disguise. It enabled his successor to carry out the much-needed devaluation, which de Gaulle himself had refused to countenance.

His dismissal of Pompidou as Prime Minister redounded to the latter's advantage, since he was able to assume the highest office later with only diminished responsibility for the débâcle which gathered momentum as soon as he was replaced.

When M. Maurice Couve de Murville was appointed Prime Minister in July 1968, he was faced with the bill for wage increases of up to 14 per cent (more than three times the yearly increase in productivity), which had to be absorbed somehow by the economy without increasing the already powerful inflationary forces. He had two courses. He could either attempt to weather the crisis by expanding out of it rather as Reginald Maudling had tried to do just before Labour took over in 1964, or he could play it safe with severe disinflation, a rise in unemployment leading possibly to further disorders as the workers and the nation as a whole were made to pay for the follies of the spring.

He chose the first course – and went from blunder to blunder. Weathering the storm by expansion entailed allowing the economy to absorb the higher wages bill by increased productivity, and simultaneously following a liberal import policy (using the gold reserves if necessary) to help keep consumer prices down, thus preventing the erosion of the wage increases to which the Government had committed themselves. It also required a quick restoration of confidence in the franc. None of these things happened. France boldly announced that the 1 July 1968 deadline for the Common Market's Customs Union and common external tariff would be kept. Foreign exchange controls imposed at the end of May were lifted at the end of July and import quotas on motor-cars, steel, textiles, and domestic appliances imposed in the early summer were removed in the autumn.

Despite every encouragement, financial and otherwise, exports did not improve at the rate needed. The trade gap widened month by month and confidence in the franc ebbed. For the Government this was the moment of truth. The dash for growth was not paying off – and the world knew it. People were speculating heavily not only against the franc (and the pound) but on an up-valuation of the D.-mark, which had gone from strength to strength since the international monetary crisis started in earnest in the spring of 1968.

The Cabinet finally bowed to the inevitable and decided that devaluation of the franc could not be avoided. Finance ministers gathered hastily at Bonn during the middle of November. Devaluation was accepted. All that remained was to fix the percentage, generally agreed to be between 12 and 14 per cent. The French, the British, and the Americans brought strong pressure to bear on the Germans to revalue, as part of a realignment of currencies, but to no effect.

In the run-up to the election, Dr Kiesinger's Government refused to revalue outright. It would only agree to a shadow revaluation by imposing a four per cent levy on exports and a similar rebate on imports in order to cut down the vast surpluses which had been building up on external current account and which by the end of 1968 were to reach $3,000m. Measures were also taken to make it as unprofitable as possible for speculators to hold D.-marks for any length of time.

When the French Ministers returned to Paris they found the General in a truculent mood. There would be no devaluation – the 'ultimate absurdity' he called it – despite the fact that in return for agreeing to devalue unilaterally, the French Government had been given credits of nearly $2,000m. over and above the July $886m. drawing on the I M F and swap facilities totalling $1,300m. Instead severe deflationary measures were adopted. Budgetary policy was tightened up and the deficit (about £124m.) – the first since 1964 – was cut by half. Bank rate, which had been raised from 3½ to 5 per cent in May was raised to 6 per cent (by the end of September 1969 it was up to 8 per cent as in England).

Civil and military expenditure was drastically cut and the money supply severely curtailed. Controls on the export of capital hit importers and exporters and French tourists travelling abroad. They were so tight that operations on the foreign-exchange market were subject to so much paper work and form-filling that they became the despair of brokers and the Paris gold market came to a virtual standstill.

And still the drain on the reserves went on. Speculators used the most ingenious methods of avoiding the controls, encouraged by an announcement that the Government intended to introduce legislation to increase death duties, and the irony was that in many cases they were using the massive short-term credits given to industry between May and November to help expansion. In one week alone in November about $1,000m. worth of francs found their way to Zurich or Frankfurt.

By the end of the year the published reserves, despite all the official credit arrangements, stood at only $4,200m. compared with $6,108m. in December 1967.

At the start of 1969, the French economy was in a state of siege. The export performance had improved during the last quarter of 1968 after industrial production picked up. But the external trade gap was still as threatening as ever.

By the spring, the cost of imports was only covered up to four fifths by exports and the deficit was running at about $250m. to $300m. per month.

This was the time de Gaulle chose to gamble on his future for the last time. Misreading the mood of the people as he had never done before, and against what advice had been proferred, he held the fatal referendum on the highly controversial administrative reforms, and lost. He resigned immediately and went off to the south-west coast of Ireland to reflect on the ingratitude of the French nation.

He left France as he had found it – on the verge of bankruptcy. When he took over in 1958, one of the first things he did was to devalue the franc. His successor did the same thing eleven years after. The coffers were empty then as they were in 1958. The *politique de grandeur* had been expensive. In July 1969, the currency reserves of the Banque de France stood at $3,594m. (a drop of $1,256m. compared with July 1968) and as opposed to $5,967m. in July 1966, during the height of Gaullist power. But not all the glory had evaporated.

A strong Gaullist rump lived on in the shadow of the General, looking to M. Michel Debré, one of his most faithful lieutenants, for spritual guidance. This rump was determined to prevent the new Government from straying too far from the paths of Gaullist orthodoxy. They were a source of some embarrassment because they were M. Pompidou's main supporters during the presidential election campaign. Indeed they constituted his majority in Parliament. There was a further difficulty. M. Pompidou himself, as Prime Minister, had been the main executor of the General's policies. To his credit, however, he had been dismissed for suggesting that the General might find it convenient to withdraw gracefully after the upheavals of May–June.

The process of dismantling the more unrealistic policies pursued by the General, both internally and externally, would obviously be a slow and delicate one, particularly as M. Debré had been retained and given the Ministry of Defence as a sop to the dyed-in-the-wool Gaullists.

Indeed the rapid deterioration of the economic and social climate at home in twelve months had been well matched over the years by the steady decline since 1967 of French influence abroad.

Eleven years of Gaullism, after the early successes in restoring

French morale, had produced an unimpressive balance-sheet; constant sniping at the 'Anglo-Saxons', sometimes for personal motives left over from The Second World War, sometimes in an attempt to break the power of the Americans, while having some effect as an irritant, hardly qualified as a foreign policy in the French diplomatic tradition. It had left France dangerously isolated and suspect among the major Western powers and irretrievably weakened in the Common Market, where the centre of gravity was slowly moving across the Rhine. The Americans were as powerful as ever – and so was the dollar – despite the tragic effects of the Vietnam war. Europe, as a third force under French leadership, had not got off the ground, nor had de Gaulle's *Europe des états* composed of an inner council of France, Britain, West Germany, and Italy. Politically, Europe was stagnating. Moscow and Washington still dealt with one another direct, by-passing Paris (and London for that matter). The Urals were still as far away from the Atlantic as they were when de Gaulle took over. The question of the enlargement of the E E C loomed larger than ever; Britain still insisted that she should be allowed to join. The Treaty of Co-operation between France and Germany, hastily produced after Harold Macmillan signed the Polaris agreement with President Kennedy, had been a dead-letter for years. Both countries had largely nullified the common agricultural policy and not co-operated at all in adjusting the parities of the franc and the D-mark. The growth of German power was potentially as threatening as ever, even after Herr Willy Brandt had become Chancellor. Britain as a counterweight was still spurned.

French defences were still as dependent as ever on American nuclear power and France's withdrawal from the military organization of the North Atlantic alliance had not added to her moral authority or to her material protection.

Charting a more realistic course in foreign and monetary affairs received strong support, surprisingly enough, from the French National Assembly which hitherto had been little more than a Gaullist rubber stamp. The Foreign Affairs Commission, presided over by a Gaullist, drew up a report recommending almost everything the General had scorned over the years. The

Finance Commission, also in charge of a Gaullist, in a pithy reference to economic and, by implication, political sanity, said: 'A long era of visionaries – Winston Churchill, Charles de Gaulle, Konrad Adenauer, Joseph Stalin, and John F. Kennedy – has come to an end. The realists are now in command.'

The new realism was very much in evidence at the 1969 Hague summit conference. Fighting a rearguard action against the Gaullist rump in Paris and picking his way cautiously into the future, M. Pompidou made two historic breaks with the past. He agreed that negotiations with Britain and the three other applicants should begin not later than the end of June 1970, provided the Six had reached a common negotiating position by then. The French Foreign Minister, M. Maurice Schumann, said he saw no reason why they should not have done so. He also accepted the need for further European integration, economic and monetary co-operation, and a Commission budget. The latter would mean that the Commission should be entitled to the revenues accruing from the common agricultural policy and eventually the duties from the common external tariff – something which de Gaulle opposed bitterly in his day. Indeed, Professor Walter Hallstein was eased out of office on this issue *inter alia*, when he was President of the Commission.

Equally important, M. Pompidou agreed that technological co-operation should begin and that fresh efforts should be made to re-activate Euratom, which had been moribund for years because of French opposition.

Nine months after the General's departure, the wheel had turned almost full circle.

M. Maurice Schumann, the new Foreign Minister, was a tried hand in politics and a staunch Gaullist in his day. His career started in journalism – in London, with the old Havas News Agency, just before the war. He joined de Gaulle in the very early days in London and was his mouthpiece for some considerable time on the BBC French services. On returning to France he joined the Mouvement Républicain Populaire. He survived many a political battle in the whirligig of French politics and gained a reputation for skill in manoeuvre – just the man to steer France on the new course set by President Pompidou.

On the home front M Pompidou, as befits a banker who has worked for the Rothschilds, saw it as his first duty to put France's financial house in order, and appointed M. Valéry Giscard d'Estaing, a dissident Gaullist and an economist of repute, as his Finance Minister.

Soon after it had taken over, the Pompidou Government took further steps to curb inflation and stimulate confidence in the franc by reinforcing the measures adopted by its predecessor in May and June. They included freezing of half of all public-sector investment planned for the second half of 1969, except what had been earmarked for education; the funds thus blocked, amounting to some £336m. or 2·5 per cent of the 1969 budget, were placed in a special fund to be released as and when the disinflation of the economy allowed. They included moneys originally earmarked for civil, military, and scientific research (but not the Concorde project).

When the foreign-exchange markets were least expecting it, the franc was devalued by 12·5 per cent, roughly what had been agreed in Bonn in November 1968 before the General's veto.

Immediate speculative pressures on the franc were thus avoided. Further stringent measures followed including a five-week price and profits freeze to prevent the effects of devaluation from being dissipated by rising costs and prices in an inflation-prone economy. Both were already rising at an annual rate of 6 per cent even before devaluation which put on another 3 per cent.

Demand control, by a combination of wage restraint and a reduction in Government expenditure, thus became the fundamental aim of the new Government – a policy already recommended by the O E C D.

Three weeks later, a new batch of measures was introduced, aimed at balancing the budget by 1 January 1970; striking a balance between national production, consumption, and investment by 1 April 1970; balancing imports and exports by 1 July 1970. This involved the State in ruthlessly restricting its own expenditure; preventing an overheating of the economy; encouraging savings; increasing exports; and ensuring equal sacrifices by measures to protect the lower-paid members of the community.

Further government cuts in expenditure would bring the special blocked funds for 1969–70 up to some £615m. The rate of state spending during the Pompidou Government – and this was a more significant commitment – would be lower than the rate of increase in GNP. Current accounts in banks were taxed, thus encouraging a switch to deposits in savings banks which enjoyed a bonus of 1·5 per cent provided they were not withdrawn before the middle of 1970. Income tax concessions were granted to the lower-paid classes and the elderly, and the guaranteed industrial minimum wage (*salaire minimum interprofessionnel garanti*) was raised by 4 per cent and geared more closely to the general level of wages and not merely to the cost of living as before.

Companies were affected in two ways: first, the amount of taxation they were required to pay during any current fiscal year was raised from 80 per cent to 90 per cent, which brought the French Treasury another £78m. in 1969, and second, the rules governing the depreciation of capital investments were altered so that amortization would be calculated from the date of purchase of the equipment and not for the whole of the year in which the purchase was made.

As a sop to those who paid the widely disliked added-value tax, the rate of taxation was reduced and its method of application simplified.

These measures were designed to administer a short shock to the economy of the sort M. Giscard d'Estaing had already given it during a previous spell at the Finance Ministry. But this time, bearing in mind how easily quick deflation can lead to an even quicker stagnation of the economy, it was administered more gradually. The measures were the preliminary to the much more drastic long-term reforms of the economy outlined by M. Chaban-Delmas's opening policy speech to the National Assembly on 16 September 1969.

Further checks to consumer spending were introduced in November 1969 when a restriction of unprecedented severity on bank lending was imposed by the Banque de France. This had the effect of limiting short-, medium-, and long-term loans at the end of January 1970 to 3 per cent of their level in June 1968. Limiting the money supply in this way was considered by some economists to be a significant break with orthodox fiscal policy and it appeared that the French were taking a leaf out of Roy Jenkins's book. The British Chancellor had tried hard and unsuccessfully to limit consumer spending by imposing a ceiling on bank lending.

By September 1969, to bolster confidence in the franc and discourage further draining of the reserves, France was forced to make stand-by arrangements totalling $3,400m. with central banks and other financial institutions.

The International Monetary Fund granted a further standby credit roughly equivalent to France's quota in the Fund of $987m., which entailed accepting I M F supervision of the country's economy, just as Chancellor Roy Jenkins had had to do when the U K was granted a $1,000m. stand-by credit by the same I M F in June 1969 – a far cry from the Gaullist heyday when the Fund and central bank swap arrangements were judged unhealthy adjuncts of an ailing international monetary system.

LABOUR UNREST IN GERMANY AND ITALY

Not that France alone had been caught up in a tide of social disorder and labour unrest. West Germany and Italy had both fallen victims to the 'English sickness'. Wild-cat strikes in major industries, such as coal, steel, automobiles, and shipbuilding had strained the economies of both countries in the late summer and autumn of 1969. In Italy, with the expiry of three-year contracts affecting about five million workers in all major industries, the labour situation rapidly deteriorated. Strikes and lock-outs led to a worsening of labour–management relations such as had not been seen in Italy since the days immediately after the war. A decade of healthy expansion, booming exports and fairly stable prices and wages in 1968-9 was threatened by strikes in almost every sphere of industrial activity. Workers were striking for wage increases which in the case of steel, motor cars, and engineering would put as much as 35 to 40 per cent on production costs. Overnight Italy's basic industrial exports would become less competitive. Confidence in the Italian lira faded rapidly, speculators began to sell lire on the expectation of devaluation.

Capital was flowing out of Italy in the early summer of 1969 at an annual rate of $3,500m., defeating all official attempts to prevent the drain. The commercial banks were even borrowing from the Bank of Italy at the rate of 3·5 per cent so that they could relend abroad at average interest rates of about 8 per cent or more – and very much more at one time in the eurodollar market. According to the Italian Ministry of Finance capital outflows during 1969 inclusive reached the staggering figure of $4,488m. (£1,867m.). Loss of production at the Fiat motor works at Turin caused by persistent strikes was put at 180,000 vehicles, equivalent to £106m. Alfa Romeo estimated their loss at 11,000 vehicles. Ignis, one of Italy's leading electrical appliance manufacturers, suffered a production loss of 100,000 refrigerators. Typewriter and computer manufacturer Olivetti lost 1·4 million work-hours, and tyre-maker Pirelli 1·6 million hours. The medium-sized and smaller firms were even worse hit.

To stop the exodus of capital seeking refuge abroad, the Finance Ministry eventually gave orders for the immediate repatriation of speculative funds and banks were forbidden to invest in the eurodollar market.

Italy was paying the price of the French sickness – fast-growing economic and political instability caused by a succession of weak governments – faithfully reflecting not only the divisions of Italian politics, but the perniciousness of a society sapped by corruption in high places, inefficient administration, and lack of moral consciousness.

Only in Germany was stability assured, partly by reason of the German character, and partly because of sound economics and good management–labour relations. Germany's economic successes, however, are no miracle. They are due to business efficiency and a high export performance. In two key industries, coal and steel, the workers are represented on the supervisory and management boards, and one of the major industrial issues in Germany is whether this system of co-determination should be extended to other sectors of industry. The trade unions are in favour of extension and so are the new ruling Social Democrats, but the Christian Democrats and Free Democrats are fiercely against it. Demarcation disputes are unknown because there is nothing to demarcate. All workers in any given industry are included in the same union, of which there are only sixteen in all, compared with Britain's 170-odd. Unofficial or wild-cat strikes are illegal and offenders can be taken to labour courts. The law requires that one-third of the members of the supervisory boards of joint stock companies should be elected by the employees (excluding the white-collar staff).

The fact that the wild-cat strikes in the autumn of 1969 did not lead to any prosecutions was because the employers were in no mood to disturb the traditional good relations between the board room and the factory floor which keeps working days lost through strikes down to a minimum – a mere 25,248 in 1968. The strikers felt they had a genuine grievance. Whereas company profits had been soaring for years, wage claims had been few and far between – not because the employers were unwilling to consider them, but because the trade unions themselves were either very slow in making them or did not make them at all. From the workers' point of view, union leaders had become so deeply involved in a combined labour–management operation to prevent inflation that they were unconsciously doing the employers' bidding, and neglecting the interests of their members.

The wave of strikes, of course, was not without inflationary effects. Workers in the major industries had been granted wage increases which would put between 11 and 12 per cent on the hourly wages bill in 1970. They had also been granted social benefits such as health insurance which were the equivalent of another 14 per cent average rise in wages.

The assumption was that the rises would be absorbed by higher consumer prices because German industry was already working almost to full capacity and could only increase production by about 6 to 8 per cent. The effect of the salary increases would thus probably have the net effect of putting wage costs per unit of production up by between 4 to 6 per cent. This would be a blessing in disguise for the German balance of payments.

Germany's major economic problem since 1965 has been embarrassingly large balance-of-payments surpluses, which in 1968 had reached the record figure of nearly $3,000m. on current account. To redress the balance the Germans were forced to export capital wholesale. They are major suppliers to the Euro-currency market and British firms and public corporations alone had obtained loans which by the end of 1969 totalled over D M. 1,000m. (£116m. at the new rate of exchange). Borrowers included the Gas Council, the Electricity Council, British Petroleum, Charter Consolidated, Courtaulds, Sears Holdings, Redland Holdings, Derbyshire County Council, and the Scottish Electricity Board. The last two loans by-passed the German long-term bond market and were raised from private sources. But this is only a fraction of the total outflow of German capital.

By the end of 1969 total German investments abroad were put at about £1,400m., most of it portfolio and loans to foreign industries such as those in Britain. So far the Germans have not felt the need to increase their direct investments abroad because of the ability of their big exporters to absorb rising production costs by reducing profit margins, thus maintaining a competitive selling price. Farbwerke Hoescht, the chemical giant, was a case in point, when it succeeded in lowering its prices to keep pace with Imperial Chemicals after the devaluation of the pound in 1967.

There is a danger, however, that rising production costs after the upvaluation of the D.-mark and the extensive wage increases granted at the end of 1969 will be too large to be absorbed by increased productivity. In this case German industry may be tempted to reverse the trend by setting up manufacturing sub-sidiaries in fast-growing markets.

In 1968 out of net exports of long-term capital amounting to £1,000m. only £180m. was invested in foreign companies, and in 1969 less than 12 per cent of Germany's exports were attributable to operations on foreign soil. But by the end of the year Hoescht – who else – had made a successful take-over bid for the British paint firm of Berger, Jenson, and Nicholson. Thus the writing was on the wall. The acquisition of a major British paint manufacturer could be the prelude to further excursions into fields hitherto held to be the preserve of the Americans and the British. If this trend should gather pace, Germany will become as tough a competitor established abroad as she is working from her home base.

Her dominant position in the Common Market is by now well established in the economic and monetary fields where the Treaty of Rome makes ample provision for co-operation. This co-operation becomes all the more necessary because since 1968 the relative strengths of the economies of the E E C countries have dramatically altered. Germany has gone from strength to strength whilst Italy has sunk deeper into industrial strife and political chaos. France is beginning a precarious convalescence and the Benelux countries are fighting an uphill battle against inflation, while trying to preserve the stability of their currencies in the backwash of three major parity changes in the same number of years. The need for co-operation is obvious.

2 Economic and Monetary Co-operation in Europe

Article 3 of the Treaty of Rome states that the economic policies of member-states shall be co-ordinated; that administrative and commercial laws shall be approximated 'to the extent necessary for the functioning of the Common Market', and that there shall be rules to prevent restrictive trading practices.

This article, which stipulates also that there shall be a common agricultural and transport policy, is the foundation stone of the EEC. It assumes that economic integration cannot be complete unless the economies of the Six are in time welded together and common rules apply among others to competition, company law, taxation, internal and external trading practices. In short, broad economic and monetary policies shall be co-ordinated in order to ensure a uniform harmonious development of the Community as a whole.

To achieve this, the Treaty of Rome set up an Economic and Social Committee of 101 members (Art. 193) and a Monetary Committee (Art. 105) with a consultative role. Later, a Short-term Economic Policy Committee was set up (1960) and also a Medium-term Economic Policy Committee (1964). All three committees can call on a variety of sub-committees to advise them, including the Committee of Central Bank Governors.

Thus the instruments for implementing common policies are not lacking. What is lacking is the will to implement them. Quite apart from difficulties which arise from the fact that the Germans are not committed planners as such whereas most other members of the Community are, governments have jealously guarded their right to pursue their own economic policies in the light of their own particular needs which vary widely from country to country. What they have admitted, of course, is that in a Community now linked by a Customs Union, a common external tariff, and common agricultural and transport policies, inflationary or deflationary pressures in any one of them are bound to affect the economies of the other members. They could hardly do less. But no state has yet been prepared to surrender powers which they consider indispensable to the proper functioning of government. This was particularly so in the case of de Gaulle's last government in France, which had to take emergency measures to deal with the consequences of the May–June riots and social unrest. The Commission, as guardian of the Rome Treaty, could do little more than acquiesce in the measures then taken to meet the situation and recommend that the import restrictions and export incentives introduced at the time and contrary to the terms of the Treaty should be rescinded as soon as possible.

Again, in the monetary field the Commission was only an observer of the dramatic events of November 1968, when the international monetary system was on the verge of collapse.

The need for closer monetary co-operation had constantly been stressed and the Commission had produced the Barre report on the subject. But individual governments considered that far too much was at stake politically, i.e. the revaluation of the D.-mark and the devaluation of the franc among other things, for the solution of these problems to be left to the Community and by implication to the Commission.

It is indeed in financial matters that co-operation is conspicuously lacking. National currencies have become the symbols of sovereignty to be defended for reasons of pride and prestige, and this is why proposals put forward by the Commission for linking the various currencies by fixed exchange rates have constantly been turned down. Ideally and logically, in an integrated economy, there should be a single currency and a European central bank but these are nowhere near acceptance.

The two staunchest defenders of parities have, ironically, been the French and the Germans. In November 1968 the French refused to devalue the franc while accepting a $2,000m. loan from the International Monetary Fund to defend it, and the Germans refused to upvalue the D.-mark while admitting that it was undervalued by introducing fiscal measures to reduce the external trade surplus (a 4 per cent tax relief on the value of imports and a tax burden of the same amount on exports and other monetary measures to make the hoarding of D.-marks unprofitable).

De Gaulle considered the defence of the franc a vital national interest and Professor Erhard, the former German Chancellor, is on record as having said that the national currency is an expression of the national will and independence. So long as these attitudes persist in the two major countries of the Six, there is little hope of achieving a common European monetary policy or a common approach to international monetary questions.

When the Six negotiated as a body in the various tariff-cutting rounds under GATT, their voice carried great weight. But on monetary problems they are divided. There is no common stand on the gold question, on the eurodollar question, on the question of exchange rates, or on the needs of the European capital market. And this arises because there is no common attitude towards the roles of sterling and the dollar and the problem of world liquidity. When de Gaulle was the dominant figure in Europe and the French franc was riding high (up to 1967) a determined attempt was made to oust the dollar and the pound from their roles as reserve currencies because the General argued that this gave both countries privileges which they did not deserve. It made them bankers to the world and gave them the power to dictate financial policy in the International Monetary Fund, the Group of Ten, and the Bank for International Settlements. There was no shortage of liquidity. The trouble was that it was of the wrong type – American deficits on balance of payments. In other words world trade was being financed by the American dollar with the pound trailing behind.

To smash this stranglehold confidence in the dollar had to be broken (confidence in the pound was fast disappearing of its own accord) and the way to do it was to start selling dollars for gold (at the official US buying price of $35 an ounce) and at the same time advocate an increase in the official price of gold. This would increase the value of the gold reserves held by various countries – among the major holders was France – and automatically devalue the dollar. This would have to be rectified by a general realignment of currencies which would favour the franc and correspondingly weaken the two major reserve currencies.

This policy – part of the General's overall onslaught on the American way of life – achieved only a limited success. It got no support from the British or the Germans and the Americans dug their toes in and weathered the storm. Their main argument against a revaluation of gold was political. They saw no reason why, in one easy move, they should revalue Russian reserves of the precious metal or give the South Africans – the world's largest gold producers – an added boost to their economy which was already extremely sound. The South Africans, however, argued with some force that it was rapidly becoming uneconomic to mine gold at the official price.

The Americans further insisted that it was not part of their policy to reward the currency speculators who had hoarded gold against the dollar and the pound. They took strong action on all fronts. They forced the International Monetary Fund to bend its rules so as to prevent the South African Government from selling gold to it at the official price – which was its undoubted right under the articles of the Fund – and at the same time wound up the London gold pool through which the central banks had agreed to supply the open market. They set up the two-tier system, the aim of which was to force the free-market price down. To do this, they obtained the agreement of the major central banks not to buy South African newly mined gold. In this way the South Africans would be forced to sell on the free market, thereby forcing the price down and the speculators would get their fingers burnt. This policy was largely successful and to the amazement of bullion dealers the free market for gold stood up remarkably well, whereas most of the experts had forecast its rapid collapse.

Lastly, the Americans forced acceptance by all the leading governments including, reluctantly, the French, of their scheme for special drawing rights on the I M F to create supplementary reserves – 'paper gold' as the pessimists called them – in order to finance the continuing expansion of international trade. This move effectively, although probably not permanently, halted the debate on the merits of raising the official price of gold. Certainly speculators slowly drifted away from the free gold market.

The Americans, under the then Secretary of the Treasury, Henry J. Fowler, were already winning the battle when the French position collapsed overnight, following the May–June riots of 1968. There is nothing to suggest that it will be renewed under M. Georges Pompidou, whose main concern when he took over was not to attack other peoples' currencies but to defend his own – in the event by devaluing it.

EUROPEAN CAPITAL MARKET

The tradition that currencies are a symbol of sovereignty may linger on for years but the need to co-ordinate the monetary policies of the Six in order to increase the flow of capital into European industry will remain. The shortage of ready capital for expansion is one of the greatest weaknesses of industry in Europe. There is no capital market on anything like the scale of those existing in London and New York. This is because the stock exchanges of Paris, Milan, Frankfurt, Amsterdam, Brussels, etc. are small beer compared with the London Stock Exchange and Wall Street.

Traditionally, no one on the Continent invests in equities to the same extent as do the British and Americans. Hence the narrowness of the markets. The small investor in France and Italy – and even in Germany – has an inborn dislike of financial institutions, which he usually associates with the professional 'insider' who brings off 'coups' at the expense of the amateur investor. He prefers to put his money into savings banks or on deposit with the equivalent of the British clearing banks where he is certain of getting a fixed return with no speculative element involved. Or, if he is less advanced than his neighbour, he will try to buy gold and hoard it under his mattress. Whatever the method chosen, the aim is extreme liquidity, i.e. he can take his money out at any time. Unless the banks or savings institutions invest his money in the Stock Exchange, it does not reach the normal capital market at all. In France and Italy, until very recently, the banks invested his money in government securities or in loans for officially sponsored housing projects. In Italy the Government virtually insisted that the commercial banks should hold large portfolios of government funds, which the authorities then used for public expenditure. In both countries, and in France particularly, the merchant banks became lenders of money to industry in the form of short-, medium-, and long-term loans. They thus got a grip on industry, which had to go to them because of the inadequacy of the stock exchange.

In France, furthermore, the banks for years laboured under the ridiculous rigidities of the law, which made a clear distinction between the clearing banks (*banques de dépôts*) and the merchant banks (*banques d'affaires*). The former were forbidden to make medium- or long-term loans and to invest in private companies and thus were of little use to industry, although they had the money to invest, whereas the merchant banks could do all these things but very often lacked the large-scale funds needed to modernize and rebuild French industry despite the fact they had a fair sprinkling on their boards of the '*deux cents familles*', who traditionally ran France. What is more, they were not allowed to open branch offices.

The result was that the clearing banks invariably channelled their deposits into government funds or officially sponsored housing loans. Banks generally were obsessed with the need for liquidity and rushed to rediscount all credit with the Banque de France, thus raising the cost of lending to industry. In any case the largest clearing banks were all nationalized after the 1939–45 war in the wave of left-wing opposition to capitalist régimes. They included the Banque Nationale de Paris, the Crédit Lyonnais, the Société Générale, the Banque de Paris et des Pays Bas, Banque de l'Union Parisienne CFCB, and the Banque de l'Indochine. They accounted for about three fifths of the total resources of the banking community.

When M. Pompidou became Prime Minister under de Gaulle, all this changed. He quickly saw the need to reform the whole of the banking system so that it could perform its proper function of supplying capital to industry in preparation for the 1 July 1968 deadline when the Customs Union between the Six came into operation. French industry would then face the full blast of competition from the other five and would need far more investment capital than could be provided by the old method of self-financing and would have to place far greater reliance on the stock exchange for new sources of capital.

The clearing banks can now take up to a 20 per cent equity share in companies and the merchant banks can canvass the small saver who still goes for the savings bank or *caisse d'épargne* type of investment or just leaves his little nest-egg on deposit.

The next problem was to revive a sagging and discredited Paris stock exchange, where the number of quotations is pathetically small compared with the London Stock Exchange, as it is in the other continental *bourses*. Few banks and commercial undertakings invested in equities, and unit trusts and pension funds are in their infancy in France. The big banks and insurance companies, who were naturally conservative with large sums to invest, played safe and went for government securities where little investment analysis was required.

Furthermore, self-financing by firms was becoming increasingly more difficult because of shortening profit margins caused by the higher wage-cost factor. The May–June riots in 1968 added anything between 10 and 14 per cent to production costs and the wage-cost factor is likely to continue to rise owing to the shortage of labour, which will probably get worse rather than better in the late 1970s. Companies will therefore have far less to plough back.

Memories of money lost on the Paris Bourse go far back to before the First World War to the Panama Canal scandal and the Stavisky affair between the wars. And the take-over battle between the old-established industrial firm of Saint-Gobain and the thrusting glass manufacturer Boussois-Souchon-Neuvesel did nothing to revive the confidence of the public in the stock market.

Nor did the somewhat savage battle between the Banque de Paris et des Pays Bas and the Compagnie Financière de Suez, for the control of the Crédit Industriel et Commercial (C I C), one of the largest of the deposit banks still in private hands, which was closely connected with regional industry through its thousand-odd branches throughout France.

There was so much in-fighting between these two houses that the Government eventually had to step in and force a truce, all of which was very embarrassing, particularly as the Banque de Paris et des Pays Bas was a nationalized institution.

In 1968 the French Government set up, under M. Pierre Chatenet, the Commission des Opérations de Bourse, which combined the general functions of a watch-dog committee, take-over panel and public relations office to breathe new life into the Paris Bourse. Also among its tasks was the enforcement of greater discipline among companies and stock-brokers and greater observance of the rules governing company accounts and auditing. One of the major obstacles to new investment was that far less was revealed in company accounts than is the case in Britain and America. This has now been changed. Within a few months of taking office the Commission des Opérations de Bourse called more than 170 firms to order for non-observance of the rules. It now vets company prospectuses.

Another move to improve the attraction of equities took place when the Government put a ceiling of $8\frac{1}{2}$ per cent interest on debenture loans in April 1969. Even so it is going to take a long time for the improved image of the Bourse to get through to the small investor, who will probably opt increasingly for the unit trust or contractual pension-fund type of investment.

In Germany and the Benelux countries, however, the problems are rather different. In Belgium and Holland they are of smaller dimensions and capital can be more readily found than it can in France and Italy. In Germany, the most powerful industrial nation in Europe, the commercial banks are in complete command and have close trading-links with manufacturers. The three main ones – the Deutsche Bank, the Dresdner Bank, and the Commerzbank – do everything from representing shareholders at company meetings by proxy to acting as brokers and advisers on mergers in firms in which they have a shareholding and whose equity issues they handle. Until recently they were even allowed to buy and sell shares under the counter, as it were, with other banks, thus bypassing the stock market.

Eventually these almost *carte-blanche* privileges were challenged and some curtailment has been accepted. Even so, like the French and German commercial firms, they contrived to reveal as little as possible to shareholders about their affairs, and by means of watertight secrecy they arranged mergers and take-over bids and then presented shareholders with a virtual *fait accompli*.

They have, however, under pressure of public opinion, agreed to curb certain activities which in Britain, for instance, would be considered highly improper. As in France and Italy, the small investor still has a lurking suspicion of high finance and prefers to put his money into savings institutions, and unit trusts.

However, the German capital market has expanded rapidly. In 1968 it was opened to foreign borrowers as a means of cutting down the embarrassing balance-of-payments surpluses. But like the Swiss market, it provides only limited semi-international facilities and the commercial banks can easily get indigestion if there is a rush to raise funds in Germany. Indeed, Professor Karl Schiller, Economics Minister under the Kiesinger Coalition Government, was not at all sure that the German banks were not exporting capital badly needed for regional development at home.

In Italy the central bank, the Banca d'Italia, is all-powerful. The governor has wide statutory powers which make him a virtual dictator of the Italian economy. More often than not the Italian Treasury does his bidding and he rules the banking community with more legal authority than the Bank of England possesses to perform the same task.

The commercial banks are only allowed to make medium-term loans to industry but they are engaged on a lucrative financing of the export drive. The central bank expects them to subscribe heavily to government funds and government-guaranteed loans, and it has ways of persuading them to do so. Thus the government gets much of the money which would otherwise go into the private sector. However, the government through the state-owned I R I (Istituto per la Ricostruzione Industriale), has a finger in every industrial pie in the country and therefore feels entitled to swallow up a fair proportion of funds flowing from the private sector.

This brief survey of capital markets among the Six illustrates quite clearly that nowhere do proper conditions exist for a flourishing European capital market. In most of them governments and nationalized institutions have priority in raising capital and they tend to monopolize the market where they enjoy special privileges such as tax exemptions, low rates of commission payable to banks for floating issues, and preferential treatment; all this enables them to jump the queue if necessary.

The Treaty of Rome calls for the free movement of capital between the Six. But such movement is impeded by a variety of barriers including double taxation, withholding taxes, and discriminatory taxation of dividend income whereby relief is granted only to residents or to holders of domestic shares. Control of foreign investment in France is severe. As part of the Gaullist policy of keeping foreign capital out of France, and particularly American capital, the French Government in January 1967 decreed that all direct foreign investment in France should be subject to the approval of the French Economics Ministry. The decree covered all new investment and increases of existing holdings. Approval was at the discretion of the Ministry and this power was exercised to prevent Fiat from taking a larger shareholding in Citroën.

The European Commission protested to the French Government that its ruling should not apply to Community firms under the Treaty of Rome. The French replied that most American subsidiaries in the Common Market were Community companies in law and that the American parent company could therefore bypass the restriction on a technicality.

Up to 1969 exchange controls on capital transactions were still in force in France and in Italy. Until most, or all, of these restrictions are removed or severely curtailed there will not be a European capital market worthy of the name. In March 1969 the Commission submitted proposals to the Council of Ministers calling for the progressive dismantling of controls and restrictions which prevented Community countries from making full use of their combined capital resources. It did not suggest an immediate return to 'total and uncontrolled liberty' in capital transactions but it did propose the abolition of the withholding tax in all countries.

But like so many proposals submitted by the Commission it fell on stony ground because integration in monetary matters, which is essential to full economic integration, means surrendering the last sovereignty and this no country was prepared to do at this stage.

THE EURODOLLAR

Meanwhile, on the international money market, the eurodollar – or better, the Euro-market for US dollars – has stolen the limelight. Eurodollars are US dollars which have not been sent back to America although, as Sir George Bolton, Chairman of the Bank of London and South America and one of the prime movers in this market, has pointed out, 'in all cases where a eurodollar deposit is made or repaid, a transfer of funds takes place either in or between banks in the USA'. It is essentially a book-keeping transaction. Eurodollars are quaintly known as 'non-resident' dollars, i.e. dollars owned by somebody living outside the USA. The London branches of American banks, where virtually all the business is transacted, qualify as 'non-residents'. Until the law is altered in the USA, dollars that have not been repatriated can change hands – and do so very swiftly – at rates of interest above those permitted in the USA and which in the spring of 1969 soared to unbelievable heights.

The market emerged in the late 1950s largely as a result of the American balance-of-payments deficits caused by progressive involvements in Far-Eastern wars. By stages it has grown from overnight money to short-term loans from one month to one year; medium-term loans from approximately two to seven years, and long-term Euro-bond issues of from ten to twenty years.

It is an expensive market for the average borrower because the dollar, despite some hard knocks in recent years, is still an eminently acceptable international currency, and when the Vietnam war is finally wound up, it will become even more so.

The market is an integral part of the foreign-exchange markets for spot and forward transactions. It is a highly sophisticated mechanism. It is used extensively by leading world banks who freely deposit and re-deposit currency with one another when adjusting their liquidity positions. This is done without any form of security beyond that provided by the impeccable standing of the banks concerned, and at rates of interest which vary according to the official rates on the London and New York money markets. But there is little official supervision of it beyond the somewhat vague control exercised by the Bank for International Settlements.

The long-term Euro-bond market has developed considerable stability and suits the big and influential borrower. It has been extremely useful to American firms, which could not raise funds in America for development projects abroad because of the severe restrictions on the export of capital imposed by the U S Treasury on balance-of-payments grounds.

The medium-term market is a relative late-comer. It is in the hands of some very large consortia of international banks. It suits the firm which needs short-term finance for a specific project, such as the construction of new factories at home or abroad, or modernization and expansion of existing installations, etc. It is in the hands of five large groups of banks, all of which contain a fair sprinkling of major British, American, and continental finance institutions. In fact, nearly all the biggest names in world banking are involved. They form the following consortia: Midland and International Bank Ltd, based in London; the International Commercial Bank also based in London; the Banque Européenne de Crédit à Moyen Terme, with headquarters in Brussels; the Société Financière Européenne, centred on Paris, and the Compagnie Internationale de Crédit à Moyen Terme, which operates from Lausanne.

Their market is likely to prove the most durable, given the financial requirements of the vast majority of European industries, which do not measure up to the international giants, but which nevertheless play an important role in expanding the economies of the Six and other countries of Western Europe. Their loans are not restricted to dollars and they will in fact provide loans in any currency chosen by the borrower including what are known as 'parallel loans', i.e. loans floated in different currencies so as to appeal to the maximum number of subscribers with the minimum of risk. Their assets are so vast that they can lend anything up to the $1m. to $9m. mark.

It is the short-end of the market which is the most volatile and the most controversial. Some economists and bankers have considered it a plague on the international monetary scene. Others have called it the international currency *par excellence* which is above local politics and governmental controls, having no nationality (beyond its basic American origin) and going to the highest bidder whoever he might be.

With sterling's role as an international currency inevitably in decline they argue that the dollar is the one currency which is absolutely universal and they are supported in their argument by the fact that the Bretton Woods agreement in 1944 specifically mapped out this world role for it. And as such it has sustained virtually the whole of the development of world trade, for which the pound today barely accounts for twenty-five per cent.

But European governments, in particular, have had very different views. First and foremost, they have accused it of drawing funds away from their own modest capital markets and generally playing havoc with the normal foreign exchange markets.

With some justification, the British, French, and Italians have complained that it has forced interest rates up in their own countries thereby depressing their gilt-edged markets and directly interfering with their national economic policies.

They have accused the Americans, as the ultimate owners of the dollars, of exporting inflation which they should have cured by adequate fiscal measures at home instead of driving American firms to call back eurodollars to make up for the shortage of funds in their own country caused by the ceiling on deposit interest rates (regulation Q of the U S Federal Reserve Board).

The mad scramble for eurodollars which took place between American banks in London in May–June 1969 pushed the interest rate on three months eurodollar deposits up to the preposterous level of 13 per cent. This, coupled with the high rate on U S Treasury bills and the record $8\frac{1}{2}$ per cent prime lending rate (the rate charged to their most credit-worthy customers) by the American banks pushed the $3\frac{1}{2}$ per cent British War Loan down to an all-time low of £36 giving a yield of over $9\frac{1}{2}$ per cent. This even depressed the Euro-bond market.

According to M. Louis Camu, President of the Banque de Bruxelles, the general estimate of eurodollars lent and borrowed is $37,000m. – an increase of 30 per cent during the first half of 1969 alone.

Little wonder that many European governments have had to take defensive measures by restricting foreign-exchange dealings and curbing the outflow of funds badly needed on their own domestic capital markets. Many of them, including the UK Government, put up bank rate (or re-discount rate) as a direct consequence of the rush on eurodollars.

But worst of all, the eurodollar market has provided a highly efficient vehicle for currency speculators. Those who gambled on a revaluation of the West German currency in 1969 – and won – took nearly $4,999m. out of the market.

By the summer of 1969 the US authorities were fully conscious of the damage this market was doing to the European economies and looked at various steps they could take to prevent it happening again. Eventually they removed the $6\frac{1}{4}$ per cent ceiling on deposit interest rates and the anomaly whereby eurodollars were not subject to the Federal Board's reserve requirements by making them carry a 10 per cent reserve.

Valid as these criticisms may be of American monetary policy, it does not alter the fact that European governments themselves must take a large share of the blame for the inadequacy of their capital markets because so many of them seldom balance their budgets, resort to deficit financing at the expense of the banks, and therefore of the public, and take money which should properly be used for the financing of industry.

In this way they have depressed their own stock markets as the Common Market stock exchanges share index shows. Between 1958 and 1961 it went up from 100 to 227 and declined steadily thereafter, the biggest falls being recorded in Italy, France, and Germany in that order.

Apart from the eurodollar and sterling, there are two other main sources of capital – D-marks and Swiss francs. But neither market is satisfactory for the long-term financing of trade in Western Europe. The Swiss banks make small loans to foreign borrowers but do not claim to be a major source of capital.

The Germans have become exporters of capital willy-nilly as a convenient method of offsetting embarrassingly large foreign-trade surpluses, According to the Bundesbank's annual report in 1968 capital exports represented 20 per cent of total domestic formation of money capital.

Clearly, exporting capital merely to balance one's foreign accounts is an unsatisfactory foundation for the enlargement of the European capital market. Most of the money goes to the United States in any case, as portfolio investment, and is not channelled into industry there, nor – until quite recently – into industry in Europe.

Moreover, not everybody in Europe relishes the prospect of the D-mark replacing the American dollar in the financing of European and world trade. Deutschmark colonization could become every bit as embarrassing and dangerous as dollar colonization after the World War I and sterling colonization before that. But in 1969 it was official policy in Bonn (although not with the Bundesbank) to encourage West German industry to make direct investments abroad, something which up to then it had only done spasmodically.

Before the Germans went into the capital export business, in the late 1960s, the French had toyed with the idea of re-establishing Paris as the centre of the European capital market – a position it had once enjoyed in the nineteenth century. The franc was probably the strongest currency in the world at the time (1965–6) and it was part of de Gaulle's battle against the 'Anglo-Saxons' that he should attempt to set Paris up as a rival to the City of London. This was, of course, wistful thinking and nothing more was heard of the idea, particularly after the 1968 May–June riots.

THE CITY OF LONDON

No European financial centre is likely in the foreseeable future to challenge the City of London as a capital-raising centre – a function it has been performing for centuries with great expertise, although New York is now laying serious claim to this position of eminence. London still boasts unrivalled commercial and financial institutions, which handle the bulk of the world's trade in raw materials, precious metals, insurance, shipping, banking, and other services, and this wide experience would be at the service of the Continental countries if Britain joined the Common Market.

True, there have been some setbacks to capital-raising in London. Because of economic austerity, a declining stock market, and extremely high international interest rates, several issues flopped badly in 1969 – even the convertibles such as Philips sterling–guilder issue and International Standard Electric's sterling–dollar loan, despite the fact that the latter provided British investors with a back-door way of avoiding payment of the investment dollar premium, which at the time hovered around 30 per cent. In all, by July 1969 underwriters were left with £193m. on their hands.

Even so, this does not detract from the attractiveness and efficiency of the City as a money-raiser. Increasingly, however, the City will be left with the expertise but not the money, as more British savings go into British industry via unit trusts, etc., and what is left into the Commonwealth. At the moment the City is doing a thriving business in the eurodollar market because of its close links not only with the four largest American banks – the Bank of America, Chase Manhattan, First National City, and Morgan Guaranty – but with some of the lesser ones like United California Bank and Crocker-Citizens National. This business can last several years and the American banks which invaded the City in recent years are here to stay. They have even opened branches in Birmingham and Manchester (Bank of America). They are here because they know that London is the ideal centre for branching out into Europe and into certain parts of the Commonwealth. But with Britain's declining financial power and sterling's dwindling use as a reserve currency, the City could easily become an appendage of the American banking community and, as such, is looked upon with some suspicion by certain elements in the Common Market. De Gaulle used to taunt us with being 'travelling salesmen for the Americans' and America's Trojan horse in Europe. Little time was wasted in countering these charges but it is nevertheless true that the City is faced with the prospect of still closer links with the USA, leading to virtual dependence, or of retaining some independence by becoming the financial centre of an enlarged European Community. This prospect does not displease all financial leaders in the Common Market, many of whom have great admiration for the City. Indeed, no other central-bank governor could do what Lord Cromer did as Governor of the Bank of England during the predevaluation sterling crisis of November 1964, when he picked up the phone and raised loans totalling $2,240m. within a few hours from the leading West European central bankers, most of whom he had known personally for years.

M. Jacques Rueff, for years de Gaulle's *éminence grise* in financial matters and the man who first put the French franc back into the top drawer of currencies, is on record as having said:

I always live under the impression that Britain is the country with the highest financial tradition and the best equipment in the field of credit. The London market is a model and for thirty years I have been fighting for the introduction of its practice in France.

Perhaps M. Rueff may be instrumental in grafting the City on to the Common Market's financial structure – not as a liability but as an asset.

In an economically, and therefore financially, integrated Europe, the thorny problems of exchange rates, international monetary pressures, the price of gold, balance-of-payments deficits and surpluses, sterling balances, etc. could be tackled with far greater chances of success than they could be in isolation, in an atmosphere of mutual distrust and suspicion with some nations willing to co-operate and others striking outmoded nationalistic attitudes.

3 Structure of Industry

Apart from a handful of giants, industry in the Common Market is fragmented, and even the giants are not very large by American or even British standards. In steel, for instance, the sales of the US Steel Corporation are more than three times those of the four German firms, Thyssen, Hoesch, Krupp, and Mannesmann, and in the world league the German firms come well behind the Americans and the British Steel Corporation. In mechanical engineering (motor cars apart) there is not one Common Market firm in the world's top ten. Nor is there in oil, if one takes into account that Royal Dutch/Shell is Anglo-Dutch. In electrical engineering the Dutch Philips Lamps and the German Siemens are sixth and seventh respectively behind the American leaders and the British G E C/E E. In chemicals, however, where Britain's I C I takes second place behind America's Du Pont de Nemours and is just in front of another US firm, Union Carbide, E E C countries are well placed with Montecatini/Edison (Italy) fourth, Hoescht (Germany) fifth, Bayer (Germany) sixth, Rhône-Poulenc/Péchiney/Saint-Gobain/Progil (France) seventh, and Badische Anilin- & Soda-Fabrik, (BASF), Wintershall (Germany), eighth.

The Common Market's best performance is in motor cars, where Fiat, Volkswagen, and Renault/Peugeot come immediately behind the three American giants, General Motors, Ford, and Chrysler and in front of the British Leyland Motor Corporation. But, apart from these few examples of European firms taking a place among the top ten, and with the notable exception of Germany, industry in the Common Market countries is unorganized and with no great reputation for efficiency. Some of the largest groupings belong, paradoxically, to the state.

There is a tradition of state ownership in Italy and France, for instance, which arose from particular economic circumstances and was not always politically motivated. The state in both countries gradually assumed responsibility for running the essential services and public utilities in keeping with the times. But in Italy the depression of the 1930s was directly responsible for the setting up of the state-controlled industrial reorganization corporation – the Istituto per la Ricostruzione Industriale – which is involved in all major industries. It is not, however, entirely owned by the state. In some of its branches private capital can amount to as much as 40 to 50 per cent.

No political party in Italy since the fall of Fascism and the Monarchy has ever thought of dismantling this vast empire, mainly because it is highly successful and constitutes a convenient tool for the injection of government funds into industry. Nor has its existence ever been questioned on politico–economic grounds. No one has any doctrinaire views about the Italian state being the majority shareholder. Similarly in France the nationalization issue has never been the bone of contention it has in Britain. No party thinks of denationalizing the banks and insurance companies which have come under public control since the end of 1939–45 war. The Régie Renault, entirely state-owned, is one of the most thrusting and efficient producers of motor cars in the world. Yet control by the state is remote.

The Director-General is appointed by the government but the day-to-day running of the firm is left very much in the hands of the management. Renault, in fact, is the barometer of French industry. It is the largest single industrial enterprise in France and its plants and factories are among the most highly automated in Europe.

Thus, over and above its role in the provision of services, the state in many countries in the Common Market has a powerful stake in a sector of the economy where it competes directly with private enterprise. This situation is unknown in Britain where coal and steel are state monopolies. The nearest equivalent is the government's 43 to 44 per cent shareholding in British Petroleum although the City has often complained of state interference in the private sector through the activities of the Labour Government's own Industrial Reorganization Corporation.

In the public sector alone Commission statistics show that within the EEC state-owned enterprises are responsible for about 25 per cent of all productive investment, 10 per cent of employment, and 9 per cent of total turnover in industry and services. Public transport and telecommunications account for more than half the public sector in all member-countries.

In its dual capacity as a purveyor of services and a large employer in industry, the state is thus in a position to exert a powerful and direct influence on every sector of the economy and this is indeed the role governments have played in countries other than Germany, where the ruling philosophy is very much one of free enterprise in a liberal social market economy.

In this capacity governments, particularly in France, have also taken a strong hand in reshaping, reorganizing, and modernizing industry so that it could withstand the fiercer competition expected in every country of the Six after the Customs Union came into force in July 1968.

At the beginning of that year the Commission submitted guidelines for the modernization of industry in the EEC to the Council of Ministers. It emphasized the need for all governments to avoid forms of state aid which distorted free markets and which gave an unfair competitive edge to national or nationalized industries. It stated specifically that governments

should play only a limited part in modernizing industries. Public aid should be confined to helping, first, a small number of particularly promising growth industries where the costs of research are too high and too risky for the firms themselves, and secondly, those industries facing severe structural difficulties which could do serious social and economic damage.

The Commission added that governments 'should not try to retard the contraction of declining industries, but should concentrate on retraining the workers and finding them new jobs'. Mergers and regroupings were an essential part of modernization and governments should take steps to improve the flow of savings into capital investment.

As far as the Italian Government was concerned, it needed no reminding of the benefits of concentration. Italian industry was already highly concentrated through the I R I and the other state corporations, the Ente Nazionale Idrocarburi (ENI) and the Azienda Generale Italiana Petroli (AGIP) with their vast interests in oil, oil refining, natural gas, and petrochemicals.

The state also had a monopoly of steel-making through the Finsider group of companies, which form part of the IRI. It later acquired, also through IRI and the other state trading agency ENI, a controlling interest in Montecatini-Edison, the giant private chemical and electrical concern, after some rather obscure dealings on the Milan stock exchange which caused a storm among shareholders at the annual general meeting of the firm in 1968.

Furthermore, the state owned a car company (Alfa Romeo) and the three largest commercial banks in Italy (Banca Commerciale Italiana, Credito Italiano, and Banco di Roma), and was the prime mover in all public-works projects now being carried out by government agencies known as *strumenti imprenditoriali*, modelled on other agencies which had achieved much success in the speedy building of some of the motorways. This new form of government-sponsored operation was designed, incidentally, to overcome the extraordinary delays caused by bureaucratic hurdles before the simplest project could get through Parliament and past the various government departments, most of which work in slow motion during the dog days of Rome and the sweltering heat of the Mezzogiorno.

In France the need to streamline industry had long been recognized. The facts, indeed, were alarming. French industry, in the words of a governmental committee's reports, just 'didn't measure up' to the standards required in international competition. The country was heavily under-industrialized and industry itself under-capitalized. It contributed only 47 per cent to gross domestic product against 53 per cent in Western Germany and 49 per cent in the United Kingdom.

The contribution of the services, i.e. the unproductive side, on the other hand, at over 51 per cent, was the highest in the Common Market. Only three firms had turnovers of more than $1,000m. per year compared with twenty-nine in the whole of Europe and eighty in the USA. Industries which should be doing most of the exporting – chemicals, mechanical and electrical engineering – represented only 38 per cent of the total export effort whereas among the other industrialized nations, they averaged 65 per cent. Only 1·9 per cent of GNP was devoted to research and development as against 2·3 per cent in the UK and 3·4 per cent in the USA. Belatedly attempts were made to retrieve the situation: France's Fifth Economic Plan allotted 2·4 to 2·5 per cent of GNP to research and development in the 1970 Budget. In September 1969, this was raised to 3 per cent. Because of recurring wage increases, production costs were the highest in Europe. Between 1963 and 1968 wage costs in France had risen by 23 per cent as against 22 per cent in the Netherlands, 17 per cent in Great Britain and Belgium, 11 per cent in the USA, 7 per cent in West Germany and 5 per cent in Italy.

The report pointed to old-fashioned ideas in administration, general inefficiency, and lack of streamlining in the face of rising competition. What was needed were thorough-going reforms aimed at revitalizing top managements and above all – and this only the government could provide – greater incentives to investment through higher profit margins and better access to new capital. The Fifth Plan (1966–70) suggested that firms should be able to supply 70 per cent of their capital needs from their own resources. Most of them could hardly raise 65 per cent in this way.

The measure of France's backwardness industrially was startlingly revealed in figures given by M. Francois Peugeot of motor car fame and President of the French Federation of Mechanical Engineering firms: if France's industrial weight in engineering (electrical and mechanical) and electronics – a fair yardstick to judge performance in the world industrial league table – is put at 100, the USA comes out at 1,230, Japan at 183, Western Germany at 178, the United Kingdom at 159, and Italy at 41.

All this had been known for years. But nothing had been done about it because of recurring political crises, largely connected with the liquidation of the old French Empire, which left each successive government weaker than its predecessor. It took de Gaulle eight years to get down to the problem of rejuvenating an antiquated economy based on family ties and class loyalties which were often stronger than the national interest. French industry had survived because it had been protected by tariffs for three quarters of a century.

The problem was tackled from two angles. Mergers and concentration went hand in hand with regional development. Financial incentives were provided for old and new industries moving into under-developed areas outside Paris. Graded subsidies were granted according to the area chosen. The plan applied equally to services such as banks and insurance in the hope that they would shift some of the burden of their operations away from Paris.

Broadly speaking, regional development was based on the natural geographical areas of France. The North was centred on the Seine valley with its natural sea outlet through Le Havre and the South on a new inland waterway system comprising the Rhône and Saône valleys, and the West around a new industrial area to be designated later. The South-West, with Bordeaux as its centre, presented less pressing problems. The Eastern regions were to have improved links with the Seine valley.

Plans are well advanced for the Rhône to be flanked by a canal by 1976 to enable it to take a large share of the traffic originating in the new industrial area to be built in the region of Fos, to the west of Marseilles. Goods that are not exported via Marseilles will go north into the heart of Europe by the new waterway system which will also provide a canal link between Lyons and Dijon-Auxonne.

The problem of industrialization in the West was particularly urgent because of the politically dangerous Breton home-rule movement, which towards the end of de Gaulle's reign became increasingly militant and rebellious. Disaffection was spread in other areas of France by 30,000 migrant agricultural workers every year, who set up Breton nationalist cells in all the major cities of France and even abroad. Strict control of development in the Paris area would help to push new industries into the other regions.

Under special emergency powers granted by the French Parliament in 1967 de Gaulle announced increased investment grants for firms in the poorer regions, tax relief on earnings received from abroad, and on a revaluation of assets following mergers, and a highly controversial profit-sharing scheme between workers and employers was made compulsory, although workers would not receive any profits for the first five years.

A rash of mergers followed. The most important were in the steel industry, where firms received special subsidies. De Wendel et Cie., one of the great names in French steel, merged with Sidelor which itself was the result of a merger between two equally famous names – the Pont-à-Mousson group and the Société Mosellane de Sidérurgie. Between them they are responsible for about 35 per cent of total French steel production. An important case of vertical integration in the steel industry was Usinor's controlling interest in Vallourec, the latter producing about 850,000 tons of tubes a year – 80 per cent of total tube output in France. The mergers in steel were clearly intended to help the French withstand strong competition from Germany and Italy.

Pont-à-Mousson, which was a holding company, hived off most of its steel-making interests when it joined forces with the Société Mosellane de Sidérurgie to form Sidelor. It then concentrated on heavy engineering and housing. In July 1969 it was taken over by Saint-Gobain which had just fought a costly take-over battle against a lesser rival, Boussois-Souchon-Neuvesel. The finance company, Compagnie Financière de Suez, has a 20·1 per cent interest in Saint-Gobain and its President, M. Jacques George Picot, one of France's leading take-over specialists who helped Saint-Gobain fight off the B S N challenge, has assumed the lead in a vast conglomeration of steel, chemical, man-made fibres, oil, and construction industries. Through mergers and cross-holdings, the biggest names in French industry are now closely linked: de Wendel/Sidelor/Pont-à-Mousson/Péchiney/Saint-Gobain/Progil/Rhône-Poulenc. Like the Italian I R I, they have a finger in every major industrial pie, with countless opportunities for 'commercial' arrangements which might cause eyebrows to be raised in Brussels.

Other mergers, or joint operating agreements, concerned electronics – Thomson-Brandt/CS F, Compagnie de Télégraphie sans Fil – and heavy electrical engineering where Thomson-Brandt together with C G E (Compagnie Générale d'Électricité) and Alsthom signed a close co-operation agreement, with the blessing of the French Government after the latter had vetoed a take-over bid by the American Westinghouse of another large French electrical firm, Jeumont-Schneider. This agreement took co-operation one stage further after Alsthom and C G E in 1965 had formed three joint subsidiaries.

In the field of domestic appliances a further move by Thomson-Brandt took over the ailing Claret; this put Thomson-Brandt in second place in Europe with 650,000 units behind the Italian firm Ignis (850,000), and in front of two other Italian firms Zanussi (550,000), and Indesit (450,000), and before the German Siemens-Bosch (550,000) and A E G/Linde (300,000). Sharp, almost cut-throat competition on the French market in domestic appliances brought about this merger. In textiles Dollfuss-Mieg and the holding company Pricel merged (combined turnover £100m.). Also, Agache-Willot acquired a 43 per cent share in another textile firm, Saint Frères, and then swallowed up two retail outlets – the well-known stores, La Belle Jardinière and Au Bon Marché – achieving a yearly turnover of more than £100m. In chemicals and petrochemicals the same trend to larger units was shown by the link-up between the semi-state-owned Total (Compagnie Française des Pétroles), E R A P (Entreprise de Recherches et d'Activités Pétrolières), and the S N P A (Société Nationale des Pétroles d'Aquitaine) through a joint subsidiary with a yearly turnover in petrochemicals of £56m. In shipping Paquet and Chargeurs Réunis merged, and in safe-making Bauche and Fichet came together to make the largest firm in this field in Europe. Further mergers were: Radio and T V sets (Cie. Générale d'Électricité, Lebon, and Lyonnaise des Eaux, with combined yearly production capacity of 200,000 sets); heavy engineering and nuclear energy (Babcock & Wilcox, Fives-Lille-Cail, and Chantiers de l'Atlantique); aluminium (Péchiney/Tréfimetaux thus fully integrating the aluminium industry); motor cars (Citroën/Berliet and Renault/Peugeot); aviation (Dassault/Bréguet). Several other amalgamations or working arrangements were reached between insurance companies and banks, many of which are in any case nationalized.

Even so, apart from Péchiney/Saint-Gobain in glass, metals. and chemicals, Compagnie Française des Pétroles in oil, natural gas, and refining, Wendel/Sidelor and Usinor in steel, Ugine–Kuhlmann in metal manufacture, Rhône/Poulenc in man-made fibres, and Dassault in aircraft, French firms are small compared with the international giants in America, Japan, Britain, and Germany.

In West Germany concentration started immediately after the war with a considerable amount of American financial backing. But most German firms were already large by international standards, particularly in steel, although here again not even August Thyssen Hütte or Hoesch is a match for the American steel companies. Integration in steel with financial assistance from the government has been both vertical and horizontal, and the industry is among the most efficient in the world. Apart from steel, the major link in German industry up to 1969 was between Siemens and Allgemeine Elektricitäts-Gesellschaft-Telefunken, both agreeing to certain engineering links without actually merging. Their combined turnover, however, at about £1,400m. a year is not far short of the Italian I R I (£1,486m.), and higher than their British rivals G E C/E E (over £900m. a year).

Another major concentration was between B A S F and Wintershall, two chemical and fertilizer giants, with a combined yearly turnover of £760m. in 1968. Other mergers in the offing in 1969 were between Chemische Werke Huels and Bayer or Hoescht, probably the former.

As a deliberate attempt to ward off co-operation between German oil firms and the Compagnie Française des Pétroles, the Bonn Government sponsored a consortium of eight oil companies and gave them a grant of £60m. to enable them to buy exploration rights and start prospecting in various parts of the world.

The mergers in steel, chemicals, and engineering have gone through with little or no opposition from the German Anti-cartel Office which has been almost completely inactive since it was set up by law in 1957. A great debate preceded the passing of the act on whether mergers, either horizontal or vertical, or both, were a good or a bad thing but the argument fizzled out when the government and industry both favoured mammoth concentrations, particularly in steel and engineering. Even so, German law still stipulates that mergers involving firms employing more than 50,000 persons between them and with a combined turnover of more than DM.500m. must be registered with the Anti-cartel Office and they can only be stopped if they 'abuse dominant positions'. Sheer size has never worried the Germans. As a people they have invariably been on the side of the big battalions. And German firms are big, at least by European standards.

In the Benelux countries mergers and co-operation agreements have been on a relatively small scale and mainly in the steel and textile industries, although in March 1969 a major rationalization agreement was announced between the big Dutch textile and chemical group A K U (Algemene Kunstzijde Unie, N V) and the U C B (Union Chimique-Chemische Bedrijven), one of Belgium's largest chemical companies. The companies did not merge but exchanged divisions. The Dutch took over all but one of U C B's fibre plants in exchange for their cellulose film division. In steel the Royal Dutch Hoogovens reached a manufacturing agreement with the German giant, Hoesch, in return for a 14·5 per cent share in the enlarged capital of Hoesch.

A Commission study of the industrial needs of the Six showed conclusively that there were many fields where the small firm could operate more profitably than the large one. This was particularly so in trades like clothing, where fashion trends change rapidly and long production lines can lead to a loss-making operation, and in services where repairs and maintenance are of paramount importance. Furthermore, the study showed that the smaller firm was often better suited to the development of the poorer regions of the Common Market, where it might prove uneconomic to set up large industrial complexes but where the small firm, requiring little capital but much labour, could operate economically.

Although the Commission has in many cases, notably in steel, relaxed its earlier opposition to large-scale amalgamations because of the need for European industry to become competitive in international markets, it has made a point of protecting the smaller firm against the depredations of the larger groupings because of their overall importance to the economy. Figures produced by the French Confederation of Small- and Medium-sized Firms show that their contribution to total economic potential is high; in Italy about 70 per cent, in France 65 per cent, in West Germany 63 per cent, in Belgium 60 per cent, and in the Netherlands 50 per cent. Their importance has also been growing since the war in the U S A, where the figure is now between 56 and 58 per cent.

But the most important amalgamations of all – the cross-frontier ones – have barely begun; Community firms co-operate across the frontiers through manufacturing and sales agreements in the normal commercial way and banks and insurance firms conduct their intra-Community affairs in the time-honoured but slow-moving ways. Apart from the Agfa/Gevaert joint German–Belgian operation in the photographic components business, there have been no complete trans-frontier mergers of any size – certainly not of the size needed to compete successfully on an international scale. And this is not likely to happen until the Six agree to give merging firms a European company status which does away with all legal and fiscal impediments to a workable amalgamation.

Meanwhile, it is a handful of American firms which operate on an inter-Community basis. In cars General Motors, Chrysler, and Ford have a 20 per cent share of production in the Common Market (as against about 50 per cent in Britain). In computers, International Business Machines outshines all the others both in hardware and software. They are able to operate on this vast international scale because of the size of their home markets, swollen by government orders for defence, space research, etc.

And it is to the Americans that European firms have turned when they wanted to expand, or found themselves in financial difficulties, rather than to their own capital markets. The American firms were quick to seize their opportunities. They have long recognized Europe as a major growth area and are ready to step in in every country of the Six. Between 1957 and 1967 U S direct investment in the Common Market jumped from about $600m. a year to around $8,000m. a year, overtaking American investment in the U K by over $3,000m.

Generally speaking, keen Common Market industrialists welcome American capital and know-how much more than do governments, which are very wary of potential American dominant positions in industries working for defence, such as computers and electronic equipment. This was at the root of de Gaulle's battle – which he lost – to prevent Machines Bull, the French computer firm, from falling into the lap of the US General Electric Company. Some safeguards, however, are obviously necessary. Few businessmen on the continent would have agreed with Lord Keynes who answered 'no such luck,' when he was asked what the chances were of Britain's becoming the forty-ninth state.

What worries the Common Market countries is not so much the size of American investment but its selective nature. The vast majority of it goes to France and Germany and about half into manufacturing industry – in sectors where a high degree of technical know-how is needed.

However, except for France, most Community countries encourage foreign investment, particularly American. They offer a wide variety of inducements including government-backed loans on favourable terms, reduced interest rates, accelerated depreciation provisions and the carrying over of losses. And they will give special inducements and investment allowances and make special loans to firms willing to set themselves up in areas of low employment or in need of greater expansion.

Only in France have any serious steps been taken to curb the activities of American investors. Under de Gaulle the Government tightened up on the conditions which foreign investors must observe when setting up in France.

French law stipulates that no foreigner shall acquire more than a 20 per cent interest in a French firm without government permission. If a new company is formed then a certain number of directors must be French.

If control of existing companies passes out of French hands, approval of the transfer of shares may be withheld for a variety of reasons, not only connected with defence but with the future of industry in France and with plans the government may have for its reorganization and modernization. A touch of Gaullist economic nationalism was carried over to the Pompidou régime when the President vetoed the American Westinghouse's attempts to gain control of Jeumont Schneider, one of France's largest electrical engineering concerns. The argument in this case was that if control was lost to the Americans it would have a damaging effect on France's efforts to build up a French national nuclear industry.

On the other hand, if the investment is likely to contribute to the government's industrial and regional development plans with no ill-effects elsewhere, then favourable consideration may be given.

Professor Walter Hallstein, the Commission's President in 1965, summed up the E E C's attitude, when he said,

Restraint in direct American investments abroad would be helpful. A common attitude towards this problem within the Community is also needed, and we are working on it. Our purpose, of course, cannot be to keep direct investments out of our countries. Europe and the Community have derived great benefit from such investments. They have often contributed to more rapid progress and helped to put an end to the long years in which there was a shortage of capital in Europe. What is really needed is to avoid excess.

Much of the resentment at American economic penetration of Europe could have been avoided if individual governments in the Six had earlier adopted less nationalistic attitudes and concentrated on the overall interests of Europe as an integrated economic unit. This lack of integration coupled with Britain's exclusion has been the direct cause of Europe's indifferent performance in the field of technology.

4 The Technological Gap

Technological co-operation, 'a common policy in the field of research and technology, including the nuclear sector', was named in the report of the Common Market Commission (30 September 1967) on the British application as one of the four major issues to be negotiated before Britain's entry. The others were improvement in Britain's balance of payments; agreement on financing the Community's activities including the agricultural policy; agreement on the relationship with EFTA and the Commonwealth countries.

A month later Robert Marjolin, Vice President of the Commission, warned the European Parliament:

If the six European Community countries remain, as they probably have done for a generation, the world's main importers of discoveries and its main exporters of brains, they will be condemning themselves to a cumulative underdevelopment which will soon make their decline irrevocable.

An alarming technological lag was revealed in 1967 in a report by the Organization for Economic Co-operation and Development; this showed that the US spends six times as much on research and development as the EEC and three times as much as Western Europe. The survey showed gross national expenditure as follows:

Gross National Expenditure on Research and Development

	$m.	Financial Year	Proportion (%) from govt	business	other
United States	21,075	1963–4	64	32	4
United Kingdom	2,160	1964–5	54	42	4

	$m.	Financial Year	Proportion (%) from		
			govt	business	other
Germany	1,436	1964	41	57	2
France	1,299	1963	64	33	3
Netherlands	330	1964	40	54	6
Italy	291	1963	33	62	5
Belgium	137	1963	24	71	5
Japan	892	1963	28	65	7

Besides spending more, the US was also getting better value for the money spent, which was devoted to well-defined ends, whereas that of European countries tended to be spread too thinly over many unrelated areas and even lost altogether in abandoned projects like the TSR-2 in Britain and various joint enterprises which became too expensive.

Somewhat late in the day the Council on 31 October 1967 agreed that the Six's scientific and technological research in certain fields should be co-ordinated as progress had been less rapid than in countries outside Europe, particularly the US, and 'Europe's lag creates a serious risk for its medium and long-term development'. A first report was ordered on possible co-operation in the fields of data-processing and telecommunications, development of new means of transport, oceanography, metallurgy, air and water pollution, and meteorology.

The merger of the executives of the three Communities itself focussed attention on the virtues of co-ordination and the first report of the medium-term economic policy committee and of the inter-executive research group both emphasized the need to eliminate wasteful overlapping of effort and expenditure.

In a forceful and historic speech at the Lord Mayor's Banquet in Guildhall on 13 November 1967 Mr Wilson offered the Community his seven-point technology plan as a basis for joint action. Referring to the American near-monopoly in the strategic growth industries of Europe, he called for urgent action if Europeans were not to be left in industrial terms as 'hewers of wood and drawers of water'. His proposals were:

1. Bilateral talks on computers, electronics, and the civil application of nuclear energy.

2. Multilateral discussions on the same subjects.

3. Co-operation between the CBI (Confederation of British Industry) and their opposite numbers, the employers' associations towards this end.

4. The setting up of a multilateral European Institute of Technology to study the areas for action.

5. The creation of 'European' companies.

It is a telling reflection on all of us in Europe, that apart from a handful of established organizations such as Shell, Unilever, and Philips the only companies which transcend Europe's national frontiers are the American-owned corporations in Europe in such industries as automobiles and computers.

6. The Board of Trade would examine the field of patents, monopolies, restrictive practices, and company law to fit in with this wider economic integration.

7. The Trades Union Congress would co-operate in furthering these objectives.

We can create a vast and powerful European technology. The immediate task is to stop the gap from widening. The next step is to narrow it.

Clearly the EEC has not given the Six the framework in which technological progress could be made enabling Europe to make a great leap forward to bring her, if not level, at least within measurable distance of America and Russia. Or if the framework is there, the nations are not ready to build within it. Only CERN (Centre Européen de Recherches Nucléaires) set up in 1951, long before the Common Market, can be counted a complete success. CERN is a pure research organization in the field of nuclear physics and not involved in production. It is at the production stage that national, political, and economic antagonisms begin their destructive work.

Britain, her financial problems complicated by the devaluation of sterling, decided amid storms of protests from scientists to withdraw from a major project of CERN – the 300 GeV accelerator project – in June 1968, while agreeing to maintain her present subscription of around £6m. to CERN's annual budget. The cost of the 300 GeV accelerator was estimated at £180m. over the eight years it would take to build and Britain's share of this would have been about one fifth; but she had to take into account the enormous escalation of costs which had been the pattern of past joint efforts in ELDO, etc., and that a similar American machine might be available sooner, making the 300 GeV obsolescent before it came into use.

The failures are there for all to see: the near-demise of Euratom and of the space organizations ELDO and ESRO; the dependence of Europe's airlines on American civil planes, and of Europe's defence forces on American military planes and weapons; the dependence of Europe's satellites on American launchers; the American computer empire in Europe. The take-over bid for Europe in the technological industries gathers momentum from day to day.

It is impossible to make any neat assessment of where to lay the blame for Europe's technological lag except to say that it is unlikely that it would have developed so fast if Britain and EFTA had been admitted to the EEC at the time of the first application. Much is involved of history, of philosophy – of politics. When Europe was picking itself up from the ruins of World War II, physically, financially, and emotionally worn out, America, comparatively untouched, was embarking on a huge programme (military and civil) of research and development in space and nuclear energy. Russia, war-torn like Europe, was in the grip of Stalin, who, spurred on by hatred of the Americans, by love of military success and determination to stay in command, was prepared to see his nation deprived of even the smallest creature comforts provided that he could keep pace with the American military and nuclear machine.

Great Britain was obsessed by domestic social problems – the establishment of a National Health Service, of comprehensive education, and of the Welfare State – and paid scant attention to the great and stirring explorations in space, except to opt out on the philosophical grounds that since nuclear force could never in fact be used militarily there was no positive loss in being a non-starter. France was a prey to splinter groups and a series of vacillating coalition governments. Later De Gaulle could see the prestige-value of keeping 'right up there' with the Russians and Americans but was blinded by his dislike and fear of the

'Anglo-Saxons' from taking the step that could have made this possible – admitting Britain and E F T A to the E E C. Clearly it was not because the Russians and Americans are cleverer than Europeans that they went ahead; they each acted as one consolidated unit, and each had the will, the money, and the motive.

A Europe united in the E E C would have had the same advantages but in 1969 her lack of progress towards true co-operation can be measured by the size of the gap in the technology based industries, which is greatest of all in computers.

COMPUTER 'COLONIZATION'

'Europe's technological lag is greatest in the field of computers and is so severe that backwardness in other areas seems of minor importance. In fact we have almost reached the point of no return in computer technology.' This was the conclusion of a long comparative study made by the O E C D in 1968. Yet the computer industry is destined to become a major industry, if not the major industry, of every modern state, and its influence will be felt throughout the economic, industrial, and social structure of Europe. As an instrument of analysis, management, and decision-making, the computer will dominate industry by 1970 and is then expected to be the biggest single investment expense for a company, at least ten per cent of its total investment. Sales of computers (I B M's 1968 revenue was nearly $7,000m.) are growing at a breathtaking 20 per cent – twice as fast as cars at around 10 per cent.

Computers are at the very heart of industry: the Diebold Research Programme indicated that in 1969 40 per cent of consumer companies were using computers as a primary source of information and that this would rise to 75 per cent by 1973; the figures for industrial companies were lower – 16 per cent in 1969 rising to 42 per cent by 1973. It would be foolish to ignore the dangers of computer colonization by America. In 1968 I B M had around 75 per cent of world computer business and three other American firms – Univac, Honeywell and Control Data – had between 4 and 6 per cent each, next came International Computers Ltd (British) with 3 per cent. I B M controlled 63 per cent of the German market, the largest in Europe, and over 40 per cent of the British market, where despite an improved performance by I C L, imports were gaining. Figures for 1968 were: imports £50m. (£29.4m. in 1967): home production £74.3m. (£60m. in 1967). Exports of British machines rose to £40m. in 1968 (£35m. in 1967) so that imports were outpacing the British export effort.

The enormous sums involved in research and development largely explain why America has gone ahead so much faster than the rest of Europe (far from America having been first in the field scientifically, she was a late-comer and even then she did not realize the tremendous impact computers would have on industry and society; the British realized the immense possibilities much earlier). But America was in a position to provide money from her own resources and to borrow it (much of it from Europe itself). Some idea of the huge sums involved can be gained by considering that over a four-year period I B M alone invested 5,000 million dollars in its third generation computers (based not on tubes or transistors but on integrated circuits) – a sum equal to the total annual space budget of the U S Government.

Europe has lagged. Stung by the take-over of Machines Bull by the American General Electric, the French launched their Plan Calcul (100m. dollars) in 1967 attempting to build up the French Compagnie Internationale d'Informatique and followed this up in 1968 with an agreement worth 80m. fr. to help three firms make peripheral electronic components over a period of five years and another for 20m. fr. a year for five years to assist C S F (Compagnie de Telegraphie sans Fil) and Thomson Houston to make micro-electronic components. But even when a national computer has been produced, a marketing organization must be established and this puts France effectively out of the running for several years. Philips in Holland were too pusillanimous to accept the challenge of I B M, dallied for three years and announced that with Electrologica it would go ahead in 1968 with a full computer range, but it had missed the boat by several years. Germany is almost entirely in the grip of America; the market there, the largest in Europe and 25 per cent greater than Great Britain, is split as follows:

American	Market (%)
IBM	63
Univac	8·4
Siemens/RCA	8·3
GE/Bull	8·1
Honeywell	2·3
Other	9·9

In Italy Olivetti's computer division is owned by General Electric.

The only European country with an independent computer industry is Britain where I C L (International Computers Ltd, the £100m. company formed in 1968 by the merger of International Computers and Tabulators Ltd, part of the English Electric Co. Ltd plus money from the government and from Plessey Co. Ltd) is by far the largest company outside the U S A specializing in commercial and scientific computers (and through Plessey in the manufacture of telecommunications equipment). It has a major share of its home market, a good order book and with the establishment of International Computers (Canada) is starting on a policy of aggressive expansion. Sales of computers in Britain are expected to soar by 35 per cent a year from £125m. in 1968 to £450m. in 1972. Britain's Mintech estimate for 1972 is even higher – a market of £600m.

It is a cut-throat market as the Americans are prepared to sell at a loss to establish themselves in a particular market, knowing that with their worldwide coverage, this loss can be made up in another market and that once they are well and truly established in the first market they can make the market pay its own establishment costs in the form of higher prices. For instance I B M's prices were nearly 10 per cent lower in the United Kingdom than on the continent where competition was not so fierce. Honeywell, the Scottish-based American computer firm, are prepared to lose up to £10m. over three years to establish a marketing force in the E E C countries. I C L have to win back customers from an I B M allegiance, big customers such as B O A C, Rolls-Royce, I C I and the Central Electricity Generating Board, but they are assured of government purchases for their new 1908A, a computer twenty times as powerful as any existing

British machine; and the enhancements offered to update the 1900 and System 4 ensure continuity with existing customers. The prize is huge: in 1968 the capital value of computers rented or sold in Europe was put at £1,000m. compared with a figure for the Commonwealth, excluding Canada but including South Africa, of £100m. Success will mainly be found in Europe for the next few years. It is estimated that sales of British computer and related equipment at home and overseas might stabilize at some £1,500m. a year in the 1980s. With her strong telecommunications and software know-how, Britain should get a good share of the time-sharing systems involving central machines linked to slave units, such as branch offices, laboratories, and factories, which are expected to make up half of the market in the 1970s.

But ICL's resources in 1968 were still only roughly equal to those of the smaller American companies such as National Cash Register (NCR), Burroughs, and Honeywell and the logical policy would be, even at this late date, for Europe to pool all the resources she can muster, perhaps using the British nucleus with immediate support from German, French and Dutch units. But the difficulties of reaching any such agreement are deep-rooted. IBM has ten plants, seven laboratories, and 55,000 staff throughout continental Europe, and three of these plants, employing 16,000 workers, are situated in Germany, a country which normally follows a policy of buying the German product and, in default of that, buying the product manufactured on German soil by another nation (usually America), or lastly buying from an 'outside' European power.

The Germans are working on a national computer plan of their own; the West German Government has given the equivalent of $25m. each to Siemens and Telefunken. Siemens is tied to the American RCA but might find a formula for getting free. Telefunken, strong in communications and having a world marketing network, would make an extremely useful partner for ICL

The position is humiliating. The European vice-president of IBM even suggested that Europe might be better advised to invest in stimulating the use of computers (IBM naturally) in industry and other fields rather than to try to strike out on her own. Here, indeed, would lie the fifty-first state – Europe. The danger is real because of the impetus the American computer industry already has; it is too late for Europe to establish the legal restraints and quotas by which the Japanese have contrived to cut I B M down to size and keep some of their own market for themselves.

I B M suffered a severe blow when in January 1969 the U S Government Justice Department filed an anti-trust suit against the giant firm (two such suits had already been filed by trade rivals and another was filed subsequently). Allegations were that when I B M sold or leased a computer, it quoted a single price for the hardware (machine itself), software (programming, etc.) and for support (education of operators, etc.). This was said to have inhibited the development of independent software and support industries. Maintenance agreements were another bone of contention – it was alleged that I B M charged exorbitant prices for I B M parts to users who had refused to sign a maintenance agreement. Other allegations were that I B M was prepared to take 'unusually low profits' in highly competitive markets, basically the 'high-street' policy of loss leading.

This setback for I B M could be Europe's opportunity to set her house in order. Even if Philips, Plan Calcul, and the Germans did eventually come up with their own range of national computers, the time-lag might mean that they were already obsolescent and there would have been unnecessary duplication of effort and expense. By regrouping and by establishing common objectives Europe could compete. Most EEC and EFTA countries will need computers to sort out the increasingly complex social security payments, to pay the armed forces and police, for hospitals, for education, for transport planning. A prearranged specialization and an agreed European buying policy would appear to give Europe the best chance of making a worthwhile, if belated, appearance on the world computer scene.

An EEC Computer Consortium of Philips (Netherlands), Siemens and Telefunken (both of Germany), Olivetti (Italy), and Cie Internationale Informatique (France) began consultations with ICL (Britain) in May 1969 on a scheme to build a giant computer. The initiative was taken by a specialist committee set up by the Commission and other European manufacturers might be invited to join.

In July 1969 IBM announced the System 3, a new low-cost computer system designed for the small businessman with as few as a hundred employees; it was aimed at the upper end of the market at present making do with calculating machines. A European computer consortium, had one been in existence for long enough, could well have scooped this market.

NUCLEAR ENERGY – EURATOM A COSTLY FAILURE

The story of the ten years of Euratom is the story of the decay of the European idea in the field of nuclear energy.

The European Atomic Energy Community (Euratom) was set up in 1957 and came into force on 1 January 1958 at the same time as the EEC. Euratom was concerned only with the peaceful uses of nuclear energy and had no responsibilities in the military field. During the negotiations it had looked several times as if Euratom would cover both peaceful and military applications of nuclear energy but the French were bent on having control of their own national military programme and so the fatal dichotomy was built into the EEC; the Six nations (except for West Germany which had undertaken in 1954 not to manufacture nuclear weapons) were to contribute to Euratom while simultaneously undertaking a vast expenditure of men and money on national ventures.

Euratom was organized on the same lines as the EEC with a Commission of five as the executive body, the mainspring of the Community, supervising the day-to-day running of the Community's work and planning its future by preparing proposals on the basis of which the Council of Ministers took decisions sometimes by unanimous vote (for instance, if they wanted to alter the Commission's proposals) and at other times by a weighted majority vote. Its budget for the first five years, 1958–62, was $215m.

The chief aim was to finance and develop nuclear power for industry in Europe (chiefly to meet the constantly rising demand for electricity, consumption of which was doubling every ten years). It would promote research and training of atomic scientists and technologists, draw up common investment plans, and set up atomic installations of its own, besides contributing under contracts of association to approved national programmes. It would also act as agent for the import and distribution of nuclear fuel and maintain a team of inspectors to make certain that Community plants and nuclear fuel were used for peaceful purposes.

Britain did not join. She was in any case well ahead owing to her scientists' wartime contribution to the atom bomb, in return for which she was given the vital nuclear secrets (though not as much information as she would have liked on their industrial application) on condition that she would not divulge them to third parties. This led to Britain turning down a French request in 1955 to build a fuel-enrichment plant for them; the French canvassed support in Europe without success and had to tread alone the difficult path the British had already taken. Not till 1967 after gargantuan expense and tremendous setbacks did the French plant at Pierrelatte come on stream.

In 1957 Britain joined E N E A, the European Nuclear Energy Agency (the nuclear club of the seventeen-nation O E E C, now O E C D). Euratom was also a member and participated in the development by Britain of the Dragon high-temperature gas-cooled reactor at Winfrith, Dorset. The U S–Euratom agreement signed in November 1958 provided for a joint power and research programme, and the subsequent financing and building of American-type reactors in Europe helped to transfer know-how quickly.

The first programme got under way successfully though it soon became apparent that members were tending to identify with national needs rather than to subscribe whole-heartedly to a joint venture. When de Gaulle came into office he insisted on the replacement of the pro-E E C president of Euratom, M. Étienne Hirsch, by the Gaullist, M. Châtenet, because M. Hirsch had been seeking to introduce a system of qualified majority voting on research programmes so that members would have to reach an agreement among themselves instead of constantly wrangling. (A parallel situation arose in the Commission of the E E C where de

Gaulle challenged Professor Hallstein on the same issue; de Gaulle would not give up his right of veto.) This, unhappily, set the pattern. As far as France was concerned, national considerations would always be paramount. From then on it was each man for himself.

The second programme 1963–7 got under way, its research budget of $425m. nearly double that of the first programme. This was cut back by the Council in June 1962 and by 1963 dissensions were rife. France and Germany were going ahead with their own fast-breeder programmes; this duplication was exactly what it had been hoped Euratom would avoid. The flow-back of information from the contracts of association was suspected, particularly by the Italians, of being much less than the whole truth.

By 1967 when the third programme should have been prepared, Euratom was in a state of crisis. The Italians not unnaturally did not see why they should not be as nationalist as the two big powers; the Belgians thought the whole thing was getting far too expensive; the Euratom staff were looking for other jobs.

At the December 1967 meeting of the Council to decide the future fate of Euratom, it was necessary to arrange a bridging budget for 1968, so that the four research centres – at Ispra, near Varese, Karlsruhe, Petten and Mol – wholly owned by the EEC could continue in being. It appeared unlikely that Euratom would continue to participate in national programmes and in the development of industrial prototype reactors; in short, it would no longer play its appointed role of co-ordinating nuclear development in the EEC. It was agreed that 1968 should be a sandwich year with a budget of $80m., half to finance the Community centres and half to finance Community participation in the national programmes (association contracts), though the choice of the beneficiaries stirred up such hostility between the French and Italians that for a time all association contracts between the EEC and member-states were suspended.

There were about twenty of these association contracts involving work in thermonuclear fusion, biological research, etc., but easily the most valuable and vital were those concerned with fast reactor work, chiefly in France and Germany. The basic

French grievance was that she thought most other EEC states adopted minimum national programmes, relying heavily on the EEC joint programme and therefore on France, one of the biggest continental producers of nuclear energy, whose research work in conjunction with Euratom automatically became available to them. It is all too easy to cast the French as the villain of the piece in the failures of the EEC but often it is all too true. In this case the French had not formally renewed their fast reactor association contract with Euratom when it expired at the end of 1966 (although work continued) and they had been still more high-handed in refusing to agree to the inclusion of an Italian project on fast reactors in the Euratom–Italy association. The Italians were understandably more than a little annoyed.

Even if it is conceded that most of the EEC nations had been trying to get more out of Euratom than they put in, the true reason for French intransigence goes much deeper. In nuclear energy, as in all other fields, de Gaulle objected as a matter of principle to Community overlordship and to Community financing. At the December 1967 meeting the French were able to get agreement to *ad hoc* arrangements by interested member-states on specified projects, an agreement which is the very negation of all Euratom stands for – a genuinely shared European effort. These *ad hoc* arrangements were already undermining ELDO and ESRO.

By 1 August 1968 initiative had already largely passed from Euratom's hands. A consortium to market (and construct) high-temperature nuclear reactors developed from Dragon and under construction at Winfrith Heath, Dorset, was announced. Four countries were involved, Nuclear Power Group of Britain, Belgo-Nucléaire, Gütehoffnungshütte of West Germany, and SNAM-Progetti of Italy. Another consortium, comprising Belgo-Nucléaire, Siemens Schuckertwerke and Interatom in Germany and Neratoom of Holland, was studying joint participation in a prototype sodium-cooled fast breeder reactor with a 300 Mw capacity.

A side effect of the breakdown was that the US, which had been supplying plutonium and enriched uranium (U 235) to Euratom (a quota of 1,000 kilograms of plutonium and 145 tons of U 235 was agreed for 1968–73), might not feel inclined to do so to individual nation-states. The suggestion that the EEC should build its own gas-diffusion plant did not find favour with the French, who thought it would be preferable to extend their own Pierrelatte plant. Not surprisingly, the other five did not wish to be dependent on supplies from France and the debate continued.

In 1968 disillusion was complete. The grand idea had failed on yet another front: Europe had demonstrated on the nuclear plane as on so many others that she was not yet politically ready to lose her separate national identities in an overall European programme. Differences had still not been resolved in March 1969, when a further interim budget was agreed, principally to keep Euratom's research centres ticking over but even in this it did not succeed; 382 redundancies were declared, mainly at Ispra. Instead of a mini-budget of $69m. proposed by the Commission, the Council agreed to one of only $47·8m. – $24·3m. for the joint programme and $23·5m. for the association agreements.

The impotence of the European Parliament was shown when it totally rejected the reduced allocation, bitterly pointing out that the $24·3m. for Europe's joint research programme was 1 per cent of the cost of the common agricultural policy for 1969 and half the amount to be spent in 1969 on subsidizing EEC rice-growers. But this protest went unheeded ...

The Commission too protested. They said that when drawing up the programme for several years, to run from July 1969, it would rule out participation in *à-la-carte* association agreements altogether, as these damaged the integrated EEC effort and dissipated money needed for it. Already when drawing up guidelines in March 1968 for an abortive programme (designed to start in January 1969 and run for five years) the Commission had stressed the need for a more integrated nuclear policy. While in the United States orders for 50,000 Mw of nuclear capacity since 1966 had been shared between four constructors, the 5,000 Mw ordered in the same period by the Community had been shared out among twelve. Wastage would be inevitable unless larger, multinational groupings were formed, purchasing policies coordinated and a wider market obtained.

The failure of Euratom is the more dangerous because Europe

is a fuel-starved continent which vitally needs nuclear energy. The EEC's dependence on imported energy is growing; for the first time in 1967 over half the EEC's energy requirements were imported. Oil, most of it imported, provides over half of consumption and demand is growing by around 10 per cent; the use of coal continues to decline; natural gas which provides around 5 per cent of total energy is growing rapidly – by around 25 per cent.

Energy Produced in EEC and Energy Imported (%)

	1960	1967	Estimated 1970	1980
EEC-produced energy	73	48	44	41–48
Imported energy	27	52	56	59–52

With such large imports of energy, which in turn condition economic and technological development, small wonder that attention is focussing on the generating capacity of the Community's nuclear power stations which by 1969 were providing only a very small part of total electricity generated in the Community (about 1·8 per cent). This contrasts with a US estimate that nuclear power will provide the US with more electricity in 1980 than coal does. It is precisely there, where the biggest advance is needed, that progress has been slow, hamstrung by rising costs and political difficulties.

Energy Requirements of the EEC

	Share (%)			
	1965	1966	1967	1968
Coal	37·7	33·7	31·3	29·8
Lignite	5·7	5·6	5·4	4·7
Oil	45·3	48·4	50·9	51·6
Natural Gas	3·8	4·4	5·2	6·9
Primary electricity	7·5	7·9	7·2	7·0
Community sources	53·2	50·4	48·2	39·1
Imports	46·8	49·6	51·8	60·9

European Community Bulletin

In the generation of electricity from nuclear energy Britain has a commanding lead over any country in the EEC. By 1972 the Community is expected to have nearly 9,400 Mw of capacity in operation (3,100 Mw in France, 2,500 Mw in Germany, and 1,300 Mw in Italy). Britain will have over 6,000 Mw. Long-term estimates for the EEC are 40,000–60,000 Mw by 1980 (compared with the US Atomic Energy Commission's forecast of 150,000 Mw for America). To maintain her lead and to exploit it, for example by a massive programme of small steam-generating heavy reactors for export to countries which cannot make economic use of the huge advanced gas-cooled reactors, Britain needs partners. Whether or not any atomic plants are sold (and in 1969 the likelihood of the sale of an advanced gas-cooled reactor, AGR, to Germany was good), research and development costs on Britain's four existing atomic-power reactor types will be well over £100m. for 1970–75. On other projects too large for one nation to take on single-handed such as construction of a large diffusion plant and isotope-separation plants, co-operation is needed. It is one of Europe's major post-war tragedies that Britain's know-how was not brought into a European pool; for quick production of nuclear energy is essential for the EEC economy, which is over-dependent on oil with all its notorious political and economic uncertainties.

A fantastic growth in world demand for nuclear fuel is forecast in the next decade; in 1970 the world market could be worth £100m. and by 1980 it could easily top the £1,350m. mark. The main demand will be for enriched uranium – whose natural content of the fissile isotope 235 has been stepped up from 0·7 to something over 2 per cent. Up to 1969 the only well-tried way of enriching the isotope was by a gas-diffusion process, the drawback being that gas-diffusion plants are of necessity enormous and need huge inputs of electric power to feed the compressors – the cost of this electricity is about half the cost of enrichment. Britain is well ahead in this race; her diffusion plant at Capenhurst is being expanded and when ready in 1970 will be the only specially designed nuclear-fuel plant, but the Americans have the advantages of scale and of cheap hydro-electricity and of cheaper finance in their ageing diffusion complex (Oak Ridge, Paducah, and Portsmouth). The only other fuel-enrichment plant in Europe is the French Pierrelatte, which although it may have cost four times as much to build as Capenhurst is two to three years at least behind in adaptation to civilian nuclear use.

More significant is the announcement that Britain is to go ahead with the development of the gas-centrifuge system of fuel enrichment together with Holland and West Germany, who have made great advances in this method. The gas-centrifuge system is a far more efficient method of enriching uranium than gas diffusion is. The plant does not need to be so vast and involves the use of only a fraction (about one-tenth) of the electricity to operate it. Moreover, Britain had a crucial piece of know-how to trade in – the use of carbon fibre, the new wonder material, developed by Rolls-Royce, which is immensely strong and stiff but light and enormously resistant to heat and which could be used to overcome some of the engineering problems encountered.

In May 1969 the Commission reported on the future of Euratom: 'As is also the case with most advanced technology industries, the nuclear industry has so far reaped scarcely any benefit from the Common Market.' It detailed the follies of the past – the dissipation of Community nuclear efforts over an impossibly wide front – two high-temperature reactor projects, four heavy-water reactor variants, and three separate fast-reactor programmes, fifteen nuclear power plant constructors (as compared with four or five in America), thirteen fuel elements manufacturers (whose total production is equalled by Westinghouse alone), ten turbine makers (compared with two in the States and two in the United Kingdom), and so on.

French lack of co-operation and *folies de grandeur* had led to the wastage of several hundreds of millions of pounds on abortive French projects and brought Europe close to the status of a dependent territory in the mighty American business empire; at the end of the day Europe might be forced into abandoning her own paths and buying her way into nuclear technology by licensing from the Americans, thus helping to 'consolidate a supremacy that will soon defy all assaults'.

The Commission called rightly for a political commitment to bring about an independent nuclear industry in Europe. Without this basic declaration of intent, piecemeal negotiations will only scratch at the surface of the problem. On both the major recommendations of the Commission the admission of Britain to the Common Market would be of vital importance. On the choice of reactor types Britain's experience and know-how would be invaluable; on the joint policy for fissile material, especially enriched uranium, Britain could speak with the voice of the acknowledged leader in this field in Europe.

In the great monetary assessment that has to be made when Britain joins the EEC (quite apart from political and defence considerations), the estimate of her earnings from technology and especially from nuclear systems will count on the credit side and could do much to offset losses on the agricultural policy.

France, especially, could be interested in a deal. It was clear by the end of 1968 that her civil nuclear policy had collapsed: only about half of the 2,500 Mw called for in the French Fifth Plan (ending in 1970) would have been provided. France had concentrated on gas-graphite reactor technology (largely for political reasons – gas-graphite reactors burnt natural uranium widely available in France and the franc zone and so obviated the need for France to humiliate herself by buying from the United States the enriched uranium fuel used in other systems). Besides the very serious engineering difficulties, the falling cost of conventional fuel, especially oil, was making the whole gas-graphite system commercially uneconomic. In October 1969 M. Boiteux, head of Électricité de France, admitted that St Laurent I, the gas-graphite reactor on which France's nuclear energy programme has been based, was uneconomic (the average cost per therm of energy produced from conventional power stations would in the early seventies be two-thirds cheaper than St Laurent's therms). The likelihood was that France would purchase or manufacture under licence a number of American-designed light-water reactors. And so the whirligig of time brought France back to depend on the American overlord – she had shaped her own destiny by refusing to admit Britain to the EEC, and by consistent lack of team-work in Euratom.

Undaunted, the Commission drew up an ambitious plan, Euratom 1970–74, and submitted it to the Council in April 1969.

Towards One Europe

The plan streamlined the activities of Euratom and gave more prominence to the industrial application of nuclear research, recommending that Euratom should also undertake contract research, world demand for which is growing fast, and that this research could be on non-nuclear projects, such as combating pollution. The total cost came out at $391·6m.

Euratom's Third Five-year Programme – Proposed Budget

Activities	Personnel	Budget $m.
Reactor development		
Fast reactors	175	29
High-temperature reactors	185	45·2
Heavy-water reactors	490	55·9
Fuel-cycle problems	220	25·3
Public-service activities		
Central Bureau for Nuclear Measurements	180	24·9
CETIS (Scientific Data Processing Centre)	117	16·3
Control of fissile materials	40	3·2
Nuclear-plant safety	47	3·8
Biology and health physics	112	38
Training and instruction	9	7
High-flux irradiation	90	20·9
Basic research		
Thermonuclear fusion	94	45
Condensed-state physics	180	29·7
Non-nuclear field		
Combating pollution	103	8·2
Data processing	105	11
Community Bureau of Standards	189	15·3
Research total	2,336	378·7

To the research total various other charges were added.

	Personnel	Budget $m.
Research total	2,336	378·7
Public-service activities to be charged to operating budget		
Uses of radiations	9	0·9
Information	119	12
Grand total	2,464	391·6

Far from this plan being adopted, the Council could not even reach agreement in October 1969 on a compromise proposal costing $154m. spread over 1970–73. The French said this was far too expensive and they thought research co-operation should take place within industry rather than in Euratom. Belgium asked for a basic reappraisal of E E C nuclear policy with the collaboration of Britain; this, they thought, could take place before Britain was a full member and they wanted the suggestion placed on the agenda of The Hague summit conference. Without the intervention of a miracle of some sort, Euratom was seen to be on its death-bed. Outside headquarters, redundant personnel from the Euratom research centres and the Commission demonstrated with banners saying, 'Euratom is dying, Europe too.'

EUROPE'S HANDICAPS IN THE SPACE RACE

When Neil Armstrong and Buzz Aldrin set foot on the moon on 20 July 1969, it was an illustration of man's courage and endurance in the face of the unknown but still more a triumph for American technology. The moon landing was the end product of a $24,000m. NASA experiment involving over 300,000 technicians and eight years of trial and error.

Europe had played a part. Apart from Wernher von Braun, the world's greatest rocket expert, and about 125 scientists and technicians working for NASA, West Germany's contribution on the industrial side was a Siemens-produced dashboard-lighting system for Apollo 11's cabin and for the lunar module which gave out practically no heat and used very little power; Schott, formerly an East German firm, supplied a special quartz type of lens glass for the cameras used by the American astronauts, and also the special mirrors for the laser-beam reflector left on the moon. A Bavarian firm supplied the tantalum condensers and coil resisters used in communications between Apollo 11 and the base at Houston, Texas.

The French firm, Thomson-Brandt, made the remote-control measurement equipment for the relay satellites and for the ground-communication system, and Angenieux, of Saint-Étienne, was responsible for the zoom television-camera lenses used on the moon's surface. The well-known Swedish firm of Hasselblad, which has supplied equipment to NASA since 1962, made special camera equipment for use in space.

The Swiss chemical firm CIBA supplied the heat-resisting resins for the nozzle of Apollo 11, which had to survive temperatures of over 2,000° centigrade on re-entering the earth's atmosphere. Swiss watchmakers supplied many of the precision recording instruments.

The UK's contribution consisted mainly of the cupola for the space-tracking and guiding station on Ascension Island in the South Atlantic and electronic equipment supplied by GEC/EE.

To achieve anything comparable to the American (and Russian) space epics, Europe would have had to combine her brains and her money and to create a 'European will'. This she had not been able to do. A month before the moon landing Britain's do-it-yourself rocket Black Arrow had veered off course and had to be destroyed off Woomera; the path of European co-operation was littered with the debris of wrecked projects and broken promises, of political and financial quarrels.

Of space President Johnson said, 'It is really a battle for the first place in the world. The English dominated the world in their day because they were masters of the seas. Those who are first into space will inevitably be the first in the world of to-morrow.'

Europe explored the *terra incognita* in past centuries; in this century it has been left to America and Russia to explore space. They were motivated by urgent ideological and military passions at a time when other advanced nations were intent on exploring the possibilities of a return to normal life on earth. To compete, Stalin denied his people the basics of civilized housing, clothing, and food.

While America and Russia jockeyed for position in the space race, war-torn Europe was slowly picking herself up and trying to mend her shattered civilization. The space race was the least of her worries. Britain, however, got away from the starting post with her nuclear missile, Blue Streak, but had to withdraw as the economic going got heavier. Later de Gaulle saw the prestige value of entering France for the space stakes; he was more intent on giving France *la gloire* in space than on giving individual Frenchmen the things that they wanted for themselves such as a modern liberal education for their children. Even if France was a late developer, she must be outstanding in Europe. To some extent he succeeded. The French satellite AI launched in November 1965 by the missile Diamant was the first wholly European space venture – the British satellites Ariel I and Ariel II and the Italian San Marco had been put into orbit on American launchers.

Apart from purely national ventures, the EEC had agreed to channel the Community space effort for peaceful purposes through two main bodies, ELDO and ESRO. The European Space Vehicle Launcher Development Organization (ELDO) convention was signed in 1962 and came into operation in 1964; there were seven members; the Six, minus Luxembourg, plus Britain and Australia, the landlord partner with its Woomera range available for use by all partners. ELDO was largely the result of a British initiative; Blue Streak born of Britain's somewhat pretentious post-war plans and by 1960 dropped from her military programme, would conveniently form stage one of a joint European rocket programme of which the French could well provide the second stage (Coralie) and the West Germans be persuaded to undertake the third stage (Astris). Italy would produce the first pay-load, Belgium the guidance stations and the Netherlands telemetric links. The first budget was fixed at $196m. for 1964–9, the British paying the heaviest share, 38·8 per cent as against 23·9 per cent for France; 22 per cent for West Germany; 9·8 per cent for Italy; 2·8 per cent for Belgium; 2·7 per cent for the Netherlands, and the use of Woomera for Australia.

It seemed that Europe might have discovered a workable formula for channelling the national space effort into supranational projects; but already in 1965 the Italian Minister of State for Foreign Affairs was complaining that it was the practice in ELDO to assign most of the work 'on the basis of cost and technical arguments', which favoured the more advanced nations. A year or so later the House of Commons Estimates Committee pointed out in their second report (1966–7) that ELDO was foundering because member-governments, afraid that they were not getting fair-dos, kept changing their minds about the programme. Money squabbles loomed as large as the ballot boxes which periodically cast their shadows over one or other of the governments; the electors must be seen to be getting their money's worth.

An early difficulty was that the timetable was for ever slipping, which added to the cost; this was technology of the most advanced kind and to some nations it was quite new. The French met with repeated failure in their attempts to provide the second-stage rocket. By 1965, too, Early Bird had shown that communications satellites might be a way of enabling space programmes to pay at least in part for themselves and the French wisely asked whether the original programme should not be expanded to take this into account and include communications satellites. Real trouble followed in 1966 when Britain questioned the organization itself, criticizing the failure to keep to schedule and the escalating costs. A compromise was reached – geostationary communications satellites, the hoped-for money-spinners, would be launched under a complementary programme – ELDO PAS (ELDO Programme for Applications Satellites). As a *quid pro quo* France and West Germany agreed to share the financial burden equally with Britain. The new programme would cost $330m. to which had to be added the $196m. voted on the original five-year budget, which had had to be given a $100m. supplement because of increased costs, making in all $626m. for the first two programmes.

At the time that ELDO was founded to undertake the rocket launching, there came into being the organization which was to provide the pay-load – ESRO, the European Space Research Organization. Britain played a large part in the founding of this too. Its aims were at first purely scientific and it included the Six, plus Great Britain, Switzerland, Sweden, Denmark, Spain, Austria, and Norway, each country contributing roughly according to national income. ESRO aimed at firing smallish rockets carrying each nation's individual experiments and, after three years or so, at putting two small satellites carrying nationally conceived projects into orbit. Finally, it was hoped to launch by about 1968 at least one large astronomical satellite (LAS), a space observatory, which would need a launcher of about

ELDO PAS size. The first eight-year budget of $400m. was not accepted and the one of only $300m. ultimately approved meant a good deal of cheese-paring. ESRO, however, was more immediately successful than ELDO; it established common research facilities and excellent installations – a sounding rocket range at Kiruna in Sweden, a computing centre in Darmstadt (West Germany), and central laboratories at Delft (Holland). LAS was still in the melting-pot in 1969 though still strongly advocated by Britain, who was to supply the equipment making up her pay-load.

Meanwhile events on other fronts were overtaking the slow-moving European organizations. In 1963 CETS, the European Conference on Satellite Communications, consisting of eighteen European countries, had been founded to speak for Europe in Intelsat, the new world organization for communications satellites, in which the voice of America was predominant. Votes and financial contributions to Intelsat were allocated according to the use made of the satellites, so at first the US, paying for 61 per cent of traffic, had that proportion of the voting power, though qualified majority voting on some issues ensured that the European users' voice was heard. Intelsat rents channels on the satellites to all members of the International Telecommunications Union at rates which compare favourably with those for cable-borne traffic. America gets most of the $200m. worth of contracts, mainly because of her imposing lead in space technology. As the Intelsat arrangement was due for revision in 1970, Europe was anxious to establish a good bargaining position. Though in the event the US announced that they would take only a 40 per cent share-holding, the French and West Germans had already consolidated their position; France, who had been working on two experimental communications satellites, Saros I and II, saw the wisdom of pooling resources with West Germany, who was working on a television satellite it hoped to have ready to relay the Olympic Games from Munich in 1972. Jointly they would develop a satellite, Symphonie, to be launched in 1970 with an ELDO PAS rocket before the Intelsat meeting. Unfortunately this pre-empted similar CETS proposals for a satellite with very much the same specifications.

Dissensions grew. Britain wanted to press on with LAS (an ESRO project) but the French refused to support this – their share of Symphonie was beginning to bite into the national budget already under pressure for other reasons such as the *force de frappe*. The French and West Germans were more interested in keeping ELDO PAS going.

In July 1968 Britain refused to agree to the financial ceiling for ELDO PAS being raised; her attitude was caused by balance-of-payments difficulties and by growing frustration at France's refusal to admit her to the Common Market.

In 1968 Britain announced that she would withdraw altogether from ELDO in 1971. This was a bombshell largely caused by the Causse report, a full-scale plan for Europe's role in space, setting out exactly what the objectives should be. The work of ELDO and ESRO would be combined and ESRO competitive tendering for contracts, which had proved more successful than the ELDO direct contract system, would be adopted. An ambitious ten-year programme was outlined, including schemes for a big launch-vehicle capable of putting seven-ton satellites into a low orbit or two-ton satellites into a geo-stationary orbit (stationary over the equator in relation to a fixed point on earth) by 1978. These would innovate direct-broadcast television (i.e. direct from satellites to roof-top aerials); this would revolutionize TV services and help to open up under-developed countries by beaming educational programmes to them and would have the incidental but important effect of preventing the telecommunications market from being dominated by the US and USSR (with its grave threat that only their propaganda and their teaching would reach the outposts of civilization). This, with a family of smaller launchers for meteorology, navigation aids, air-traffic control, and general scientific research, was costed at £1,200m. over ten years. The British Government's view was that development costs would far outweigh the immediate economic returns and that it must look to fields where there would be a quicker financial return – such as civil aircraft, computers, machine tools, and nuclear power. It also disagreed with the proposal of ESRO and CETS (Conférence Européenne des Télécommunications par Satellites) that the pay-load for the Europa II space rocket being built by E L D O should be an experimental television relay satellite. Britain agreed to honour its standing agreements covering development of E L D O rockets up to 1971 (not including escalation costs which threatened to add another $100m. to the agreed $626m.). Italy, too, decided to limit her financial contribution.

Ostensibly, the U K withdrew from E L D O on the grounds of expense – on a short-term evaluation of cost-effectiveness; it was calculated that it would be much cheaper to buy launch-capability from America as and when needed than to develop a European launcher. It has been argued that Britain should have stayed in because of the prestige involved and because E L D O offered actual projects to work on and so provided a concrete challenge to some of the rather theoretical laboratory-based space research. But prestige can be bought at too high a price; besides, the British Government, for ever taunted with being unfit or unready on economic grounds to enter the E E C, and seeing the lack of cohesion and constantly escalating costs of an E E C-dominated organization, could have been suffering mildly from pique. Certainly they saw no reason for undertaking an open-ended commitment which seemed to redound to the greater glory of one nation, France, and incidentally give her the lion's share of the work involved. The decision cannot be divorced from the political context.

Britain's withdrawal left E L D O with only France, Germany, and Belgium as customers and, clearly, the proposed launch facilities at the equatorial space centre of the French national space programme in French Guiana, which replaced Woomera after 1969, would become grossly uneconomic unless development continued after the six or so Symphonie communications satellites planned had been launched. Although the E L D O countries, except Italy, agreed to make economies and to consult on absorbing Britain's proportion of costs, E L D O was brought to the point of collapse (and the French set-back of May–June 1968 was a further blow). But the structure had been tottering from the day the foundation stone was laid – no nation was whole-heartedly working towards its success. While the nations of Europe were bickering, America and Russia surged ahead. In

1966 the space budgets of Western Europe combined amounted to $216m. as against $5,152m. for the USA and a comparable amount for the USSR. Apart from the huge difference in emphasis and in achievement, the technological fall-out is more difficult to assess.

Space research is unique because, owing to the great technical difficulties posed by space conditions, research is stimulated in areas which would otherwise not be explored and a very wide span of industries becomes involved. Innovation is stimulated continuously and often results in the direct transfer to commercial use of products, processes or materials originally developed for space (such things as miniature radars enabling the blind to 'see', miniaturized electro-cardiograms, even completely heat-proof oven tops). Harder to measure is the intellectual feedback. It must be considerable, for space research is the meeting place of many technologies, which instead of concentrating on one narrow project interact one on another and produce a ferment of creative advance not achieved in unrelated research projects.

By 1969, however, Britain was taking another look at ELDO. There was the possibility of going it alone in a small way. Westland Aircraft has developed the all-British Black Arrow three-stage satellite launch-vehicle, which is regarded as a solid foundation on which a UK aerospace industry could be based and, together with Blue Streak, make a viable combined Black Arrow–Blue Streak launcher project. But experience had shown that escalating costs were part and parcel of space projects, and, beside Europa II and Saturn V, Black Arrow cut a very small figure. On reconsideration, the cost of implementing M. Causse's proposals, put at between $200 to 300m. per year, did not seem so outrageous when compared with the West German calculation that by 1980 communications licensing and other fees to America would cost almost exactly the same amount per year. Business considerations, too, were involved; the British Government was heavily backing the British computer industry and from America came statistics showing that the growth in the communications business there was mainly from data communications (computer speaking to computer). Was it sensible to opt out of applications satellites at a time when Lockheed of Los Angeles already had a communications-satellite link with Rolls-Royce? Was not this the pattern of the future?

The Spaey Committee set up to try to reconcile the positions of Britain and the Six discovered, buried beneath the antagonisms, a true wish by Britain and the Six for a genuine European NASA (the US National Aeronautics and Space Administration). The Belgian President of ELDO Council of Ministers, Theo Lefevre, admitted that, in retrospect, it had clearly been a mistake to set up two separate organizations and that the optimum would have been a European NASA. Both sides wanted a well-co-ordinated scientific and applications programme and were agreed on a two-ton direct TV satellite in the 1980s. Britain still held out for American launchers, however, while the Six wished to be sure of having their own launchers before building up a fleet of satellites; Britain, they thought, was putting the cart before the horse. It costs the comparatively small sum of $4m. to hire a launching pad from the US but outsiders naturally go to the back of the queue and when free launches were arranged for ESRO I and ESRO II, they were only free in exchange for the information obtained by the satellites. The danger of relying on US technological achievements had been brought home to Europe on several occasions, notably when the US Government vetoed the sale of a Control Data Corporation's giant 6600 computer to the French Ministry of Defence and when they refused to allow the UK to sell to the USSR computers which had any parts manufactured on licence from the US (the US itself was prevented by Federal laws from trading with a Communist country).

The Spaey Committee tried to overcome differences of opinion by suggesting that there should be a minimum programme excluding the launchers, which would be invoiced in the scientific and applications projects. But here again opinions differed; Britain wanted the invoicing done at market price. i.e. the American price, whereas the Six wanted to strike a price mid-way between the market price and the actual cost of the European launchers. In January 1969 the Minister of Technology announced that Britain would allocate more money to ESRO; negotiations continued and it seemed that some sensible joint solution might still be reached. It was agreed that ELDO and ESRO should be merged into a single European Space Authority in the spring of 1970 and that a draft convention should be ready for study by 1 October 1969.

An important side issue is that space studies help to halt the brain drain. The dedicated scientist must move to the country where his intellectual hunger drives him; a full programme of space projects, guaranteed against cut-backs by large centrally administered funds, would help to keep Europe's scientists in Europe.

Britain estimates that nearly 35 per cent of the physicists and incidentally about 40 per cent of the doctors and biologists who qualified in Great Britain in 1964–5 emigrated, generally to the USA. (In 1964–5 11,000 interns out of a total of 41,000 in American hospitals were graduates of foreign medical schools.) The Commission estimates that the EEC loses between 10 and 20 per cent of its newly qualified engineers each year, with France being the least-affected country. But the evidence is that the brain-drain is more serious in quality than quantity. An OECD report stated that 'Probably only about 5 per cent of the total stock of American scientists and engineers were trained abroad but 21 per cent of the 631 members of the United States National Academy of Sciences were born abroad and 18 per cent were trained abroad.'

Such scientists do not want to be at the mercy of schemes which are constantly being chopped and changed as the political wind veers; they must have security of tenure for their work. It has been suggested that since, in the space business as in the other technological industries, the state is the major buyer, some central procurement scheme for all the technological industries is what Europe really needs. Mr McNamara has brought to a fine art the use of government purchasing power to promote industrial advance and Europe could do the same. The question is one of management: it has been said that the only technological gap in Europe is the gap between the nations and nowhere is this more true than in the space effort.

AIRCRAFT

Despite the euphoria surrounding the take-off of Concorde, the European aircraft industry is in danger of being virtually eliminated within the next five to ten years by the much larger industries of the US and USSR. The way in which, although once the most powerful in the world, it has succumbed to American competition shows conclusively the folly of European nations trying to go it alone in the great new technology-based industries. Planning as usual on a long-term policy the Boeing Company of America, which had first concentrated on the 707 inter-continental jet, decided in the 1960s to enter the European-dominated medium- and short-range field with the 727 and 737 both derived from the parent 707. Standardization had been brought to the airlines of the world. Boeing had done a first-class research, production, and marketing job and reaped the rewards.

Lufthansa was the first big European airline to move over to the idea of a complete range of Boeings to facilitate the supply of spares, simplify training, and bring down costs. Instead of a motley fleet, Lufthansa would have a homogeneous Boeing fleet but at a cost – the cost of making Germany's national airline entirely dependent on American aircraft.

Other European lines such as Air France which had been using French or British middle- or short-haul planes, switched to the Boeing 727; and Alitalia, Iberia, KLM, SAS, and Swiss-Air, too, using DC8s for long-haul services became convinced of the merits of standardization and ordered the smaller DC9 for shorter distances.

The effect was disastrous for the plane-makers of Europe; however good their product, it would not sell. The jet-propelled BAC 1-11 was agreed to be a worthy successor to the famous four-engined turbo-prop Viscount; it was well timed and lower in price than the American equivalent but found all too few buyers; even where the merits of the BAC 1-11 were admitted, these were outweighed by the advantages of possessing an all-purpose homogeneous fleet. The same fate awaited the Dutch F28, successor to the highly successful two-engined turbo-prop Friendship.

The Americans also scooped the market with their jumbo-jets; Boeing announced the 747 four-engined jet-propelled long-range giant to carry 490 passengers and Pan American ordered twenty-five, thus forcing other airlines to follow suit to avoid being undercut. The maintenance alone of the jumbos threatened to be so enormously expensive that Europe's airlines decided to form a 'jumbo club' to share out the maintenance work (Air France all air-frame work, Lufthansa all engine work, etc.) for the group. (Britain with eleven jumbos felt self-sufficient.) This forced collaboration may be an object lesson to Europe on the virtues of co-operation. Concorde, the Franco–British jet which has cost over £500m. to develop, should scoop the supersonic pool; it is well ahead of American competition, though not of Russian. Yet such is the American hold on the market that even before the US had decided which company was to build the American supersonic airliner more than a hundred orders for it had been received. That Europe can successfully co-operate is also shown by joint engine-programmes under way for the VFW 614 short-haul (M45H turbofan engine by Rolls-Royce and SNECMA, France), for the Jaguar supersonic strike-trainer (Adour turbofan by Rolls-Royce and Turbomeca, France), the V/Stol strike fighter (RB 193 lift-cruise turbofan by Rolls-Royce and MAN Turbo, Germany) and the Breguet Atlantic Transall C-160 being manufactured by a consortium of Rolls-Royce, Fabrique Nationale (Belgium), Hispano-Suiza (France), and MAN Turbo (Germany).

Europe is also learning the wisdom of establishing the widest possible market in advance of production. In 1968 a new company, Airbus International, was formed by the European A-300 airbus consortium specifically to arrange sales. Without a marketing organization Europe will have little chance of selling its productions, let alone financing new designs. The inevitable brain-drain is setting in, with highly skilled engineers and designers from Germany, Italy, France, the Netherlands, and Britain migrating to the US.

The explanations and excuses are many. Whereas the British and French aircraft are produced for a comparatively small home market and in the hope of picking up a few foreign orders, the American companies are assured of very large initial home orders owing to the longer distances flown. US airlines purchase about 60 per cent of all world civil aircraft and this in turn brings down the price for export. Vast US military expenditure benefits civil aircraft as well; US armed forces use 52,000 aircraft while those of Western Europe use only 25,000 and of these only 60 per cent are of European origin. In Europe there is no unified home market and the small national home markets cannot absorb enough of the nation's aircraft to justify the huge sums spent on research and development. Europe has built-in problems such as short distances, bad weather, strong competition from rail and road, highly seasonal operations and many border problems. This is a weak base on which to work.

US firms too benefit from economies of size in manufacture. In Europe only four companies, Hawker Siddeley, BAC, Rolls-Royce and Sud Aviation, employ more than 20,000 workers compared with twenty US aviation companies who do, and one of those, Boeing, employs 128,000 – more than the French and Italian aerospace industries combined. Four US companies each have annual sales exceeding those for the whole of the British aviation industry.

There have, of course, been many bilateral projects; late in the day European plane-makers realized this was the obvious way to split research and development costs. In any one year there are nearly fifty projects on the go in Europe involving two or more countries. Some, like the variable-geometry plane, are abandoned (by France in July 1967), others are known as the paper planes because they never get beyond that stage. Some succeed, like the Anglo–French Jaguar supersonic jet advanced trainer-strike aircraft (a pact was signed in January 1968 to produce 400, – 200 each by 1971), Concorde and the ACA, Advanced Combat Aircraft, for Belgium, Germany, Italy, the Netherlands, and Canada (1,000 were ordered to replace the Lockheed F 104). Many smaller projects are undertaken jointly such as air-to-surface guided missiles and helicopters.

The MRCA project (UK, West Germany, and Italy), the biggest multi-national aviation venture ever undertaken, exemplified the way in which politics impinge on high-technology industry. The German Government who wanted 600 (UK 385 and Italy 200) preferred the Rolls-Royce RB 199 engine to the American Pratt & Whitney design and approved Britain's plan for the MRCA project to be the base for an integrated European aero-engine industry. But the Americans made it clear to the German Government that when it came to reckon up offset payments for American occupation troops in Germany, very considerable allowances would be made if the Pratt & Whitney design were adopted. In the event, chiefly because of better work-sharing proposals, Rolls-Royce won the contract, estimated to be worth eventually over £600m. The Dutch Government, which withdrew from the project, agreed to co-operate on research and development until at least May 1970.

True integration is preferable to *ad hoc* arrangements because of the time taken to dovetail each agreement in the first place and the time taken to get to know other people and their methods. Then there is the time taken in keeping a wary eye on each other and, alternatively, reassuring one another. And when the partners in *ad hoc* arrangements are changed frequently, it is more confusing, time-consuming, and so expensive. The costs of collaboration have been put by M. Ziegler of Breguet at between 10 and 20 per cent of the cost of an aircraft.

Delays lead to soaring costs. When the project definition agreement for the A-300 airbus was signed in 1967, the cost of engine development was put at £52m. and of the airframe at £130m. These figures had risen by July 1968 to £70m. and £215m., making the total £285m. instead of the £192m. budgeted for. A decision to go ahead was then dependent on firm commitments from the airlines to buy at least a total of seventy-five. The British Government decided to pull out but the British firm, Hawker Siddeley, joined as a private-venture partner, putting in its own money.

The creation of common defence requirements would make a huge contribution to rationalization of the aircraft industry. But, even within the UK, the Royal Navy and the RAF could not arrive at a joint specification for an interceptor plane, so it is hardly surprising that the seven governments in the Western European Union (Britain and the Six) have failed to reach agreement on a joint arms programme, though its Standing Armaments Committee exists for the purpose of bringing about co-operation in arms procurement. The British, with overseas commitments, and the French, with their *force de frappe*, imagined that their defence requirements were incompatible with those of any other nation; the West Germans, wishing to spare their economy the burden of heavy defence production, had built up an aircraft industry which was a direct subsidiary of the U S aircraft industry; the Netherlands wished to protect the freedom of action of its resident giant, Philips. So no agreement has been reached on standard specifications, on joint manufacture, or on common procurement with the result that all are being forced to rely on the U S as the sole supplier of their major military equipment.

Europe is belatedly making efforts to put its aircraft industry in order. The Bundestag decreed in April 1968 that 'government spending would depend on the industry's success in rationalizing itself', and the result was a joint grouping of the four biggest companies – Messerschmitt/Boelkow, Vereinigts Flugtechnische Werke, Hamburger Flugzeugbau, and Dornier Werke. They aim to work out an independent German aerospace policy and make the German aircraft industry competitive, although on a long-term basis the Government is perforce thinking in terms of international rather than national projects; government officials are sitting on the steering committee to make joint proposals on research and development and production. In Britain the Plowden report revealed that Europe's aviation industry had been feather-bedded for the past fifty years and should now take its place in the national economy on a cost-effective basis. There would have to be a drastic realignment to match up to the new defence policy; if self-defence was no longer a feasible economic proposition for each individual state of Europe, neither was self-indulgence in the manufacture of strictly national weapons – such as aircraft. European co-operation should be organized on a permanent basis.

There will be a dramatic upsurge in air traffic in the 1970s – B O A C reckoned to double its size over the five years 1967–72. Ahead of the supersonic aircraft lies the hypersonic jet – about 10,000 m.p.h. – which could appear in the 1970s and which would probably be built on a world-scale partnership, which Europe would be entitled to join if she had settled her own difficulties and achieved really close co-operation. AICMA (Association Internationale des Constructeurs de Matériel Aérospatial), with members from Britain, Belgium, France, Germany, Italy, the Netherlands, Spain, Sweden, and Switzerland, has set up working parties to study the financial, technological, managerial, legal, and tariff obstacles at present hampering closer working. One of the more obvious obstacles is that 'drawing offices do not speak the same language'. Although actual language difficulties are minimal, different units are used, different standards and regulations are referred to, and there are different relationships with government technical departments; design standards and methods of testing need to be made uniform. Also the needs of various partners and their clients need to be reconciled at an earlier stage.

The turning point in the fortunes of Europe's aircraft industry could come if a successful joint UK-European VTOL (vertical take-off and landing capability) plane is achieved. Development costs would exceed £100m; three possible projects are being debated and marketing studies undertaken. There is unlikely to be a big enough market in the UK alone, but British requirements plus those of Western Europe should provide a big enough market, and using cost-sharing and work-sharing procedures Europe could prove herself self-sufficient in this field.

Mr Wilson referred to the history of European co-operation as 'a desert littered with the dry bones of joint projects'. Some projects obviously are doomed to die on the drawing board or shortly after but others choke to death in the atmosphere of suspicion and fear which inhibits action by the European governments and manufacturers. The Lockheed air-bus has been given at least a two-year lead while Europe fiddled. It is the British and French who have to resolve their differences; many British manufacturers believe the French aim is to secure a monopoly in air frames so that they can dictate what engines will serve their purpose; the French bitterly resent the British lead in engines which always preempts the position in joint bargaining; when Rolls-Royce got the contract to supply its fan-jet engines for Lockheed's rival air-bus in March 1968, it was in French eyes almost an act of *lèse-majesté* From the earliest days of aviation, the aircraft builders and flyers of both countries have been very friendly; the differences are not on the production and technological side, but on the political. The atmosphere has been poisoned by the non-admission of Britain to the Common Market. Once a political decision is taken for a united Europe, joint defence requirements would follow logically and from that would stem joint procurement and joint manufacture of military aircraft. This in turn could not fail to influence civilian production.

EURO-COMPANIES

One way of overcoming the fragmentation of Europe's technology-based industries would be the formation of genuinely European companies from the various national firms. In 1958 the Treaty of Rome was concerned with the danger of monopolies (Article 86) but the problem ten years later was rather how to bring into being the larger European or international company able to challenge the American giants which, with their longer production runs, their saving on wasteful duplication, their pooling of research and development costs, and their rationalization of services and marketing facilities, bestrode the European economy. Worse, Europe herself had been contributing to the American onslaught owing to the ease with which American corporations had been able to raise loans on the European market – investors and bankers appreciated the advantages of size. The answer was clear – if they wanted to stand up to the American giants, European mini-firms must combine. The importance of business mergers across national boundaries became all the more desirable to the Brussels technocrats as they had been thwarted on political unity. They saw the creation of Euro-firms as a step towards industrial unity, good in itself, but which could also hasten the coming of true political unity.

Despite the huge and undisputed advantages of trans-frontier organization, the difficulties, too, were very real. The great national companies such as Fiat in Italy, ICI in Britain, Philips in Holland, and Nestlé in Switzerland had long ago outgrown the small domestic market but had not outgrown strong national affiliations and loyalties. Moreover, some of the newer firms and organizations, especially those in the new technological industries, had been created with the active support and, often, capital of their governments. Yet these were the very ones where owing the ballooning of research and development costs, cross-frontier mergers were most to be desired. Such companies may be bound to their governments by extensive defence contracts (in America firms with such contracts, that is many of the biggest ones, are forbidden by Federal law to have foreign directors on the board).

Yet, whatever the difficulties, the advantages of mergers could not be denied. In Britain, Mr Wilson referred specifically to this as one of his seven points in his speech at the Lord Mayor's Banquet in 1967 (p. 87-8) and in that same year the Industrial Reorganization Corporation was set up and financed with government money specifically to bring about suitable large-scale mergers (such as the creation of International Computers Ltd, from ICT, English Electric, and Plessey). Seminars and conventions devoted to the subject multiplied and in the corridors of power of the *joyeuse entrée*, Euro-companies were one of the big talking-points of 1968.

But in France there was less enthusiasm. M. Amboise Roux, vice-president of the French Employers Federation (Conseil national du patronat français) referred to Euro-companies as a myth and as virtually useless. Other equally eminent industrialists referred to them as legal fictions and certainly no panacea for the industrial integration of Europe.

In memorandum (66) 1250 on 'the creation of a European commercial society', the EEC had come out in favour of concluding a convention, separate from the Rome Treaty, to provide for the establishment of 'Community-law companies', able to operate freely and uniformly throughout the member countries and open to non-members. The Commission turned down an alternative suggestion to form such companies under the provisions of the Treaty on both economic and legal grounds. A third proposal, by the French Government, was that each member country should enact uniform provisions for the formation and operation of 'Community companies', which would operate alongside companies incorporated under the national law and would themselves be subject to such national law within each member state. The Commission thought such pseudo-European companies would not achieve real legal identity and would leave the main problems untouched. i.e. the difficulties involved in the transfer of a company registration to a new domicile and the question of under which national law the new Euro-companies should be incorporated, i.e. should an Italian–German merger be registered under Italian or German law? In January 1968 the French Government tried to force the issue by announcing that for their part they were introducing new legislation to authorize mergers or associations between firms in different countries of the Common Market and to give them fiscal advantages to compensate for the high cost of multi-national mergers. The new creations would be called European Interest Companies and the French Government hoped that other members would pass similar measures.

The Commission, however, felt that this was totally inadequate and continued in their view that a specifically new type of company under European Law but separate from the Rome Treaty should be envisaged; in this case the question of transfer of domicile would not arise and the new company would become 'Europeanized' rather than lose or gain any one particular nationality. Further detailed studies were called for, not only of the company law position but of the tax, financial, and social implications; the latter were important because employees of some countries have the right under national law to sit on managerial boards (Germany) and to share profits in one way or another (France). It was widely felt that company tax should be based on the already adopted added-value system.

Taxation in the EEC

After the transitional period in 1970 there will be three basic forms of revenue-raising in the EEC: (1) a harmonized value-added tax, plus a limited number of harmonized excise duties; (2) a corporation tax with uniform rates throughout the Community. and (3) personal income tax, the rates of which could vary from country to country.

The most controversial tax is without question the value-added tax (V A T) because it is considered by many to be a direct incentive to exports and this point has been taken up by the Americans, who argue that it gives the Common Market unfair trading advantages because the tax is rebated to exporting firms.

Value-added tax is a widely spread indirect taxation system – far more so than purchase tax in Britain which can be, and usually is, highly selective and applied directly against consumption, although there is no reason why it cannot be extremely widely spread as a matter of monetary policy. V A T, like purchase tax, is a consumer tax, and those who for economic policy reasons dislike taxes on consumption will disapprove of V A T.

But V A T is a very handy instrument against tax evasion because the manufacturer or trader, in a sense and in his own interest, becomes the agent of the tax collector. So that he can have his own tax assessed properly, he has to get written evidence – usually on invoices - of what the previous handler's tax was so that he can deduct it from the figure he has to pay.

Little wonder that V A T originated in France where there has never been any great rush to pay taxes, or reveal true incomes. The way V A T works is simplicity itself: A sells goods to B worth £100. Assuming that V A T has been fixed at 20 per cent he bills B with £120. B then sells the goods, or the goods he has made from the materials he has bought, to C for £200. He adds on 20 per cent, or £40, bringing C's bill to £240. C sells to the retailer for £250 adding on 20 per cent or £50, bringing the final price to the consumer up to £300. The deductions in payment of tax start with B who instead of paying to the taxman the full £40 he has passed on to C, only pays £20 because he has A's invoice to him showing that £20 has already been paid. C does the same. He has B's invoice showing that £40 has already been paid, so he only pays the difference between £40 and £50 i.e. £10.

So we have the tax collector getting three separate payments:

A pays £20
B „   £20
C „   £10
——
£50

which is his 20 per cent of the final selling price before tax. So, it may be asked, since both are consumer taxes, why not levy it in one lump on the selling price in the same way as purchase tax (except that for convenience sake purchase tax is levied at the wholesale stage instead of the retail stage), thus avoiding several collecting points? The reason, again, is that it is an extremely efficient way of preventing tax evasion.

In 1969 the Conservatives came out in favour of VAT as part of a general reform of British taxation and a Neddy report (HMSO, 4 August 1969) supported the view that VAT could help improve Britain's industrial efficiency and improve her balance of payments. From industry's point of view VAT does not have a direct impact on industrial costs as happens with SET. The report estimated that, if food and public utilities are exempted, the replacement of SET and purchase tax by VAT should not cause a rise in the cost of living of more than 2 to 3 per cent and adjustments to wages or other benefits could compensate the lower-paid workers. Twenty 'little Neddies' up and down the country representing various industries were in favour but wanted VAT to be incorporated in a new taxation deal.

The balance of payments should benefit because any VAT entering into the costs of the export at an earlier stage may be recovered so though VAT does not, strictly speaking, subsidize exports, it certainly makes them cheaper. Already the UK is doing some 40 per cent of its trade with countries mostly in the EEC, who have VAT or are going to adopt it, and she might have to agree to introduce it herself if she joined the EEC.

Drawbacks are the high costs of collection and administration. Unlike purchase tax which is collected in a lump sum at the wholesale stage, VAT is collected in fractional instalments and there would need to be some two million collecting points (as compared with 65,000 for purchase tax) and over 5,000 additional civil servants. There could be a single rate of something over 10 per cent (in some countries the rate reaches 15 per cent) or a two-tier system. The danger is that, since VAT is basically a consumer tax, it could trigger off wage and salary demands which would offset the benefit to industry's costs. This was why the Trades Union Congress came out against it in August 1969, while agreeing to reconsider it in the event of Britain's joining the Common Market.

In October 1969 the Commission proposed the postponement of the date on which VAT should apply throughout the EEC by one year i.e. to 1 January 1971. France, Germany, and the Netherlands had already introduced it and Luxemburg could keep to schedule but both Belgium and Italy were unable to meet the deadline of 1 January 1970. Belgium asked for one year's delay but Italy for two years pleading that she was involved in a programme of fundamental fiscal reform, but this was refused. Moreover, the Commission proposed that countries taking advantage of postponement should reduce their export tax rebates. Italy's further request to be excused from introducing VAT right down to retail level was also turned down. The Commission made the one year extension conditional on all the Six agreeing to harmonize their many different national rates of VAT by the beginning of 1974; it wanted each country to move as early as possible towards a maximum of two different VAT-rates.

One problem which might arise is that Euro-companies could exceed optimum size for Europe in order to compete with American companies, which are of optimum size for the much larger US market. But in 1968 fragmentation was the danger not monopolistic tendencies, which in any case can be guarded against by applying the anti-monopoly powers of Article 86.

The debate continued and was enlarged to deal not just with Euro-companies but with international companies as a whole. These were classified by Professor Howard V. Perlmutter of the Institute of Management Studies at Lausanne as of the ethnocentric type i.e. nationalistic, where even the most trivial decisions have to be referred back to headquarters in the base country; polycentric where, although relying on locals to run the subsidiaries in other countries, headquarters still keeps a tight hold on the purse-strings and sees to it that no outposts get to know the inmost secrets of markets and research – most international companies come under this heading; and geocentric, where the various subsidiaries are allowed complete autonomy except for safeguards against duplication of plant, research, and marketing, including competing with each other in third markets. In a geocentric company research is carried out on a genuinely international basis and the business is run by the best men wherever they can be found (he instanced R T Z – Rio Tinto Zinc – where overseas directors are directly involved in the formulation of policy). I B M is trying to create a geocentric image and boasts of the international character of its research, with seven laboratories in Europe and nineteen in the U S, but it is still a very American empire.

While nothing concrete was achieved in the way of legislation on Euro-companies, one result was to direct attention to Articles 85 to 94 (rules of competition) which outlaw agreements which distort competition or improperly exploit a dominant position within the market. These articles had been implemented by Regulations 17 and 27 (1962) requiring notification of all agreements involving price-fixing, sharing of markets, production limitation, etc. to the Commission for decision as to whether or not they are permissible. At one time in 1968 it was estimated that 30,000 such agreements had been notified to the Commission without any decision having been taken on them. The field had been clear for sole-agency agreements in specific areas of the E E C since 1 May 1967 but beyond this nothing was clear. In June 1968, however, the Commission adopted a more flexible attitude towards inter-company pacts. It approved three agreements: the first, Alliance des Constructeurs Français de Machines-outils, establishing joint marketing and product specialization between a number of French machine-tool producers; the second, Socemas, establishing joint buying for sixty French food-retailing concerns; and the third approving for five years a research and development, manufacturing, and sales agreement between the Belgian electrical engineering group, A C E C, and Berliet, the French heavy-lorry manufacturers. The Commission stated that it favoured agreements especially between small- and medium-sized companies where this clearly made economic sense, and that even for large concerns such agreements would not necessarily be frowned upon if the forces of competition were not thereby restricted. They also implied that no agreement should be banned under the Treaty if the total market share of the companies involved was negligible or too small to affect trade and competition in the EEC. This 'total market share' was not defined and would probably differ from sector to sector.

Such clarification was welcomed and it was also learnt that the Commission was submitting an individual case on joint-research agreements to the Council which, if agreed, would give block exemption to over 1,000 agreements of this type which had been held up in the pipeline. The regulations in force under Articles 85 to 94 are still complex and decisions arising from test cases in the courts have also to be taken into account in trying to assess the position, but at any rate with regard to the smaller- and medium-sized firms the bogey of the cartel seems to have been laid.

However, on 23 July 1969 the Commission showed its teeth by fining six major quinine-producers a total of $500,000 for having rigged the Community market in quinine and quinidine, so infringing Article 85 of the Treaty, which strictly forbids cartels. They were alleged to have taken legal advice warning them that they would be infringing Article 85 but had nevertheless gone ahead, trusting to secrecy with various ploys (limitation of production, price-fixing, and market sharing) bteween 1960 and 1965 (in 1964 their selling price was increased by around 50 per cent) but market developments, mainly increased demand for quinine because of the war in Vietnam, made subsequent arrangements unnecessary. The Commission considered the offence the more serious because the six companies between them controlled about 80 per cent of the Community market and over half of the world market. The Dutch firm of Nedchem was fined nearly half the total, $210,000, the German firm, Boehringer, $190,000, and the four other partners, Buchler (Germany), Pointet-Girard (France), Nogentaise (France), and Pharmacie Centrale (France) accounted for the remaining $100,000.

On 24 July 1969 the Commission made history by fining ten leading European chemical companies a total of $485,000 for alleged price-fixing in the aniline dyestuffs markets – for the first time the Commission fined firms from non-member countries: ICI (Britain) and the three Swiss firms, CIBA, Geigy, and

Sandoz were each fined $50,000, as were the German firms of Bayer, BASF, Hoechst, and Cassella, and the French Société Française des Matières Colorantes; the Italian firm, Acna was fined only $35,000. These companies were said to have agreed price-increase deals between 1963 and 1967 involving as many as sixty companies, some of which dropped out when investigations began and others were not proceeded against because they were considered by the Commission not to have been free agents. The four German firms had already been in trouble – early in 1969 they were fined for price-fixing by the German cartel office, and as they had also received an EEC fine they appealed to the Court of Justice in Luxembourg pleading that they should not be fined twice over i.e. by their national court and the EEC Commission, but their plea was rejected.

All the companies, except CIBA, appealed against the fine: ICI on two counts, that the findings of the Commission were wrong and that the Commission had no right of jurisdiction over a company based outside the EEC. CIBA would not even appeal to the Court of Justice saying this implied recognition of the powers of the Commission: she would, if served with a 'proper notice' have recourse to 'appropriate legal procedure'.

There have been few truly international mergers of any significance within Europe since the war. In July 1964 the German firm of Agfa and Belgium's Gevaert, threatened by America's giant Kodak organization, merged their photographic concerns; both companies continued to operate within their own national boundaries, but the boards are identical and profits are shared on a fifty–fifty basis. In January 1968 Zanussi, one of Italy's largest electric appliance manufacturers, formed a new joint production company with the German giant, AEG Telefunken, to 'better cover the European-Community market' as well as non-community markets such as Britain. One of the advantages was that marketing would be through a combination of both sales organizations, thus avoiding wasteful duplication and competition.

Although each EEC country is busily encouraging mergers within its national boundaries, the EEC as a body is still shying away from the genuine cross-frontier merger. Yet this is the only way to get large viable units able to absorb the huge research and development costs inseparable from the new technology-based industries. Even if it is too early for the genuine Euro-company, owing allegiance to no one country, the EEC knows it must find the will – and the way – to join forces in this field as in so many others.

A small step towards co-operation was taken in May 1969: seventeen European countries met to discuss a new European patents convention. Chaos reigned in the patent offices of Europe where the patents had been piling up since the Republic of Venice started issuing letters of patent in the sixteenth century. . . . Patent offices were years behind with their work and this was seriously hampering the smaller innovating firms (the bigger ones often ignore the whole business hoping to keep so far ahead of the game that they can safely ignore patents). The head of the German Patent Office dubbed the proliferation of patent systems in Europe economic nonsense. Well he might. The German Patent Office has over 2,000 employees, including 800 engineers to oversee a file of four million patents. France, where patents could be obtained in less than a year but without benefit of examination, realized in 1969 that the newness of some of these registrations was in serious doubt and passed a law introducing formal examination of novelty and utility. Holland, since 1964, has deferred examination until the inventor has had time to assess the potential commercial worth of his patent.

The Commission took the initiative in 1959 of calling for an examination of the whole question of patents which led to the publication in 1962 of an initial draft convention which set out to achieve a single-application and a single-issue procedure which would protect inventions equally in the six member-countries. But the whole issue was put aside when the French wished to draw up an EEC patent system as a *fait accompli* to which other European nations would be allowed to accede; this Holland doggedly refused to allow, maintaining that Great Britain and other applicants for membership should be consulted before definite decisions were taken – Holland wanted the writ of the new patents to run in as wide an area as possible. Now a full report on legal aspects of a European patent office will be submitted for further discussion in January 1970 and a European patent of real international significance and validity could result from the joint efforts of the seventeen nations.

EDUCATIONAL GAP

Although the technological gap has been immeasurably widened by the non-integration of Europe and especially by the exclusion from the EEC of Great Britain, the most technologically advanced nation in Europe, it was made inevitable by the failure of Europe to keep up with the educational advance of the US and USSR. Only recently has education been regarded in Europe as an investment in the future. Such a statement still sounds vulgar to many European countries with their long tradition of a liberal and classical education to prepare an élite to become the policy-makers and the professional cadre of their country. On philosophical grounds, too, many young people find the concept distasteful; they want to develop their potential as individuals and not to be regarded as so much 'economic-plan fodder'.

Yet if the EEC is to hold her own with the USA and the USSR, she must adapt her educational systems to enable them to produce the men and women to lead the greatest researches, man the great technological industries, and perhaps more important to administer the fast-moving political and social machinery. The USA with its 'go-go' economy can attract most of its young people into higher education and the USSR makes no bones about directing them. Europe still has to find a way.

The Poignant report of 1966 drawn up by an international committee studying the relative positions of educational achievement for the Institute for University Studies of the European Communities laid the blame for the imbalance between the number of graduates produced in US and USSR and the EEC on a faulty system of European secondary education, which produces the university intake. In the US, the USSR, and Japan half the children finished the long-option secondary education to the age of seventeen or eighteen whereas in the EEC fifteen per cent or less did so. Most European countries are faced with the need for greater social justice in the selection of potential graduates i.e.

those taking the long secondary course. Most are trying to overcome the difficulty by postponing the selection of those taking the long course to a later age so that inequalities of family, social, and economic background may to some extent be ironed out by the school influences. The need for broadening the base is shown by the fact that whereas in the US more than half the college students are the children of manual workers, in Germany the percentage is only seven per cent.

To make the best use of their human assets, Italy has moved over to a comprehensive system; Belgium also to a comprehensive system, though retaining the division into sections (grammar, modern, and technical). Germany is making it easier to change streams between different types of schools by setting up reception classes; in the Netherlands the first year of secondary education must be identical in every type of school to facilitate horizontal switching between the different types of school. The French are continuing selection through their observation classes from ages eleven to thirteen. In time this should ensure that the feed-pipe to university level becomes unblocked and that there is a clearway to all, irrespective of social origin, to the university.

Meanwhile the Poignant report stressed that the EEC was not drawing on the whole population for its brain-power. Children from the higher social classes (4 to 5 per cent of the population) make up between 32 to 45 per cent of the student population; but children of the much more numerous agricultural, industrial-skilled and semi-skilled workers accounted for only a small percentage: 12·6 per cent in France, 11·5 per cent in Belgium, 10 per cent in the Netherlands, and 7·5 per cent in Germany. (The figure for England and Wales was 30 per cent). A detailed breakdown of university students by social background gave the following picture for France:

Social background	Population (%)	Student population (%)
Professions and higher management	4·3	30·2
Executives	6·2	17·7
Employers	9·2	15·2
Manual workers	29·0	8·3
Clerical workers	7·0	8·2

Social background	Population (%)	Student population (%)
Farmers	10·4	5·5
Domestic staff, etc.	2·4	1·2
Agricultural wage earners	2·8	0·7
Others	28·7	13·0

Service de Presse et d'Information,
Bulletin Mensuel Series 10 No. 7

There is a great diversity in Community schools; children generally enter school at the age of six (U K at the age of five) and the age of transfer to secondary education varies between ten (Germany), twelve (Belgium, Luxembourg, the Netherlands), and eleven (France, Italy and the U K). The leaving age also varies from sixteen (France – and Britain with effect from 1970) to fifteen (most Länder of Germany and the Netherlands) and fourteen in Belgium, Italy, and Luxembourg, but in these countries encouragement is given to stay beyond the statutory age on a voluntary basis.

In the E E C specialization comes later than in England; Greek and Latin studies which are still compulsory in many continental grammar schools have been drastically cut down in the U K. In France the examination system is particularly highly organized; each stage of education is completed by a certificate or diploma enabling the student to move on to the next stage or to enter a particular trade or profession. There are certificates at the end of primary education, certificates for various levels of technical competence, and a short-course leaving certificate for those who do not stay on to take the *baccalauréat*, which gives automatic right to enter any French university (though this right may be modified). In the May–June 1968 student riots, students objected, among other things, that this documentation tied a label round their neck for life, and that their teachers and tutors were remote and pedagogic, making no attempt to know them personally, to consider their opinions, or to bridge the generation gap.

Meanwhile the Poignant report showed that in absolute figures the E E C produced hardly a quarter of the number of American graduates and one-third of the Russian total, each year.

133

Community	100,000 out of a population of 180m.
USA	450,000 out of a population of 190m.
USSR	345,000 out of a population of 223m.

Since the USA awards degrees for many subjects which would not rank in Europe, e.g. home economics, poultry farming, etc., gross figures are not strictly comparable; on the other hand, with the trend to greater specialization, such degrees probably make a very real contribution to the national economy.

The report then established what proportion of university graduates was produced each year from the total population in the relevant national age-groups and obtained these percentages:

EEC	4	
UK	5·7	(9 if various non-degree levels which rank in other countries are counted)
USA	19·6	
USSR	8·2	

The report went on to assess the percentage of the various age-groups emerging as graduates in science and technology and noted a wide difference.

	Percentage of relevant age-group	*No. of graduates in Science and technology*
EEC	1·1	25,000
UK	2·7	17,000
USA	3·9	88,000
USSR	4·0	140,000

The report pointed out that in fact the gap is even wider, since in most EEC countries graduate science-teachers are included in this category, who in the USSR and USA are included under education.

The number of students qualifying at technical institutes to become technicians, far from redressing the balance, shows the EEC again well behind the USSR and Britain. Moreover, the report warned that the lag was not compensated for when the number of advanced research workers was calculated. Simply comparing the number of higher degrees awarded as a percentage of relevant age groups in the USA, USSR, and France, the percentages were:

USA (1963)	0·55	(level: PhD., D.S.)
USSR (1963)	0·30	(level: candidature – this percentage may have nearly doubled by 1970)
France (1961)	0·15	(level: doctorate)

As far as integration of education is concerned, very little has been attempted or achieved. In 1963 the EEC, implementing Articles 41, 118, 125, and 128, adopted the general principles of a common training policy very similar in effect to the UK industrial training act. The principles were designed to make it possible for 'everyone to receive adequate training, ensuring freedom to choose occupation, establishment, place of training, and place of work'. Although two vocational training programmes were drawn up, one general and one relating to agriculture, no decision was taken as to whether they should be implemented at EEC level or at national government level. As in the UK, although in principle training should apply up to top management in practice it is likely to begin and end at the apprentice stage where it is easier to organize a useful course of training.

However, as a by-product of the European schools for the 6,000 children of Community officials at least two useful harmonizing measures have been achieved in education: one, the establishment of the international *baccalauréat* giving entry to any European university, which it is hoped will be generally recognized; the other, a harmonization of history textbooks. These are often sources of cultural and racial prejudice and give the history of wars rather than the history of peace. The new textbooks attempt to reconcile the view that Italy discovered America, because Columbus was born in Genoa, and that Spain did because King Ferdinand employed Columbus: that England had the best of the Hundred Years' War because of Marlborough's victories, and that France did, because of the mysterious victory at Denain, passed over in silence in English schoolbooks.

Educational backwardness can then be identified as one of the factors contributing to Europe's technological backwardness. The Poignant report warned that the EEC's position would be worse relatively to that of the USA and the USSR by 1970 because from their already viable secondary school launching-pads the USA is forecasting 6·5 million students at college or university in 1970 while the USSR aims at eight million by 1980.

WOMEN IN TECHNOLOGY

The lack of women taking up scientific and technical careers has often been deplored and no doubt many more women would take up such careers if they were open to them and were reasonably well paid. In the USSR 35 per cent of all new engineer graduates are women. In France the percentage is 2 per cent but in Britain only 0·1 per cent. This probably reflects reasonably accurately the degree of prejudice against women entering a man's world.

The whole question is tied up with that of equal pay, Article 119 of the Rome Treaty. The deadline adopted for Community-wide equal pay was 31 December 1964 but although the principle is accepted in every country, no single country had in fact consistently applied it by October 1967 when a special inquiry reported back to the Commission. The UK which has always paid lip service to equal pay has also shrunk from the economic and social implications; the Department of Employment and Productivity calculated that the cost of equal pay would be an additional 6 per cent on the nation's annual wage-bill. Not only is pay unequal but opportunities for promotion for women are extremely restricted and nowhere more so than in the technology-based industries. It is not a change of heart that is needed, for both the Six and the UK protest that they are totally committed; it is a change of practice and until this comes about, there will be no improvement in the comparative statistics for the USA, the USSR, and Europe.

MANAGEMENT GAP

The importance of management and management studies has only recently been brought home to the EEC and the UK. More than 80 per cent of Japan's top industrial managers have had university education compared with 30 per cent in Britain. Half the members of the Praesidium in Russia are qualified scientists. The USA has 160 business schools and 24,000 management consultants; Britain 3,000 management consultants; France, 1,000; Holland, 400; and Germany, 300.

Robert S. McNamara, former US Secretary of Defense, goes so far as to say that the gap between Europe and the US is not technological but managerial; pointing out that the brain-drain itself is witness to Europe's ability to bridge any technological gap, he suggests that top brains seek the US because they find there more modern and effective management.

Certainly most UK 'drainees', when interviewed on their reasons for emigrating, mention the better resources for research and the better use of the results of that research; their work will not be destined for automatic pigeon-holing or be solely paper research. They also mention better housing; a better salary structure; better education for their children.

McNamara defined management as 'the gate through which social, political, economic, technological change, indeed change in every dimension, is rationally spread through society'.

For centuries in Europe management has meant a board of directors many of whom hold pluralities; in England his title alone would justify a peer's name on the letter-head and put a director's fee in his pocket. It is not impossible that a man may be such an outstanding manager, that his presence is vital to the managing boards of twenty or more different firms producing widely assorted products – but unlikely. In France concentration through cross-holdings was so great in what were once called *les deux cents familles*, that businesses were ruled secretly and autocratically rather than managed. In Germany huge family and private firms did not have to reveal the secrets of their balance-sheets; Europe was a close company.

America with her more democratic development had none of

Europe's built-in problems of social order; her 'aristocrats' had won their spurs in the efficient management of her industry.

Management in Europe has lagged. But its importance is increasingly recognized and schools of management studies and business schools on the Harvard pattern are multiplying. Although students protest about over-management, alleging that institutions and bureaucracies reduce them to depersonalized ciphers, Europe suffers from under-management. Her haphazard educational systems and unco-ordinated town planning are two obvious examples. Management will need to involve students and workers in decisions reached – and be seen to be doing so.

The urgency of the problem is shown by a comparison of the output of the British workman and his opposite number in America. Presenting the awards for the Council for Industrial Design, the Duke of Edinburgh said, 'Turnover per man employed in British manufacturing is £2,500 a year compared with £8,000 a year in America. This is a measure of the technological, managerial, and design gap.' The Elstub Committee's findings (October 1969) were not far different.

Measured by value added for each of its employees, the British aircraft industry's productivity is approximately one-third that of the American industry. It is not inferior to that of the French industry, its other main competitor.

It attributed most of this productivity gap to the small scale of air frame production in Europe. Allowing for the difference in production runs,

the ratio of productivity in the US and Britain is found, by several independent methods, to be between 1·2 to one and 1·5 to one. This is the true ratio of the effectiveness of manpower in the two countries.

5 The Common Agricultural Policy

Seldom has a plan been so carefully devised by so many dedicated experts as the CAP; seldom has a plan failed so abysmally. Within six years (1962–3 to 1968–9) its cost increased by an astronomical eighty times; as a result of misguided farm policy, a surplus of about 400,000 tons of butter had been produced by October 1969; six million tons of excess grain, and one million tons of excess sugar were being produced each year, and money had to be poured into the Farm Fund to prop up prices at home, to destroy fruit and vegetables, to store butter, and to subsidize agricultural exports.

The CAP antagonized almost every country with agricultural interests outside the EEC; they objected to its blatant protectionism. It was used as one of the main deterrents to the entry into Europe of Great Britain in 1962, so helping to set back European unity by perhaps a decade; it split the EEC itself into six angry nations quarrelling over the workings of the Farm Fund and carrying over the ill-will so generated into other sectors of the EEC; and, final irony, even its main beneficiaries, the farmers themselves, turned against it when it became clear that it would drive many of them from the land they had worked, known, and loved into a rootless urban existence.

The CAP, aspects of which finally came into effect in July 1969, was nonetheless a considerable achievement. Thousands of hitherto unheeded farming problems were thrashed out round the negotiating table; after hundreds of gruelling sessions, day and night, the politicians and agricultural experts were able to settle on an overall policy for agriculture in Europe, as required by Articles 38–57 of the Rome Treaty, which stipulated that internal barriers to trade in agricultural as well as in industrial products must be abolished by July 1969. And the CAP, although a bone of contention, proved to be the strongest link between the EEC members during the many crises of the Community.

About the need for a policy there was no dispute; the pattern of agriculture in Europe had not altered basically for centuries and it played a vital role in the economy of Europe and in that of most member-states; Community farms accounted for between 6 and 14·5 per cent of the national incomes of the members, supplying over 10 per cent of the EEC's combined gross domestic product. The vital importance of agriculture to France and Italy is seen clearly from the table below; between them they control three quarters of total EEC arable land and have easily the largest proportions of their total working populations employed in agriculture; many more are involved through ancillary trades and processing industries.

Arable Land in the EEC*

	Total arable area (sq. km.)	Proportion (%) of EEC arable area	No. employed in farming and forestry (1964)	*Proportion (%) of total work-force (1964)*
France	346,330	46·7	3·7m.	19
Italy	209,650	28·3	5·0	25
Germany	143,320	19·4	3·0	11
Netherlands	23,100	3·1	0·4	10
Belgium	17,340	2·3	0·2	6
Luxembourg	1,380	0·2	0·02	14

*Basic Statistics of the Community 1965.

One of the greatest handicaps suffered by Community agriculture was the extremely small size of most farms; two thirds are virtually small-holdings with an area of less than 25 acres; the average size of a Common-Market farm is 27 acres (compared with 67 acres in Britain); only 3 per cent have an area of more than 125 acres, these are chiefly in the Plaine de Beauce, Central Provence, and Northern Italy. In Germany many farms consist of plots of land which are not contiguous and this makes for still less economical working. There had been for generations a shortage of the capital necessary for modernization. The consequent low level of productivity compared with that of industry caused farm incomes to lag far behind those of industrial workers and the gap was steadily widening. Even by dint of working a seven-day week, taking no holidays, and using his wife and other biddable members of his family as unpaid labour, the average farmer could still not obtain a wage comparable with that of the townsman; the position of the farm-worker *vis-à-vis* the industrial worker can be compared to that of the developing agriculture-based countries of Africa and South America *vis-à-vis* the industrial giants of the West – in the technological age agriculture cannot obtain the same rewards as industry; the rich grow richer and the poor poorer. This was an especially grave problem for the EEC because such big numbers were involved; although 400,000 workers had left the land every year since 1950, it was calculated that in 1968 there were still about 11,500,000 (about 16 per cent of the total work force), compared with about 863,000 in Great Britain (3 to 4 per cent of the work force).

The planners spoke with enthusiasm of the many benefits to be gained by tackling agriculture within a common framework. The wider consumer market would improve sales prospects and enable farmers to specialize; thus economies of scale would be achieved and, with farming organized in larger units, there would be a drop in the under-employed on the farms (Dr Mansholt, Vice President of the Commission, estimated that as many as 80 per cent of Europe's farmers, while tied hand and foot to their farms, were chronically under-employed in an age of mechanical aids). Modernization schemes could be co-ordinated better within a common policy which would also play an important part in stabilizing international trade in agricultural products. The Community, though becoming more and more self-sufficient, was at the time of the inception of the CAP the biggest importer of edible and non-edible farm produce in the world, slightly above Britain; its actions would closely affect the equilibrium of world markets but all this would be kept under the watchful eye of the top planners.

So ran the argument.... The problem of how to protect a backward agriculture was not new; it is common to most industrialized countries. Governments have tackled it with every weapon to hand and come up with some very ingenious ones: price regulations, marketing boards, crop limitation, import quotas, seasonal bans on imports, discriminatory health regulations, and discriminatory bilateral agreements. The weapon chosen by the Commission was a managed market protected from outside competition by levies on imports, to bring these up to the price prevailing within the Community.

The ball was set rolling by the Cereals Regulation of 1962 which embodied the thinking underlying the whole organization of the common agricultural market. First, protection of national markets within the Community was to be phased out and a single market in each product would be established through the Community. To ensure reasonable returns to the producer, a target price was laid down for the various cereals and if prices fell below this, support-buying could come into play at an intervention price (some 7 per cent below the target price); the money to finance support-buying would come at first from the national governments and the Farm Fund and later from the Farm Fund only. This single Community market was insulated from the lower prices in the world outside by levies at the Common Market frontiers on all food imports; these variable levies payable by the importer were designed to raise the price of imports to at least the target price. As for exports, since E E C prices were subsidized at well above world price levels, member-states wishing to export surpluses could apply to the Farm Fund for export subsidies to bring their price down to or below world price levels.

Theoretically the system is a perfect closed shop; it cannot be interfered with from outside and, once the delicately balanced machinery was set in motion, it would keep running *ad infinitum*. What the planners had overlooked was that their brilliant machine was put together from old rusty ill-assorted bits and pieces so that what emerged was a Heath Robinson structure, grotesque and even to those not trying to control it at times amusing.

A stream of regulations for organizing the single-market stage for each commodity duly began; common target prices for cereals came into force in July 1967 and for milk in April 1968 (though implementation was delayed to June 1968 owing to difficulties). Common guide prices for beef, cattle, and calves were established by April 1968 (also delayed); a common target price for sugar was achieved in July 1968 and norm, target, and intervention prices for olive oil in November 1966 and for oil seeds in July 1967. Common basic prices were fixed for most fruit and vegetables in January 1967 and the single market stage for pigmeat, eggs, and poultry was reached in July 1967.

Unfortunately, as farmers and small-holders made up such a large proportion of the EEC population and work-force, agricultural lobbies were very strong in all European parliaments and from the first it became clear that when the Commission had a decision to make on a single common price for any product, it would be forced to establish a price very near the highest existing price for that product rather than take the average of all prices. No farmers anywhere would agree to a cut in prices and when, to avoid a glut of butter, it was suggested that the common price for milk should be reduced, angry farmers converged on Brussels from all parts of the EEC. So high prices were to be the order of the day; this was to lead to gross over-production, all of which had to be paid for out of the Farm Fund, and, to iron out the difference between the high Common Market price and the low world price, export subsidies would have to be very high – another heavy burden for the Farm Fund and another cause of bitter dissension when it became clear that the surplus-producing countries, mainly France, were easily getting the best of the deal, since the Farm Fund was paying out to them far more than they put in.

The financing of the CAP was a difficult issue. The basic hope was that the concessions made by Germany, the biggest food-importing country, to help French agriculture (the biggest surplus-producer) would be balanced by concessions to German industry. But the balance of advantages did not work out like that. France was able to step up its exports of foodstuffs to Germany from $170m. to approximately $500m. between 1960 and 1966 but Germany was not able to establish a comparable advantage in industry. This caused Germany to take a much harder look at her contribution to the Farm Fund.

Farm Fund (F E O G A)
The balance sheet to 31 December 1968 ($m.)

| | Contributions | | Repayments | |
	Guarantee	Guidance	Guarantee	Guidance
Belgium	156	23	95	15
France	436	82	875	44
Germany	538	87	168	56
Italy	413	64	306	150
Luxembourg	5	1	1	3
Netherlands	200	27	303	16
Total	1,748	284	1,748	284

The beneficiaries and losers

	Guarantee	Guidance
Belgium	−61	−8
France	+439	−38
Germany	−370	−31
Italy	−107	+86
Luxembourg	−4	+2
Netherlands	+103	−11

This has two parts: the guarantee section which finances support buying for the various commodities when markets are depressed and provides subsidies for exports; and the guidance section, which finances improvements in the structure of agriculture in the member-countries. Until 1966 guidance expenditure could amount to one third of the sums paid out by the guarantee section, but as these guarantee sums were escalating madly, the Germans suggested that a ceiling of $285m. should be put on guidance spending and this was adopted.

As originally agreed the Farm Fund's share of the expenditure on both the guarantee and the guidance section was to rise by stages. In 1962–3 it contributed one sixth of eligible expenses under the guarantee section (the rest being financed by the member-governments themselves), in 1963–4 one third, in 1964–5 one half, in 1965–6 three fifths, and in 1966–7 seven tenths. As soon as the single-market stage in any product was achieved, i.e. for most products between 1 July 1967 and 1 July 1968, the Fund would be responsible for all eligible expenses and after the end of the transition period, i.e. from 1970 onwards, the full cost of the CAP would be borne by the Community.

Escalating Costs ($m.) of the Farm Fund (FEOGA)

	Guarantee	Guidance	Total
1962–3	29	9	38
1963–4	51	17	68
1964–5	163	54	217
1965–6	240	80	320
1966–7	370	124	494
1967–8	1,313	285	1,806
1968–9	2,012	285	2,437
1969–70 (estimate)	2,770	285	3,124

Figures for 1967–8, 1968–9, and 1969–70 include special compensation to German, Italian, and Luxembourg farmers to offset decreased prices for grain.

The financing of the Farm Fund has been calculated by a variety of methods. For 1967–70 the Six reverted to calculating contributions in two parts; one part (covering about 45 per cent of total expenditure needed by the Fund) to consist of 90 per cent of the amount received by the member countries as levies on imports of agricultural products from non-member countries, the remaining 55 per cent to be provided by member countries according to a fixed scale:

Fixed scale (%) for non-levy contributions to Farm Fund
1 July 1967 to 31 December 1969

Belgium	8·1
France	32·0
Germany	31·2
Italy	20·3
Luxembourg	0·2
Netherlands	8·2

The chief expenditure from the guarantee section has been for export subsidies (77·3 per cent of the guarantee budget in 1962–3, 81·8 per cent in 1963–4 and 79 per cent in 1964–5) with price support for the Community's internal market taking up the balance. Both payments are first made by the national governments who are later reimbursed from the Fund. In July 1969 the Commission took Italy before the Court of Justice as she had not paid these recoverable export rebates to her farmers since 1 July 1967; she had also not complied with the speeding up of payment of contributions to the Fund and owed it $150m. The chief expenditure from the guidance section has been for structural reforms (amalgamation of farms, land drainage, reafforestation, etc.) and for improvements in production and marketing (e.g. new silos, slaughter-houses, fruit stores, vegetable auctions, refrigeration plants). The guidance section contributes up to 25 per cent of the cost of any particular project (or up to 40 per cent in special cases) with the remainder being found by the government of the member country in which the project is situated and by the immediate beneficiary of the improvement.

In February 1970 it was agreed to retain the ceiling of $285m. a year on the guidance part of the Farm Fund, but the Council could raise it for any year after 1972, by majority vote. The Italians, the main beneficiaries, wanted the ceiling abolished but the Germans, the main contributors, insisted on it being kept. (It is of course a mere flea-bite compared with the estimated $2,500 per annum which Mansholt's far-ranging structural reforms would entail, averaged out over 1970–80.) The decision was part of a package deal by which the tobacco policy was set on foot (France and Italy to relinquish their monopolies by 1976 and the common market to emerge by 1980), the wine policy set up, and complex formulae governing parliamentary control of the Community budget agreed. The standstill was a wise decision since the EEC could hardly show a calm and united front at the negotiating table while quarrelling over the height of ceilings.

By 1968 the CAP was in serious trouble. High prices had produced massive surpluses, especially of butter and sugar. These surpluses were being subsidized by the Farm Fund, whose bill soared accordingly: from $1,800m. for 1967–8 to $2,400m. for 1968–9 – it is expected to reach $3,000m. in 1969–70. By 1978 it could reach $6,000m. In October 1969 it was agreed that

France and Germany should sell off 20,000 tons of butter and Holland 7,500 tons at a reduction of one third on the EEC floor price (the Farm Fund paying two thirds of the difference and the individual governments one third). But this was a mere flea-bite as the *Butterberg* was then estimated at 400,000 tons – a 'catastrophe' in the words of Dr Sicco Mansholt, Commission vice-president for agriculture, who thought it vital to solve the dairy-surplus problem before tackling the farm-finance regulations. In October 1969 he estimated it would cost $750m. to eliminate the dairy surplus.

In the spring of 1968 the Italians, who have no butter surplus, insisted on a ceiling being fixed for the EEC dairy policy, any expenditure in excess of this being contributed to on a separate scale, which would be more heavily weighted against the surplus-producing countries. This was regarded as a dangerous precedent not only in the field of agriculture, as, if a country were to elect to support only those facets of Community policy of direct benefit to itself, the whole concept of the Community would be at risk. Europe would be back at square one, with every man for himself. This understandable action of Italy did in fact lead to reprisals against herself. In October 1969 when the olive-oil agreement, of particular significance to Italy, came up for discussion, the other five countries insisted on a similar ceiling being placed on EEC spending on olive oil.

There was no doubt that Germany, Belgium, and Luxembourg were the three countries coming off worst from the operation of the Farm Fund. On the guarantee part of the Fund, Germany was putting in some 31 per cent and receiving back between 15 and 18 per cent and although she might benefit under the new milk organization, this would be offset by the new single market organization for wine, tobacco, and fish, where Germany is a minimal producer and will again suffer. On the guidance section, Germany was putting in 31·2 per cent and receiving back 20 per cent. Germany's expenditure on agriculture is the highest of all EEC countries; in 1967–8 when Britain spent $343m. on deficiency payments and other measures equivalent to those covered by the Fund's guarantee section, Germany spent $408·6m. as its contribution to the Fund alone, excluding its direct domestic expenditure – and withal German food prices were much higher than those in Britain.

The CAP was not only stirring up trouble at home, it was spreading alarm and despondency among the farmers of many lands. The Danes diagnosed the CAP as a disaster for Denmark and took energetic steps to put their house in order by a shift of emphasis to industry and by increasing exports of farm produce to other EFTA countries (these rose by 55 per cent between 1958 and 1968). The CAP bore especially hard on the traditional Danish exports of livestock to the EEC, which dropped from over $50m. in 1958 to $30m. in 1968; on poultry, which dropped from over $8m. to $2·5m., and eggs which fell from $41m. to $1·6m. Total sales of farm produce fell during the ten years by over 17 per cent forcing some 7,000 independent farmers off the land. In 1968 President Tito roundly blamed the EEC for the stagnation of Yugoslav agriculture; although Yugoslavia is the third largest beef-exporter to the EEC (after Denmark and Argentina), Tito said protective tariffs made it increasingly difficult to sell beef even to its traditional customer, Italy, and made veiled threats of counter-measures. New Zealand expressed 'dismay' at the effect the levy system and exports subsidies were having on international dairy trade. To them the EEC was an unabashed 'dumper'. Butter costing 70 to 80 cents a pound in Holland and France was offered in South-East Asia and Peru at fifteen cents a pound, seriously undercutting the new Zealand product. Industrialized countries, New Zealand affirmed, would not tolerate a similar policy in manufactured goods and she called on the Commission to enter into talks for a world dairy agreement.

With a runaway financing plan and supplies of butter and sugar which threatened to submerge the economy, it could have been hoped that at least the beneficiaries, the farmers of the EEC, were happy. But they were not. Since the subsidy is fixed to the product and not to the individual farmer, the money does not iron out social inequalities but reinforces them. The subsidy is not in direct proportion to the size of the farm; the farmer who works less than twelve acres of land gets £50 while the man working 250 acres gets £2,500. Despite the input of taxpayers' money, the average farmer's buying power fell during 1968 by nearly 4 per cent. Soon there was much adverse publicity, even in France, the main beneficiary, for the agricultural policy of the EEC; the amount spent by France on supporting agricultural markets in 1969 would, it was alleged, be around that spent on scientific research; the reorganization of the milk market alone in 1969 would cost the French Treasury as much as the war in Algeria in 1959; the sacrificial stabilizing operations i.e. storage, destruction, or sale at cut prices would rise to as much as one quarter of the gross income from genuine sale of farm produce.

Community policy was seen to be in a vicious circle by 1968; for political reasons the manipulation of the price structure had had to be begun at the highest point and as prices rose, so did production and so did the cost of the CAP. If any attempt were made to peg or reduce prices, the farmers' only reaction would be to produce more to compensate them for the drop in their incomes. The only way out was that proposed by Dr Mansholt – a structural change in Common Market agriculture coupled with a drastic reappraisal of price levels for 1969–70, which would encourage a change in the pattern of production so that the surplus in some products would be gradually eliminated.

Farm Prices Proposed by the Commission for 1969–70

		Present	Proposed
Wheat (not durum)	Target price	105·25	106·25
	Basic intervention price	98·75	97·75
Barley	Target price	94·44	94·44
	Basic intervention price	87·97	86·98
Rye	Target price	97·50	97·50
	Basic intervention price	91·00	90·00

(in dollars per metric ton)

These grain prices were due to come into effect on 1 August, but although there was little change, except that in each case the basic intervention price had been fixed at a lower level, agreement was not forthcoming and the previous year's prices continued into the 1969–70 marketing year.

The savage cut in butter price (by one third) was essential because of the enormous stocks building up, but the farmer would be compensated for this by the increase in prices for other uses of milk – the intervention prices for powdered skimmed milk and cheeses would rise and outright aid for skimmed milk be increased greatly.

The price cuts for sugar would be accompanied by a reduction in the basic quotas because production for 1967–8 had exceeded consumption by 14 per cent and it was hoped that these measures would establish a balance between supply and demand by 1970–71. But here again agreement was deferred and the old prices continued with a few minor adjustments.

Farm Prices Proposed by the Commission for 1969–70

		Present	Proposed
Sugar	Minimum price for sugar beet	17·00	16·00
	'Half fat' price for sugar beet	10·00	9·00
	Target price for white sugar	223·50	221·70
	Intervention price for white sugar	212·30	211·70
Milk	Target price for milk	103·00	103·00
	Intervention price for		
	butter	1,735·00	1,110·00
	powdered skimmed milk	412·50	712·50
	Grana	1,248·00	1,428·00
	Parmesan	1,480·00	1,668·00
	Outright aid for skimmed milk:		
	powdered	82·50	382·50
	liquid	15·00	42·50
Beef and Veal	Guide price for bullocks (live weight)	680·00	680·00
	Guide price for calves (live weight)	915·00	915·00

(in dollars per metric ton)

Coupled with these price adjustments, was Dr Mansholt's blueprint for EEC agriculture by 1980. The main recommendations were that EEC agricultural land should be cut in area by 12 per cent; from 175m. acres to about 160m. by 1980. This land might be used for afforestation or for recreation. Workers would be encouraged to leave the land, either to go to jobs in industry or to retire on grounds of age. It was estimated that 4·7m. people would have left farming between 1960 and 1970 and that five million of the remaining 10 million would leave between 1970 and 1980, bringing the active farming population of the Community in 1980 down to 6 per cent of the total working population compared with 15·7 per cent in 1965 and 20·7 per cent in 1960.

Agricultural Employment in the Community

	Actual		Forecast	
	1950	1960	1970	1980
	20m.	15m.	10m.	5m.
Total workforce (%)	28	21	14	6

Dr Mansholt's rationalization of farming land and the farm population had tremendous repercussions not only throughout the E E C but in Britain, Ireland, and America. A whole philosophy was being tampered with. The land still held an almost religious significance for most Europeans; it represented all that the country stood for; it was the land of our fathers, the land that we are prepared to fight for. The farmer himself stands for the eternal truths. Dr Mansholt was called a second Stalin, though Stalin terrorized the peasant population into accepting his programme of collectivization whereas Dr Mansholt declared categorically 'there will be no coercion'.

Mansholt, a farmer himself for many years and a former Minister of Agriculture in the Dutch Government, put the position plainly; the farming pattern had already changed. 'As many as 80 per cent of farms in the Community are too small to provide enough work for one man on a rational basis,' he declared. Two thirds of the farms had less than five cows. He proposed minimum sizes which would ensure a living wage; a farmer growing grain or root crops would need at least 200 to 300 acres; a dairy farmer would need at least 40 to 60 cows; a beef farmer at least 150 to 200 animals; an egg farmer at least 10,000 hens in lay and a poultry farmer a turnover of at least 100,000 birds a year. The appropriate number of pigs for a pig farmer would be between 450 and 600. These would be the minimum sizes to qualify for subsidies after 1975 and should give one man with modern facilities a livelihood comparable to that of the townsman.

He proposed only to accelerate and make less painful the natural process of change. To do this, he would offer attractive pensions to farmers over fifty-five (and half the E E C farmers are said to be above this age), he would offer training grants to younger farmers willing to train for other jobs and special scholarships to the children of farming families to help them to move away from a life of relative hardship and poverty. He thought that the official lead in the direction of mergers, take-overs, and co-operatives would be followed by a number of voluntary moves towards creating modern farm enterprises. Once farmers saw the advantages to be gained from working farms of a viable size (e.g. more and better equipment, and more companionship) they would not hold back from better working hours and free time and better social conditions generally. All moves towards amalgamation would be encouraged by subsidies, investment grants, and guaranteed credits.

As a result of implementing 'Agriculture 1980', the cost of supporting farm prices within the E E C should be reduced to about $750m. a year after 1980 (of which $250m. would be on the dairy sector). This compares with a figure of over $2,000m. for 1968–9. But the cost of the reforms was put at $2,500m. a year (averaged out over the ten years 1970–80), to which had to be added $2,000m. to create new jobs in the framework of the Community's regional policy and $480m. for the cost of retraining labour.

By April 1969, however, the report from Brussels was 'no progress'. It seemed that the most the six agricultural ministers could agree to was the prolongation of present price levels into the coming farm year. They knew full well that this was not tackling the root cause of the Six's agricultural difficulties – overproduction; prolongation was in fact only putting off the evil day. But time and tide were not right for concessions, let alone the launching of so ambitious a scheme. The European idea was running out of steam. Frustrations and suspicions generated throughout the Community by the continued non-admission of Britain and the EFTA countries were reflected in the negotiations where the six member-states fought hard to protect the sugar, butter, and cereals price. Europe was back to an 'every man for himself' interlude.

In one of those heroic marathons which have come to be synonymous with progress in the EEC, all the vital political decisions necessary to allow the common agricultural policy to continue were taken in day and night sessions ending triumphantly on the night of 22 December 1969. The main object was gradually to transfer the financing of the farm policy from the national governments to a central Community treasury having its own independent resources. This was to be done by a three-tier system. All levies on agricultural imports and all customs duties (common external tariff) were to be paid over automatically to the EEC, bypassing national parliaments, and so giving the EEC for the first time an embryo federal budget. As even these payments would not be sufficient to finance the CAP, the sums so received were to be topped up by a fraction of each nation's revenue from the value-added tax.

The sums were worked out as follows:

By 1975 the CAP would be costing	$4,000m. (or more)
But farm levies would yield only	$800m.
And Customs duties provide only	$1,400m.
Leaving a deficit of	$1,800m.

By 1975, however, it was expected that VAT rates would have been harmonized throughout the Community and a levy of 1 per cent of VAT, paid over by each member-country, would provide $1,900 (something over the $1,800 estimated shortfall).

The package deal included an agreement from France to lift the quota system then in force for wine allowing it to circulate freely throughout the EEC and to the formulation of a tobacco policy. The Italians had made this a pre-condition of their co-operation, contending that wine, one of their chief agricultural products, received much less generous treatment than, say, butter and wheat.

Obviously the new system involves a loss of income for national budgets and bears especially hard on Germany and the Netherlands with their high customs receipts and on Italy, a big importer of foodstuffs, with a high level of farm levies. France, in any case the chief beneficiary of the CAP, would have been the only country paying less than its whack in terms of relative GNP under the new system. The Netherlands insisted that there should be some correlation between a country's proportion of the EEC's total GNP and its contribution towards farm expenditure. The French resisted this and were bent on making all payments into the fund automatic so that it would never run dry.

The compromise took account of both views: the move to fully automatic contributions was to be staggered.

For 1970 there were to be no direct payments of levies or of customs dues. The contributions were to be based entirely on a national key specially devised for the immediate emergency.

Key for Contributions (%) to Farm Fund for 1970 only

Belgium	8·25
Germany	31·70
France	28·00
Italy	21·50
Luxembourg	0·20
Netherlands	10·35

These figures average out the share of each country in the EEC's GNP and its contribution to the EEC budget under existing keys.

From 1 January 1971, all farm import levies will be paid in to a central fund, but only a proportion of customs dues; the shortfall between the cost of the Farm Fund and the amount of levies plus import duties being made good according to an interim key.

The proportion of customs dues payable, however, would gradually be increased each year during the period January 1971 to January 1975, though safeguards were devised to prevent total contributions moving away from the 1970 key by more than 1

Interim Key of National Contributions (%) to Farm Fund
(January 1971 to January 1975)

Belgium	6·8
Germany	32·9
France	32·6
Italy	20·2
Luxembourg	0·2
Netherlands	7·3

per cent per annum (up or down) until the end of 1974; and from then until the beginning of 1968 by more than 2 per cent per annum. A proviso was made that 10 per cent of customs and levy receipts should be paid back to each nation to cover the cost of collection (the 'administrative rebate').

On 1 January 1978 all safeguards are withdrawn and all customs and import levies must be paid over, though the 10 per cent rebate will continue in force.

Interim measures will be made for budgetary control of these contributions and it was agreed that from 1975 onwards the European Parliament should have stronger budgetary powers; in theory it should have the last word on the Community's budget (but it will not be able to increase it above a maximum laid down by the Council).

The effect of the new regulation on the cost of entry to Britain is almost impossible to assess – especially if the three other candidates are also admitted. As far as customs dues are concerned, Britain, as a member, would no longer pay duties on imports from the EEC, and in any case duties on goods from outside the EEC will fall as the Kennedy Round tariff cuts take effect. The level of Britain's farm import levies depends on imponderables. Will farm imports from the EEC increase? What arrangements will be made for New Zealand? Will there be a dramatic increase of production by Britain's own farmers? The incentive will be there. What part will Ireland play? And, if the EEC does succeed in eliminating her monstrous surpluses, will the cost of the Farm Fund be as astronomical as was feared?

One thing is sure, the principles of the financial system have now been defined and can only be changed by a unanimous vote.

Britain will, once she is a member, not be able to back out of shouldering a major part of the burden of financing European agriculture. It would also seem that V A T will become obligatory, although presumably if an equivalent sum were provided from purchase tax and excise there would be no objection, especially in the short term.

It is no exaggeration to say that the future of the E E C depends on whether the problem of agriculture can be solved. The common agricultural policy (C A P) is crippling the finances of the Community: it accounts for nearly 95 per cent of total expenditure.

E E C Expenditure 1969

	$m.
1. *The Commission*	
European Farm Fund (F E O G A)	2,549·5
European Social Fund	33·4
Carrying out common policies	1·9
Salaries and administrative	
costs	95·8
Total Commission	2,680·6
2. *Council of Ministers*	9·9
3. *European Parliament*	8·9
4. *Court of Justice*	2·0
	2,701·4

That is the size of the problem. Originally it had been hoped that the levies on imported foodstuffs plus the receipts from application of the common external tariff, would provide enough to pay for the C A P but these hopes were sadly disappointed as the cost of the C A P leapt ahead of such potential revenues; even if all C E T receipts as well as the levies on agricultural imports were paid over, it is estimated that in 1973 these would total only $2,680m. to meet a total Community bill of $3,838m., leaving $1,158m. to be provided from the national budgets of member-states.

As the E E C neared the end of the transition period, 31 December 1969, by which time the financing of the C A P according to the Treaty of Rome should have been agreed, it was obvious that the whole edifice was in danger of collapsing. The devaluation of the franc and revaluation of the D.-mark had played havoc with the carefully erected but unsoundly based common price system. If total disintegration of the C A P were to be avoided, very serious thought indeed would have to be given to the monetary relationships between the E E C countries.

Common farm-prices are paid in units of account, i.e. in the equivalent of the dollar or gold; when the French devalued the franc in August 1969, their farmers would have been getting a handsome bonus (it needed fewer units of account to buy a franc). There was the risk of a serious inflationary spiral starting in France, so the Council of Ministers decided on an 11·11 per cent reduction in the guaranteed prices paid to French producers. France was to pay 11·11 per cent levies on agricultural exports to other member-states (except for beef and skimmed milk where rates of 7·33 and 6·25 per cent were fixed). On exports of fruit and vegetables, no levies were to be paid (though Italy objected that this gave the French an unfair advantage). The French market was isolated for up to two years by which time her farm prices were to be brought back into line. This was a serious breach in the C A P wall.

A more serious situation arose when the D.-mark was allowed to float immediately after the German elections. Obviously the prices paid to German farmers would come down by the amount of any revaluation (it would take more units of account to buy a D.-mark). Meanwhile, Germany was threatened with a flood of agricultural imports and the German Government imposed border taxes of 8·5 per cent without consulting her partners (she could in fairness retort that France had not consulted her before the secret August devaluation). The Commission denounced these unilaterally imposed taxes and the European Court of Justice, hurriedly summoned on a Sunday, held them to be illegal but the Council of Ministers had to compromise and agree to the taxes remaining in force pending revaluation.

When this was finally announced, to take effect from 27 October 1969, the effective rate being 8·5 per cent so far as the Common Market itself was concerned, the German Government faced a grave problem. How were the German farmers to be compensated for their losses, calculated at DM. 1,700m. a year? The Commission's plan was that the 8·5 per cent border tax should be dropped as from 8 December and direct aids be granted to German farmers by the German Government, but these were to be temporary and on a reducing scale. A ceiling of DM.1,590m. was suggested for the 1970–71 farm season falling to DM. 1,480m. for 1971–2 and DM. 1,370m. for 1972–3 of which the EEC Farm Fund (the Agriculture Guidance and Guarantee Fund, known in the EEC by the initials FEOGA, and established on 14 January 1962) would contribute respectively $90m., 60m., and 30m. At the end of 1973 the German farmers should receive no more direct aid but could be given compensatory social benefits such as family-allowance increases. The German farmers had earlier angrily rejected a solution which called for manipulation of the value-added tax and a measure of direct compensation and called for the suspension of the whole system of common farm-prices until European currency policies had been harmonized.

So events had demonstrated what many observers had seen as a basic flaw in the CAP – this ambitious structure was built on shifting sands because there was no solid monetary base to support it. The EEC had put the farm cart before the horse. This was largely the fault of de Gaulle who had pressed ahead relentlessly with supranationalism in the shape of the CAP (France stood to gain handsomely) while refusing point blank to subscribe to any supranationalism in other sectors of policy, such as monetary policy. It is difficult not to see something of the Maginot-Line mentality in the whole organization of the CAP; the CAP line was turned by monetary and financial difficulties which could have been foreseen. The pet theory in Brussels that agricultural integration would of necessity involve monetary integration was seen to be a monstrous piece of wishful thinking. France had been the chief architect of the CAP – the price Germany was made to pay to secure the concessions of tariff removal which she wanted in the industrial sector. It turned out to be a very heavy price and one which was not compensated by the industrial advantages received in exchange by Germany.

For the EEC the advent of Britain could be a godsend. In 1962

Britain was technically debarred from membership of the EEC because her agriculture could not be reconciled with the CAP, but by 1969 it was clear that EEC farmers and politicians alike were casting covetous eyes on this large off-shore market which could so conveniently absorb the suffocating EEC farm surpluses and in doing so substantially reduce the ever-increasing cost of financing them. Britain imports 40 per cent of the temperate foods she needs and could absorb all the EEC surpluses of butter, cheese, grain and sugar. The snag from Britain's point of view is that the EEC price levels are far above (almost double) world market prices, and on supplies imported from countries outside the EEC or from any new member of it Britain would have to pay an import levy to bring the price up to EEC prices, these levies being remitted to the Farm Fund. To take butter as an example, Britain uses 480,000 tons a year (about 50,000 tons home-produced and 430,000 tons imported). The EEC price is about £700 a ton compared with an average 1968 market price of £300 in Britain, i.e. there is £400 a ton difference. Britain could either pay this huge price for EEC butter or she would have to make good the difference between cheap New Zealand and Australian butter and the expensive EEC product. The British Government cannot lightly abandon its cheap-food policy, and the balance of payments would be adversely affected if food formerly bought with sterling had to be paid for in other currencies.

Meanwhile agriculture had become a crucial bargaining point of the EEC summit meeting called for 17 November 1969 but postponed to 1 December. France, under M. Pompidou, made it clear that she would insist on a permanent settlement of the financing of the CAP before agreeing to negotiations for enlargement being started. He had before him the drastic Vedel Committee proposals that over a third of arable land in France should be abandoned, that about one million older French farmers should be pensioned off by 1985, and that the intervention price of grain and sugar should be greatly reduced. But would Europe be willing to bear the burden of restructuring French agriculture? Could France exact this heavy price as a condition of enlargement?

M. Pisani in his report to the Monnet Committee of July 1969 stressed that the application of the present financing rules would be manifestly unfair to Britain as she would have to bear more than half of joint expenditure on agriculture although her national income would represent only a quarter of that of a seven-member Community. Transitional arrangements would be necessary and he concluded that there was no insoluble problem if agriculture was not 'obsessively treated in isolation' but in the context of a wider dynamic economic union.

It would be pointless to spell out the pros and cons for British agriculture when the C A P itself is in disarray and when the terms of entry have not yet been agreed, but there are a few useful general observations.

The impact on the cost of living would be considerable; acceptance of the C A P would involve bringing the prices of all foodstuffs, home-grown or imported, up to Community levels, but obviously there would have to be a reasonable transition period. Since the British system of direct support to farmers (deficiency payments) would be abandoned, the taxpayers' money, about £450m. at present used for this, would be available to cushion the shock of higher food prices for low-income groups.

But the main problem is the impact of the E E C agricultural policy on Britain's balance of payments. The E E C Commission estimated that Britain would have to pay to the Farm Fund about £215m. a year in levies on her imports of agricultural produce from 1970 on. (Unilever earlier produced the lower estimate of £165m., a figure which took account of the increase in British farm output which would probably occur. The surpluses piling up in the E E C which is nearing self-sufficiency in most farm products certainly support this theory.) In July 1969 anti-Marketeers were making big play with speculative stories of the probable cost of entry to the balance of payments put at £593m. (*Guardian*) and cost to the consumers put at £844m. (*Financial Times*). The Government spokesman did not deny that in May 1967 the cost to the balance of payments had been assessed at between £175m. and £250m. a year and that the trend would have been for these figures to rise, but he did point out the futility

unt of the levy is adjusted to the world-market
ry day in the case of grain, fortnightly for dairy
 quarterly for pigmeat.
n to move to a common price level for grain ahead
original deadline was 31 December 1969) meant a
in prices for some Community farmers for whom the
npensation scale was worked out.

Table for Cereals $m

1967–8	1968–9	1969–70
140	93·5	46·75
65	44	22
1·25	0·75	0·5
206·25	138·25	69·25

xporters of cereals, subsidies (sometimes called export
restitutions) are paid from the Farm Fund. France
e main beneficiary. In 1967 the difference between the
non Market price and the low world price entailed
f $52 a ton, but even this was not enough to allow
ender for the sale of wheat to China, and in January
tra $11 a ton was approved to help France dispose of
ns of wheat to China. By 1969 France was willing to
neat (and the threat that it could bring swine fever into
 part payment for 800,000 tons of soft wheat to be
China by January 1970, undercutting the minimum
e International Grain Arrangement (to which China
ubscribe) and calling on the Farm Fund to underwrite
 the tune of about $52m. (The deal was negotiated at
 the lowest intervention price in France, to which had
d transport costs.) In an attempt to lessen the dramati-
g stockpiles of wheat, France was also given increased
s in 1968 to enable her to ship some of the surplus to
o the annoyance of the United States who had at no
weaned the Japanese from their traditional taste for
roper regard for wheat.
s came to a head in July 1969 when the EEC, having

of drawing up estimates either of food prices or balance of payments costs when the CAP was due to change radically from the end of 1969, and before it was known when and on what terms Britain might join. Gains to British industry would have to be set against losses on the agricultural side.

Special arrangements would still have to be made for New Zealand and Australian farm produce but since the time of Britain's first application diversification, especially by Australia, has eased this problem. New Zealand would still be a special case; it is thought that in the 1962 negotiations the EEC put on offer only a three-year concession during which New Zealand dairy produce would be given a special quota. In 1966, 1967, and 1968 New Zealand exports to the United Kingdom as a percentage of her total exports were 49, 52 and 48 per cent. The United Kingdom takes 85 per cent of all New Zealand butter, 66 per cent of cheese, and 90 per cent of meat (though exporters of lamb now have to send 15 per cent to countries other than the United Kingdom). Britain would ask for this trade to be phased out slowly, not only for New Zealand's sake but for her own, since all these supplies are now being paid for in sterling.

British agriculture, employing, at most, 4 per cent of the working population, is structurally sounder than that of the EEC countries. There seems little doubt that it could expand dramatically, if given the chance. Under the provisions of the agriculture acts of 1947 and 1957, the Ministry of Agriculture in consultation with the farmers' unions determines each February guaranteed prices for fat cattle, sheep, pigs, eggs, wool, milk, cereals, potatoes, and sugar-beet. If prices realized are less than these guaranteed prices, then the difference is made good by a government deficiency payment usually distributed by the appropriate marketing board (Milk, Potato, British Wool, etc.). The estimate of this support for 1968–9 was £317m. to which has to be added £114m. paid out in production grants (for fertilizers, drainage, improving breeds, improving farm buildings, silos, etc.) Under the 1967 agriculture act, the government may also make grants of 50 per cent of the approved costs of voluntary amalgamations of small farms and pay to the outgoing small-holder lump sums or annuities.

The National Farmers Union in early 1969 still preferred the present deficiency payments to the EEC levy system, although the latter was then official policy of the Conservatives. The NFU do not quarrel with the import-levy part of the EEC set-up but do not see how home prices are to be maintained; the Tories have not yet definitely declared that they favour the intervention-price method and, if so, whether they would support an intervention level of about 7 per cent below the guaranteed price, as in the EEC, or some other level. The Tories would perhaps experiment with cereals (the import mechanism already exists as part of the minimum price system for cereals); as about one third of all cereals are imported, this would provide a handsome sum in import levies and the deficiency payments made on cereals have always been proportionately higher than those on other agricultural products, indicating a field for reform. The grain-growers would probably be willing to accept an intervention level price for all their crop, which a marketing board would resell to the trade at a higher price, the equivalent of the guarantee or EEC target price, because they would be sure of a firm price. But the NFU is anxious because only 12 per cent of sales off British farms are cereals against 60 per cent livestock, and as grain is the basic feeding stuff for the livestock any change would have repercussions on pigmeat, eggs, poultry, and beef and might lead to higher prices for the consumer.

Yet, in agriculture as elsewhere, it would be folly to reject the years of patient work and to start again from scratch. Some idea of the feats of organization involved in the various sectors can be gained from the following progress reports.

CEREALS

Much realistic thinking and rethinking, bargaining and give and take had to take place before the single-market stage was reached in cereals and this was a vital sector, accounting for a very large proportion of farm production and internal and external trade, as well as directly affecting the prices of pigmeat, eggs, and poultry where cereals are a basic feeding-stuff.

The difficulties were enorm
traditionally very dear in Ger
first idea, a good one, that each
and lower limits within which
fixed and the gap between these
failure because for political reas
with high agricultural costs (Ge
to an annual drop in the prices
the end of 1964 was agreed on a
ministers and foreign minister
package deal by which, in retu
vegetables, Italy was won over
Deadline and package-deal solut
decision-making practice. The p
established uniform price levels
munity to take effect from 1 Ju
Community levies on feed-grain
would disappear.

Wholesale target prices for whe
fixed, taking as reference point
centre of the area in the Communit
supply and therefore dearest. The
the Farm Fund, through its officia
cereals that cannot be sold at or ne
Duisburg at 7 per cent below th
prices for other market centres thro
from the Duisburg price, allowanc
costs between areas of surplus and ar

To protect the producer from im
a single threshold price for the wh
separately for wheat, barley, maize,
This threshold price is the target price
and handling charges between the po
Variable levies are charged on lower-p
ments to bring their price up to the thr
payable by the importer and 90 per cen
the Farm Fund; by 31 December 196
levies are applied to all imports of each

been notified by the US and Canada that they were making cut-price deals to get rid of some of their wheat, retaliated by increasing the amount of export refunds payable on EEC wheat so that it would not be left behind in the scramble to unload.

Speculators took a hand in destroying the rationale of a common price for cereals in 1969 when they bought in huge quantities of French wheat with weak forward francs, so undercutting the price payable to German farmers. Normal sales of French wheat to Germany run at about 6m. tons a year but in the year ending July 1969 this had jumped to 12m. tons, leaving Germany, traditionally a wheat-deficit country, with 2·5m. tons of her own wheat on the Government's hands (this wheat had to be bought in at the intervention price). Lacking storage the German Government offered a subsidy to farmers who would store the wheat in their private silos, only to be told that this was contravening the CAP rules.

BEEF AND VEAL

The single-market stage for beef and veal took effect on 1 April, 1968. Here the mechanism for the internal market was the guide price, i.e. the estimated average price which producers might expect to receive for all their output in a normal year. Intervention prices are calculated at between 93 and 96 per cent of the guide price and member-states buy in live cattle (but not calves) and certain qualities of beef when the internal market price reaches or falls below the intervention price.

To protect the EEC against imports, there is a common external tariff of 16 per cent on live cattle and calves and 20 per cent on beef but over and above this, if the price at importation (plus these tariffs) is still lower than the guide price, variable import levies are charged according to complicated rules.

In March 1969 it was announced that the British Ministry of Agriculture had under consideration a similar scheme for curbing beef imports, i.e. a target-indicator price on a seasonal scale a little below the British guarantee price. When farmers are getting less than the target price, minimum import prices and levies would be imposed on imported beef. The Conservative Party had already announced that it was part of their policy to make a transition from the present British system of guaranteed prices to an import levy system on the EEC pattern, not just for beef but for most sectors of agriculture.

To help exporters member-states may grant export subsidies to compensate for the difference between internal prices and prices in non-member countries: these subsidies are refundable by the Farm Fund.

MILK, BUTTER, AND MILK PRODUCTS

The trouble with the EEC cows is that there are far too many of them and no one seems able to control their numbers; and people in the EEC do not like to drink milk – they are not 'pinta'-minded like the British. Statistics show that in 1968 there was an increase of 0·8 per cent in the number of cows over 1967.

Community Cows (millions) 1968

1. France	8·76	
2. West Germany	5·88	
3. Italy	3·43	
4. Holland	1·87	
5. Belgium	1·10	
6. Luxembourg	0·60	
Grand total	21·64	

Worse, these 21-million-odd cows are not in the seventy-plus size herds that Sicco Mansholt would like to see, but gathered together in twos and threes (two thirds of Community farms have less than five cows). The Commission had to point out to small-holders in France who persisted in referring to their few tethered cows as their *troupeau* that it really could not consider anything under five cows as a herd. Yet 24 per cent of EEC farmers are dependent on milk and milk products.

In May 1966 after much debate a common target price of 39 Pfennigs for a kilo of milk was arrived at to come into full effect in April 1968 (postponed, owing to disagreements, till 1 June

1968). From this figure was derived the intervention price for butter. But it soon became apparent that the target price for milk and the intervention price for butter had been pitched too high. The amount of surplus butter which had had to be bought in was by December 1969 400,000 tons, the forecast for 1970 was 500,000 tons and by the end of 1971–2 Community stocks, which were rapidly outgrowing the warehouses, might amount to 750,000 tons. Worse, as the butter piled up, so inevitably did the cost of the dairy policy. The cost for 1967–8 was estimated at $370m. and for 1968–9 at $800m. As Parkinson might have said: all milk production expands to meet the intervention payment obtainable on butter . . .

The suggestion that the sacrosanct price of 39 Pfennigs a kilo should be reduced to 38 Pfennigs and held there for four years and the butter intervention price lowered accordingly, even though coupled with a concession that a slaughter grant be paid of $250 a cow plus $150 towards the cost of three new male calves or $200 for three beef-producing heifers, was rejected angrily. Coachloads of farmers from all over the Community demonstrated noisily outside the Palais des Congrès in Brussels (March 1968).

How can the butter be disposed of? The Commission tried cut-price sales to army barracks and to old-age pensioners, and considered the sale of processed butter as cooking fat and as an ingredient in cattle feedstuffs. A tax on margarine (resisted by the Dutch and West Germans, who like it, and supported by the French, who don't) was another suggestion. National governments did what they could – the French singing the merits of ice-cream throughout the summer of 1968 – but in 1968 the hapless Community-housewife was paying nearly twice the average world price for butter, two to three years old from the Community's cold stores, while Community cows were licking their lips over cow-cake filled with butter-fat or at least well topped up with skimmed-milk powder.

The only long-term solution is for some of the Sacred EEC Cows to be slaughtered; nearly one million of the 5·88m. German cows are known as postmen's cows; they are a source of pin-money to the postman as poultry once was to the British farmer's wife. And a switch to beef should be encouraged. Sicco Mansholt knows this. The Commission knows it. But shall the sacred cows die? Far more than 30,000 EEC farmers will know the reason why! But if they do not, the expense of the dairy policy may get completely out of hand.

However, when the butter mountain had topped the 400,000 tons mark (the weight as Dr Schiller gloomily pointed out of the total population of Austria), agreement was finally reached (in September 1969) on an experimental scheme. This would provide for small-scale farmers to receive a $200 premium for each of up to ten cows slaughtered and not replaced, and would run until 250,000 cows had been slaughtered; the scheme was expected to cost $100m. to be financed half by the Farm Fund and half by the national governments.

Repercussions of the EEC dairy policy are felt abroad too; export subsidies are payable on exported dairy produce and a leading British farming journal complained that French cheese dumped on the British market was being subsidized at around £200 a ton. The New Zealand dairy industry, operating entirely without subsidies, was particularly hard hit by dumpings of EEC-subsidized butter at less than a quarter of its European price on the world markets, in which she was struggling to make headway. She alleged, too, that a flourishing butter switch had grown up in Belgium: East European butter was entering Belgium and other EEC countries as a duty-free raw material and after repacking and labelling was being exported to qualify for the EEC subsidy on dairy exports.

PIGMEAT, EGGS AND POULTRY

The common market within the Community took effect from 1 July 1967. The organization of the market was less complicated than that for cereals, as there were no target prices and no support buying. To protect pigmeat, eggs, and poultry from imports from non-member countries, imports are subject to a variable levy which is fixed by taking the difference between EEC feed-grain prices and world feed-grain prices and calculating how this would have affected feeding costs of EEC pigs and poultry. As an additional safeguard, if import prices are still lower than EEC prices, sluice-gate prices come into operation and the levy is increased to bring import prices up to the sluice-gate level.

The policy has been condemned as protectionist by the outside world and would seem to be leading in the direction of surpluses within the EEC; but the Commission, mindful of what happened in the case of butter, are resisting requests to set up a pig and poultry buying and storing organization. In 1968 there was a surplus of pigmeat in the first six months and poultry could quickly move into surplus in 1969–70. In 1968 imports of poultry into the EEC exceeded exports by about 20,000 tons (compared with excess imports of 55,000 tons in 1965 and 110,000 tons in 1960). Two thirds of poultry-meat production (1·53m. metric tons) is accounted for by France (500,000 metric tons) and Italy (480,000 metric tons). Besides being nearly self-sufficient in poultry, the EEC had for the first time in 1968 an export surplus in broiler chicken.

SUGAR

'The over-perfectionized system of market organizations is understood only by a handful of experts,' said Dr Alwin Münchmeyer, President of the German Bankers' Association. This is particularly true of the organization of the sugar market.

Intra-Community trade in sugar is small since all the member-states except Italy meet their own sugar requirements. The cost prices of sugar-beet and sugar varied widely from year to year, from country to country, and even from district to district, but on 1 July 1968 a uniform Community price system was established. The target price for refined sugar was fixed at $22·35 per 100 kg. and the intervention price at $21·23 per 100 kg. For other areas, derived prices were obtained. Threshold prices for white sugar, raw sugar, and molasses were laid down and a levy is imposed on imports equal to the difference between the c.i.f. (cost, insurance, and freight) price on the world market and the threshold price. For sugar-beet, minimum prices were fixed on the basis of intervention prices, provided there is a 16 per cent sugar content of standard quality.

An extremely complicated system of basic quotas and levies and two minimum prices theoretically mean that sugar manufacturers and beet-growers can obtain three different prices for their output depending on the quantity they produce, but, as the price obtained falls in proportion to the amount by which the basic quota is exceeded, only the most efficient producers are able to increase their output.

The sugar market comes under joint financing regulations and a refund system has been introduced to enable sugar to be exported from the E E C at world market prices.

Each of the member-states was allotted an overall basic quota (calculated in proportion to average production 1961–5) for allocation among its various sugar factories. The production target for the entire Community was fixed at 6·48m metric tons of refined sugar, which was 200,000 metric tons more than the expected consumption for 1968–9; this forecast proved to be incorrect. A million tons of excess sugar was produced in 1967–8 (production exceeded consumption by 14 per cent); it was admitted that the price fixed had been too remunerative thus inducing the surplus but the price cuts proposed by the Commission were bitterly opposed and prolongation of the present price levels recommended by the agricultural ministers.

Sugar Quotas in E E C Countries

	metric tons
France	2,400,000
Germany	1,750,000
Italy	1,230,000
Netherlands	550,000
Belgium/Luxembourg	550,000

These basic quotas will apply unchanged up to and including the 1974–5 season.

The cold mechanics of the system do not reveal the intrigues, the jockeying for position, and the utter neglect of consumer interests which accompanied the organization of the sugar market. It became clear that France, the most efficient beet-grower in the E E C (French prices were easily the lowest in Europe), was to be the chief beneficiary of the system and this led to a mad scramble for a share in this booming industry. Half the shares in the largest refining firm, Raffineries Say, were acquired by an international consortium (including the British firm, Tate & Lyle) and other companies merged into the 'Delta' group. These two groups each have just under one quarter of French capacity so remaining producers juggled with commercial pacts and take-me-over bids. The probability is that internal links between the two giants could make the Say boardroom the headquarters of a giant European sugar cartel.

The deal was made more attractive to the consortium (but not for the consumer) when, by the process of levelling up prices as had happened in the other sectors of the CAP, prices were raised from the low French level towards those obtaining elsewhere in the EEC. French sugar prices rose an official 11 per cent at the beginning of 1967 compared with only 9 per cent in the whole fifteen years between 1952 and 1967 and even that was only a beginning. The French refinery industry also stood to benefit from the Farm Fund support of exports of Community sugar to non-member countries.

Runaway surpluses appear inevitable unless some curbs on the sugar price, along the lines of those proposed by the Commission, are accepted. The German State Secretary pointed out that the EEC was likely to have a sugar surplus of 1·2 to 1·5m. tons in 1969 costing the Farm Fund $337·5m. of which $100m. would have to be covered by the producers themselves.

The Common Market sugar policy is a growing threat to the under-developed countries producing cane-sugar. In 1946 around 70 per cent of world production consisted of cane sugar but this percentage dropped to around 55 per cent by 1964–5. The share of total sugar production entering into trade fell from 35 per cent in 1947–8 to just over 20 per cent in 1965 and, of this 20 per cent, half was sold under special agreements so that the remaining free market is in effect a residual market where surpluses from the heavily protected beet-sugar industries of the developed countries may increasingly be dumped at low prices to the detriment of under-developed sugar-growing countries.

Special arrangements have been made for the French overseas

departments – Guadeloupe, Martinique, and Réunion – and the French Government is committed to buying two thirds of their cane sugar output. It seems clear, however, that EEC beet-producers would strongly oppose the admission of Common-wealth sugar to the market. The Commonwealth sugar agreement emerged in 1951 as the natural successor to the bulk purchases by the UK during World War II, and though Britain could provide more for herself and pays over the odds for Commonwealth sugar, she is assured of a steady supply without the fluctuations inherent in the commodity market and also feels that this is a form of aid by trade which accords with Commonwealth ideas. The agreement was reviewed in 1968 and is subject to review every three years, but assurances were written into the agreement that Britain would try to fulfil its obligations to the exporting members if she had to withdraw after 1974, i.e. she would try to include Commonwealth sugar exporters in any bargain with the EEC.

FRUIT AND VEGETABLES

Very strange phenomena attend the working-out of the common marketing system for fruit and vegetables; grade I fruit have been deliberately destroyed to keep up the price for grade III fruit ... the best cauliflowers have gone uncut out of consideration for the second-best which will then, of course, become the best and as there are more of them the net return to the growers will be higher than if.... The rules are complicated not to say devious.

Regulations to establish a single market were laid down in the autumn of 1962 and defined the standards for the various kinds of horticultural produce along the lines of the standards laid down by other international organizations. Only products which are up to standard are accepted in intra-Community trade and as imports from non-member countries. By 1 July 1968 intra-Community customs and other obstacles to trade were abolished and on that date the common external tariff was applied fully to fruit and vegetables imported from outside the EEC. For vegetables the tariff is between 10 and 20 per cent and for fruit between 7 and 25 per cent depending on the product and season.

Support buying was established by a regulation of 1966;

support measures for specified fruit and vegetables (cauliflowers, tomatoes, apples, pears, peaches, dessert grapes, oranges, tangerines, and lemons) were not intended to guarantee a price to the growers but to avoid a deterioration in price levels which could lead to a crisis or to a serious crisis. Complicated criteria distinguish between the two.

The growers' associations cope with a crisis but a serious crisis needs government action. In a crisis the growers' associations fix a reserve price below which their members' produce will not be sold and members are reimbursed for any quantity unsold from an intervention fund to which they themselves have contributed in proportion to the quantities offered for sale.

The reserve price is supposed to be adequate to deal with a crisis but a further safeguard has been established to avoid a serious crisis. For the specified products, the Commission fixes a basic price (the average of the prices quoted for the three previous years, excluding abnormal fluctuations, on representative Community markets in the surplus-producing areas where prices are lowest). From this basic price is derived a buying-in price. When the price on the representative market falls for three successive market days below the buying-in price, member-states may, but need not, buy up produce; the cost of such support operations is borne by the Farm Fund. Up to 31 December 1969 member-states were to fix their own buying-in prices, which only apply during the normal season; for cauliflowers and tomatoes these buying-in prices must be between 40 and 45 per cent of the basic price; for apples and pears, between 50 and 55 per cent of the basic price; and for sub-tropical fruits, peaches and dessert grapes, between 60 and 70 per cent of basic price. Subsequently the Commission will fix buying-in prices.

Provision is made for a limited system of subsidies on exports (export refunds). This is specially important for Italy where fruit and vegetables are the primary source of agricultural income and for the Netherlands where they represent a substantial proportion of agricultural income. Citrus fruit, grapes, peaches, processed tomatoes, and fruit juices, but not processed apples and pears, are among the chief products affected.

The policy quickly ran into difficulties. In April 1969 the

Italians told a meeting of agriculture ministers of the Community that they now had 150,000 tons of oranges stockpiled and were seriously disturbed at the animosity aroused in the farming community by the wholesale destruction of fruit. They feared the political consequences.

The Farm Fund is authorized to spend $60m. a year on support for fruit and vegetables; and for 1967–8 expenditure was about half of this amount. Most of the fruit and vegetables withdrawn from the market is destroyed, though some is given free to those in need (the proportion of this is not known).

Quantities (metric tons) of Fruit and Vegetables Withdrawn in 1967–8

	Belgium	France	Italy	Holland	EEC	Total EEC production (%)
Cauliflowers	1,080	23,700	11,800	860	37,440	2·9
Tomatoes	—	2,010	—	—	2,010	0·04
Apples	4,270	115,750	166,900	9,270	296,190	5·7
Pears	—	490	—	—	490	0·025
Oranges	—	—	31,700	—	31,700	2·5

FAT SHEEP

There is no common organization of the market for mutton and lamb. Quantity restrictions are still imposed by individual member-states and a common external tariff of 20 per cent protects against imports from non-member countries.

WINE

The wine market was still being organized in 1970. It is very important to the Community, which produces 60 per cent of the world's wines and even more of its fine wines. A system of quality control has been introduced and measures to stabilize prices and adapt supply more closely to demand are expected. Meanwhile, the wine policy is not financed by the Community and trade in wine is still subject to restrictions and to quotas both inside the Community and in trade with non-member countries.

Although the organization of the wine market was scheduled to be completed not later than November 1969 and a viticultural land register giving the type of product, size of vineyard, cultivation method, etc. has been established, the target date was not likely to be met as some of the Commission's proposals such as those on sugaring and blending met with bitter opposition from the producers and the trade.

About 2,840m. gallons of wine are produced a year in the EEC, of which about 50m. gallons are exported to non-member countries; annual imports are on average 220m. gallons, so the EEC is 90 per cent self-sufficient. Imports have fallen by nearly half over the past twelve years largely because improved husbandry and pest control in the Community vineyards have boosted output – the area under vines has not increased. But wine consumption is increasing every year, which may be a consolation to Greek, Spanish, and Algerian winegrowers who would like to improve the level of their exports to the Six.

Rise in Wine Consumption in the Six

	1948	1968	
Germany	1·2	3·0	gallons per head
Holland	0·16	0·81	
Belgium	1·28	2·12	
Luxembourg	4·85	7·5	
Italy	18·7	24·8	
France	27·5	25·0	(*fall*)

FISH

The fish market was still being organized in 1970. The Commission aimed at establishing common quality standards and certain price-support arrangements. It also wished to establish a common social policy on working and living conditions on board ship, occupational training, and social welfare.

6 Main Industries
(Steel, Chemicals, Motor)

Up to the late 1950s the European Community was the second largest steel-producer in the world, immediately behind the U S A and just in front of the U S S R. In thirteen years, between 1952 and 1965, it doubled its production, from 42m. tons to 86m. tons. Production then levelled off, as it did in most countries except Japan, and in 1966 it actually fell by 1m. tons. It was on the upswing again in 1967 with 90m. tons and in 1968 with 98·6m. tons.

Even so, by the early 1960s, it had lost its second place to the Soviet Union whose known investment plans are designed to keep it in that position for many years to come.

Excess world production and potential capacity have forced the Community to alter course. When the European Coal and Steel Community (E C S C) assumed overall responsibility for steel under the Treaty of Paris in 1953, its aims were to encourage free and healthy competition between its six members and to ban all forms of concentration which might lead to the creation of dominant positions such as cartels, price-fixing, and market-sharing agreements. In practice this meant the continued fragmentation of the industry with the inevitable lack of efficiency. Early mergers, particularly between German firms, were frowned upon and the High Authority went to great lengths to see that the letter and the spirit of the Treaty were observed. This policy inevitably had to be relaxed as the world moved into a position of glut, cut-throat competition, and dumping.

The Treaty still acts as a guideline but pressure of events has forced the High Authority into approving several important concentrations and cartel-like agreements, not only between German firms, but between Dutch, German, Belgian, and French steelmakers. It has laid down conditions which in theory at least maintain the spirit of free competition and should provide some benefit to the consumer. For instance, it now approves 'vertical' and 'horizontal' amalgamations, i.e. those where a firm or group of firms acquires greater control of the many facets of steel-making, including the supply of raw materials and those where the creation of larger production units makes for greater competitive ability through economies of scale. In short, the High Authority is not opposed to mergers and concentrations which make economic sense, provided the consumer receives reasonable protection.

This bold change of policy has led to the formation of some very powerful groups in Western Europe, none of which, however, measures up to the American giants, although they are certainly much larger than any two of the thirteen major producers taken over by the British Steel Corporation put together. Indeed, the Hoesch/Hoogovens/Dortmund-Hörder Hütte union combined has an ingot capacity about the size of the old Richard Thomas & Baldwins, United Steel, and Colvilles put together.

The line-up of firms or groups in the Common Market by production in 1966 and/or 1967, was as follows:

August Thyssen Hütte/Oberhausen/ Mannesmann (German)	12·7 m. metric tons
Hoogovens/Hoesch/DHHU/Südwestfalen (German-Dutch)	11·4
Wendel/Sidelor (French)	9·4
Finsider (Italian)	8·1
Usinor (French)	6·3
Arbed/Hadir (Luxembourg)	4·9
Cockerill/Ougrée/Providence (Belgian)*	4·2
Krupp (German-Dutch)	3·4
Klöckner-Werke (German)	2·8
Salzgitter (German)	1·8
Fiat (Italian)	1·7
Espérance/Longdoz (Belgian)*	1·5
Ilseder (German)	1·4
Lombarde Falck (Italian)	0·97

*In 1969 Cockerill/Ougrée/Providence and Espérance/Longdoz joined forces giving them a joint production of around 6m. tons.

Furthermore Arbed/Hadir and Cockerill/Ougrée/Providence are the chief shareholders in the Sidmar Group (Sidérurgie Maritime), which operates an important steel mill in the Ghent area with a capacity of approximately 6m. ingot tons per year. Other steelworks and financial houses are participants in the Sidmar complex, which is a joint venture.

The list is by no means final. The mosaic of mergers and concentrations changes from month to month. It is on the cards that production in Germany in a few years to come will be concentrated in three main groups: August Thyssen Hütte, Hoesch/Hoogovens, and Klöckner.

Hoesch could take over the ailing Rheinstahl Hüttenwerke, which produced 751,000 tons of crude steel in 1966, and co-operate with Rheinstahl's parent body, Rheinische Stahlwerke. This would considerably enlarge its already vast interests in manufacturing and commercial enterprises. In taking over Rheinstahl, Hoesch would automatically gain control of Edelstahlwerken Witten, in which Rheinstahl has a controlling interest. In 1969 the EEC Commission approved the merger of Südwestfalen Stahlwerke with Hoesch because the joint production of special steels did not represent more than 10 per cent of total EEC production.

Klöckner has been considering merging with Ilseder and Salzgitter, which would raise its capacity to nearly 6m. tons., also including special steels. Ilseder, in which the Federal Government has a quarter financial interest, concentrates on iron, coal, and steel but is a smaller producer of steel than Klöckner or Salzgitter. The latter is something of a curiosity, a leftover of one of Hitler's exercises in economic self-sufficiency. It was set up in 1937 by Hermann Goering in the middle of the Third Reich. But it only justified itself as an economic unit in times of boom in a united Germany. Today it stands isolated on the borders of West and East Germany with Volkswagen's factory at Wolfburg virtually its only customer. The Federal Government inherited it after the Second World War and has been embarrassed by it ever since. Finally it decided to revamp it and make it reasonably attractive to would-be purchasers. It wrote off Salzgitter's very considerable losses over the years, leaving it with a bare DM. 50m. as capital to which it agreed to add DM. 300m. in four annual instalments.

A merger with Klöckner and Ilseder would be the obvious solution. Ilseder is at Peine, only twenty-five miles north of Salzgitter, and Klöckner's works are in North Germany as well as in the Ruhr. The group would move into sixth place just behind Usinor.

Krupp may well hive off its steel interests and Mannesmann has agreed to collaborate with Hoesch in building a wide-strip mill at Duisberg with an initial capacity of 200,000 tons a month. At one time Mannesmann was very jealous of its independence and strongly denied that it was looking for partners. Its interests are wide, reaching deep into steel, research engineering, chemicals and plastics, merchanting, property, etc. and the decision to share a plant with Hoesch could have led to much stronger links; particularly as the two were already partners in a joint sales organization for bars and sections. Instead, Mannesmann fell to the blandishments of Thyssen.

A Hoesch/Hoogovens/D H H U/Mannesmann combination would have left Thyssen well and truly in second place among the German giants, but Thyssen's strength is that it concentrates almost entirely on steel in all its forms and is completely integrated.

Hoesch, however, set the pace in mergers in Germany by linking up with the Dutch Koninklijke Nederlandsche Hoogovens en Staalfabrieken and absorbing Dortmund-Hörder Hütte-union in which Hoogovens had a financial interest. As a result Hoogovens acquired a 14·5 per cent interest in the share capital of Hoesch, thus making it the largest single shareholder. The grouping has many advantages. In the first place it spared Hoesch the necessity of building a second hot-strip mill. Secondly, Hoogovens acquired excellent outlets for its expanded pig-iron and ingot steel production, semi-finished products, and hot-rolled coils. Furthermore, Hoesch gets cheap imported ore from Hoogovens' modern terminal at Ijmuiden on the Dutch coast just north of Haarlem, and the link with Hoogovens enables it to concentrate on finished products which it sells to customers all conveniently close at hand.

August Thyssen Hütte of Duisburg-Hamborn controlled fifty-one companies before it took over Hüttenwerke Oberhausen (H O A G). In 1964 it acquired Phoenix Rheinrohr Eisen- und

Rohrenhandel of Mülheim and at the time was the largest all-German steel group. With HOAG and Mannesmann it has a capacity of about 15m. tons per year of crude steel. Under its dynamic chairman, Dr Hans-Gunther Sohl, who is also chairman of the International Iron and Steel Institute, it has embarked on a period of new investment in plant. Dr Sohl is a firm believer in size as a means of keeping costs down.

Wendel/Sidelor is a merger of de Wendel & Cie., the Société Mosellane de Sidérurgie and Sidelor (Union Sidérurgique Lorraine – the old Pont-à-Mousson group). It takes in the Société des Aciéries de Lorraine (Sacilor), a joint subsidiary of Wendel and Sidelor. It is the largest steel group in France, combining some very famous names, and is responsible for about 35 per cent of France's steel production.

Finsider (Società Finanziaria Siderurgica) is an offshoot of the Istituto per la ricostruzione industriale (IRI), a vast state-sponsored organization having a controlling interest in a network of companies covering almost every sector of the Italian economy. It dates from the Mussolini era but has been adapted and refurbished to meet present-day needs and has been so successful that the British Labour Government took a good look at it before setting up its own Industrial Reorganization Corporation to foster concentration and rationalization in British industry.

Its main steel interests are in Italsider, Dalmine, Terni, and Breda. But Italsider is by far the most important grouping, providing about 60 per cent of Italy's total steel output. It operates the giant new integrated steel works at Taranto, spearhead of Italy's spectacular rise as a steel-producer in the Common Market, where she ranks immediately behind West Germany and France. Total production in Italy rose from 3·6m. tons in 1952 to 15.9m. tons in 1967, and in 1955, when the works at Taranto and the enlarged modernized plant at Bagnoli and Cornigliano were fully operative, Italy achieved the highest expansion rate in the world, including Japan, with an increase in production of 29·5 per cent over 1964. Dalmine, Terni, and Breda are much smaller works by comparison and are mostly concerned with seamless tubes, stainless and other specialized steels, and the processing of Italsider's semi-manufactures.

Usinor (Union Sidérurgique du Nord et de l'Est de la France) is the second largest grouping in France after Wendel/Sidelor. It merged with Lorraine-Escaut in 1966, taking on about 2·3m. tons extra capacity. Its largest and most modern plant is at Dunkirk where coal and ore can be unloaded direct into the works. It has taken a controlling interest in Vallourec (Usines à Tubes de Lorraine-Escaut et Vallourec Réunies), which followed on logically after it took over Lorraine-Escaut's four tube-producing factories. The group now produces more than 80 per cent of France's steel tubes.

Arbed/Hadir was a natural link-up between the two major producers in Luxembourg – the Aciéries Réuníes de Burbach-Eich-Dudelange, and the Hauts Fourneaux et Aciéries de Differdange-Saint Ingbert-Rumelange. The merger took place in 1966. Arbed's interests extend to coal, cement, and engineering, and Hadir has iron-ore mines at Ottingen, Rumelingen, and Differdingen which produced 3·2m. tons in 1966.

Cockerill/Ougrée/Providence is a vast network of industrial and commercial enterprises covering iron and steel, coal, iron-ore, chemicals, shipping, gas, and electricity with many investments abroad, particularly in France.

Krupp, of Essen, the greatest name in armaments the world has ever known, was ordered to be broken up after the Second World War and the parts put up for sale by the Allied Powers. But there were no buyers. Potential customers in Germany made it a point of honour not to be cast in the role of vultures gobbling up one of their most famous enterprises. The dismantling order was eventually allowed to lapse and by 1968 Krupp had become a double phoenix. It had risen from the rubble created by Allied bombers and put its financial house in order by revamping itself into a limited liability company with a capital of DM. 500m. It received considerable help from the federal government (DM. 300m.). It took on the well-known banker Hermann Abs, former chairman of the Deutsche Bank, as its chairman and renamed itself Fried Krupp GmbH, pensioning off the last remaining member of the Krupp family, Arndt von Bohlen und Halbach, son of Alfried Krupp. Herr Guenter Vogelsang, another eminent financier, returned to Krupp after a spell at Mannesmann and was made chairman of the board of management in charge of the day-to-day running of the new firm. Early in 1968 Herr Vogelsang said the new Krupp's activities would be concentrated on the engineering works at Essen, on steel at Bochum, and on shipbuilding at the A G Weser yard at Bremen. The firm would put its own house in order before thinking of mergers and, as far as steel was concerned, streamlining had already started with the new multi-purpose electronically controlled hot-rolling mill at Hoentrop, one of the most modern in the world. It is possible, however, that within a few years Krupp's steel interests will be joined with those of Thyssen or Klöckner. Krupp already co-operates with Thyssen for rolled steel as both are members of the West Ruhr Joint Sales Organization.

Fiat, one of the largest users of steel in Italy, produces about 13 per cent of the country's steel, followed by Lombarde Falck (Acciaierie e Ferriere Lombarde Falck) of Milan, with about 7 per cent. Fiat, Falck, and Finsider between them produce about 80 per cent of all Italy's steel. The rest is split up between a large number of small firms, mostly in the North.

Espérance/Longdoz (Société Anonyme Métallurgique d' Espérance/Longdoz) is the second largest Belgian producer, after Cockerill, Ougrée/Providence. It has investments in coal, electricity, iron-ore, and fertilizers.

The above firms or groups represent about 70 per cent of production capacity in the Community. They receive the bulk of the aid. This is considerable from both E C S C and national sources. In the fifteen years between 1953 and 1968 the E C S C made loans of more than $800m. to Community producers, the bulk of which was for modernization and rationalization, industrial redevelopment, and the rehousing and retraining of workers.

At national level governments have made loans to help steel concerns to rationalize themselves and to encourage mergers. The French had more leeway to make up in this respect than their great rivals across the Rhine. Like most of French industry, steel in France was fragmented and although cross-investments provided listening posts and *de facto* cartels and agreements on pricing and sales, the French steel industry was in no way capable of competing successfully with the Germans, let alone the Japanese,

Americans, or Russians. Under the 1966 steel reorganization plan, costing some 11,000m. francs up till 1976, the French Government agreed to loans amounting to 2,700m. fr. The plan called for the following total expenditure: 4,000m. fr. for new investment; 2,000m. fr. for the financing of work already in hand; and 5,000m. fr. for debt repayment. Some of this investment may have to be cut back following the vastly increased production costs arising from the government's social and economic reforms after the riots and prolonged stoppages in May–June 1968. The wages bill, according to M. Jules Ferry, President of the French Federation of Steelmakers, would go up by 15 per cent. About 1·3m. tons of steel, or 6 per cent of production during the second half of 1967, were lost during the troubles. On the other hand, the Government's quota restrictions put an upper limit of 390,000 tons of finished steel on imports until the end of 1968.

West Germany's position as the leading steel producer in the Community appears unassailable. The country produces about 40 per cent of the EEC total and more than France and Italy put together. Concentration and rationalization with government aid and encouragement started earlier than it did in France, partly because Allied bombers had left so much more to rebuild, and has been highly successful.

One of the first steps towards concentration was taken when four sales agencies were set up to handle the whole of the distribution of steel in West Germany and eventually all export sales. Previously there had been thirty-one such agencies. The scope of these organizations has been progressively widened to include the rationalization of production as well as distribution, rather as the British Steel Corporation intends to do by centralizing all orders and farming them out to whoever is best suited at the time to carry them out. They provide a stepping-stone to further mergers and cover four areas: North Germany, West and East Ruhr, and South Germany. The High Authority, however, requires that competition in sales between the agencies shall not be restricted and that the agencies shall act independently. (The BSC need observe a similar precept in respect of its own divisions only if it sees fit.) The High Authority also reserves the right to decide whether the price-basing points are in keeping with the terms laid down in the authorization.

The German steel industry was for years plagued with high costs. The need to reduce them was paramount and this has been pursued with vigour although workers in the iron-ore mines only work a forty-two-hour week, compared with forty-eight hours in other ECSC countries. The mergers entailed large-scale dismissals – 10,000 workers when Hoesch took over Dortmund-Hörder Hütte-union. But no major strikes or stoppages took place mainly because management–labour relations in Germany tend to be on a sounder footing than they are in most other European countries and are made easier by the fact that the syndicalist movement is concentrated in sixteen trade unions, as opposed to 175 in Britain for instance. In recent years German producers have had to meet increased competition from cheap imported steel, mainly from Belgium/Luxembourg but also from France. The French were able to export cheaply to Germany because of the advantages they derived from the value-added tax. This tax was introduced in Germany at the beginning of 1968, some considerable time later than in France. In 1967 and early 1968 nearly 30 per cent of Germany's consumption of rolled steel came from abroad. Costs rose again, however, when the German steelmakers conceded a 5 per cent wage increase to 200,000 workers in the Ruhr starting 1 June 1968 and a further 2 per cent to follow automatically on 1 March 1969.

With the German and French steel industries well on their way to putting their houses in order and the Italians already possessing one of the most modern steel complexes at Taranto, the European Community presents a formidable challenge to the outside world, despite the fact that it has been overtaken by the USSR and that the Japanese now produce more steel than the Germans and the French combined – 62m. tons in 1967.

Modernization has entailed an average capital expenditure during the eight years from 1960 to December 1967 of $1,423m. a year, with progressive and heavy emphasis on oxygen converters. The Community has taken two further steps towards greater efficiency by importing more high-grade iron-ore from traditional world sources like Sweden, Mauritania, Venezuela, Canada,

Liberia, Algeria, etc; and it has to a very large extent levelled out fuel costs as between steelmakers inland and those whose plants are on the coast by subsidizing local coke supplies to bring the price into line with the price of imports delivered at coastal mills. The subsidy averages $1·70 per metric ton with an upper limit of $2·20, and is paid out of a fund to which the Six countries contribute according to the relative size of their steel industries and their imports.

Ports on the North Sea coast are being adapted to take bulk-carriers of 200,000 tons and over. Holland's Europoort can already berth carriers of 80,000 tons. Even before the Second World War Krupp and Oberhausen enjoyed trans-shipment facilities at Rotterdam and Thyssen at Vlaardingen. Today Thyssen/Hoag, Krupp, and Mannesmann have formed a consortium to trans-ship ore from the new depot at Rotterdam which cost between £3m. and £4m. and is capable of handling 11m. tons of ore a year. The Dutch are building their own trans-shipment depot at Maasvlakte. France and Holland together have decided to build a terminal capable of harbouring the largest bulk-carriers liable to be built in the foreseeable future.

Where the shipment of ore is concerned, economies of scale are remarkable. According to Dr H. M. Finniston, deputy chairman (technical) of the British Steel Corporation, the difference between the cost of shipping ore in 80,000-tonners as against a 20,000-ton vessel over an average haul of 5,000 miles is about 15s. a ton and the differential is likely to rise. Put another way, it costs 8s. 6d. per ton-day at sea to ship ore in a 30,000-ton carrier and as little as 5s. 1d. in a 100,000-tonner.

On the technical side the size of plants has increased at a faster rate than in Britain and roughly on a par with Japan. In 1961 the ECSC and Japan both had only one plant with a capacity of over 3m. tons a year. By 1967 both had five, but the ECSC had made far greater progress in the 1 to 3m. ton range than the Japanese – 33 plants as against 11.

Britain was among the first to install pure oxygen converters (LD, Kaldo, etc.) but the ECSC countries have made great strides in this direction. Production by this method in the ECSC increased by over 34 per cent between 1952 and 1967. In

1967 it accounted for 28 per cent of production as opposed to 27·4 per cent for open-hearth and 31·8 per cent for basic Bessemer, the rest being taken up by electric furnace. According to present investment plans it is expected to rise by 15 per cent per annum until 1971 when it will account for 43·7 per cent of all crude-steel-production potential – almost exactly as much as basic Bessemer and open-hearth combined.

Investment in open-hearth and basic-Bessemer plant has diminished year by year with corresponding increases in oxygen converters and electric-arc furnaces. Progress in oxygen steel-making has been extremely rapid. In 1966 and 1967 it accounted for 76 per cent of the industry's total investment in crude steel-making as compared with 70 per cent in 1963, 1964, and 1965. The figures for 1968 and 1969, respectively, were 76 and 79 per cent. Total crude-steel capacity, thanks to present investments, is expected to reach 124·2m. tons in 1971, of which L D, Kaldo, etc. is estimated at 54·3m. tons or 43·7 per cent; basic Bessemer 28·9m. tons or 23·3 per cent; open-hearth 25·5m. tons or 20·5 per cent; and electric-arc furnace 15·5m. tons or 12·5 per cent. It will be seen from these figures that very little is being spent on basic Bessemer and open-hearth and still less is planned for the future.

Capital expenditure on electric-arc furnaces – used mainly for scrap – is highest in central France, the Saar, and Northern Italy. Expenditure on oxygen converters was highest in Western Germany and Belgium/Luxembourg.

Continuous casting is also gaining ground and Continental technicians have shown a keen interest in the new British spray-steelmaking process. They have also taken a close look at American methods of smelting scrap by the use of fragmentizers instead of the traditional guillotine sheaths to produce secondary ingots.

Productivity, however, is still low by American and Japanese standards. It needs about twice as many men in Germany and France, as indeed in Britain, to produce a given tonnage of steel as it does in the USA or Japan. But productivity will improve as more and more plants become automated and production computerized. During the ten years from 1957 to 1967 production in the Community increased by 49 per cent whereas manpower dropped by 7 per cent from 463,701 men in 1957 to 428,499 in 1967. Productivity in 1967 was highest in the Netherlands (284 tons of steel per year per man) followed by Italy (280), Luxembourg (231), Belgium and West Germany (204) and France (174).

Progress in concentration and rationalization has not been matched by an orderly regulation of markets. Little short of chaos exists in the steel markets of the EEC – as it does in the markets of the world. When there was a sellers' market in steel, i.e. up to the early 1960s, all was sweet reasonableness and ECSC regulations about publishing price-scales could be readily adhered to. But from 1961 onwards buyers got the upper hand and price-cutting became widespread. Producers could align their prices on those of their lowest competitors, more often than not the Japanese, without informing the High Authority of the ECSC, unless they were selling to countries outside the Community. Competition within the ECSC became so acute that prices often bore no relation to costs.

Producers resorted to all manner of inducements such as hidden loyalty and quantity rebates, which would circumvent ECSC regulations. A classic example of unfair competition was when a well-known French steelmaker was fined 160,000 fr. by the European Commission for selling cold-rolled plates to French and German clients at prices which included a rebate forbidden by the ECSC. The Community Court of Justice upheld the Commission's fine.

Over and above intense competition between the Six themselves, the steel-producers had to face an aggressive sales drive by the Japanese, who were able to export over 20 per cent of their production in 1967 at knock-out prices not only to Common Market countries but to the USA.

Price-cutting and dumping have not been the prerogative of the Japanese. Britain has been accused of dumping by the Scandinavians and vice-versa. Cases have been known where Continental buyers of British strip have been able to undercut British manufacturers of light-gauge seam-welded steel tube because they had paid less for the strip than their British rivals were paying. The irony goes even further. It appears that some of the tube made on the Continent was being re-exported back to Britain at subsidized prices.

This illustrates the almost farcical situation of world steel capacity constantly outstripping demand, despite the fact that the latter also grows. Excess capacity in 1967 was estimated at 75m. tons. When the Japanese can sell steel to the Americans cheaper than the Americans themselves can sell it, clearly some regulation of international markets is desirable. The 6 per cent rise in the US steel-workers' wages granted in July 1968 made Japanese steel even more competitive. Cut-throat exports cannot go on indefinitely, merely to sustain an unrealistic growth in capacity. And as far as the Japanese are concerned, it is not likely to diminish since two of their top firms – Yawata Steel and Fuji Iron & Steel – have merged, thereby reinforcing their competitiveness on world markets. No steel plant in the world has been working at full capacity for years. In some cases capacity utilization has been as low as 75 per cent. In the EEC unused capacity in 1968 amounted to just under 20m. tons.

Unless investment plans are revised at international level, world capacity will have risen to around 610m. tons a year by 1970, a rise of about 30 per cent since 1965. Of this total the USA are expected to contribute 162m. tons; Soviet Russia 127m., the EEC 120m., Japan 71m., the United Kingdom 37m., Eastern Europe 39m., China, North Vietnam, North Korea, and other minor producers 40m. All told, sixty-seven countries will be producing steel, sixteen more than in 1965.

The reasons for increased capacity are sometimes political. Emerging nations often make it a point of national pride to have their own steel works, just as they do their own airlines, however uneconomical they may be. In the end some of them are no longer net importers and traditional markets for the major producers dry up. Some of them begin to export, as the Japanese have been doing so successfully for years, thereby competing on world markets with the older producers. Capacity is sometimes installed without any regard for the overall picture. In Egypt, for instance, a giant steel complex is near completion at Helwan, near Cairo, costing £360m., of which the Soviet Union has undertaken to subscribe a £70m. in the form of equipment and technical services.

Thus a further 1·25m. tons will be added to world capacity and a possible 500,000 tons of steel and 250,000 tons of cast-iron per year unloaded on world markets.

In Australia the steel industry is in its infancy. But Australia is rapidly becoming the industrial base for South-East Asia in direct competition with the Japanese. The day will come when the Australians will want to make their own steel, using their own iron-ore which they now export in such large quantities to Japan. This is unlikely to reduce Japanese output, but given the vast reserves of ore in North-Western Australia Australia may well in a few years' time become a large exporter of steel herself. The British Steel Corporation was at one time interested in teaming up with Rio Tinto Zinc's joint steel-making venture with the American steel giants Bethlehem Steel and Kaiser Steel in Western Australia, where iron-ore deposits are vast around the Hamersley Range. (Most of the ore now goes to the Japanese under contract.)

Conditions on world markets could hardly have been more difficult when the nationalized British Steel Corporation started operations. Lord Melchett and his team were told to make steel pay. Yet for years the British steel industry, like its rivals abroad, had been plagued with excess capacity. In 1968 less than 80 per cent capacity was used by the BSC to produce 23 million ingot tons of steel. The reorganization of the industry which the BSC was given a mandate to perform therefore meant increasing efficiency rather than capacity. And this in turn meant altering the whole structure of the industry, still labouring under the many handicaps left by history, romantic paternalism, nepotism, uneconomic plants, wrongly sited and ill-equipped by modern standards, hopelessly outclassed by the Japanese, and as to sheer size by the Americans. The largest single plant capacity in the United Kingdom was still in 1968 only about 3m. tons, whereas in Japan there are at least four works with a capacity of 4m. tons a year each, and more are being built with an even higher capacity. The two worst handicaps for British steel were the relatively high cost of home-coking coal and of imported ore.

The trend in all countries is to import the highest grade ore. The average iron content of ore imported into the United

Kingdom is 59 per cent, whereas the iron content of home-mined ore is only on average 27 per cent. Since it takes about 1·75 tons of ore to make one ton of steel, using high-grade ore has a very distinct advantage. But the snag where Britain is concerned is that much of the advantage is lost if imported ore has to be taken on long rail journeys to the mills, frequently twenty miles or more. Only four British steel works, the Steel Company of Wales at Port Talbot, Colvilles on the Clyde, Dorman Long on Tees-side, and Guest Keen Iron & Steel at Cardiff, can unload straight from the ship to the works. Few U K ports can take ships carrying 20,000 tons of ore and not until Port Talbot in South Wales was opened in 1969 could any take ore-ships of over 35,000 tons; Port Talbot will be able to handle ships of 100,000 tons, and eventually 150,000 tons. But bulk carriers building today are in the 200,000 to 300,000-ton bracket. Even so, they will be able to use many continental ports including Dunkirk and Europoort at Rotterdam, Taranto, etc. Steelworks on the northern coasts of France, Holland, and Belgium can now compete successfully with home-produced steel in the U K.

Becoming more competitive also means getting the cheapest possible fuel. American coking coal is marginally cheaper than coal of a similar quality supplied by the National Coal Board. American producers can supply good quality washed coking coal c.i.f. Amsterdam, Rotterdam, and Antwerp at £4 16s. 6d. per ton. The B S C would expect the Coal Board to match or beat that figure. The BSC rightly points out that if the new aluminium smelters can buy coal from the National Coal Board at below market prices, it should be able to do likewise – or be allowed to import American coal, as steelmakers on the Continent have long been able to do.

Now that the capital structure of the B S C (£830m. starting capital) has been agreed with the Treasury and dividends payable to the Exchequer related to profitability, the Corporation can embark on a stable-price policy, long overdue particularly on the home market where imports have been rising steadily since 1965 (the increase in 1967–8 was due mainly to the urgent demand for pipelines for North-Sea gas). But pricing on international markets is a delicate exercise. How delicate can be seen from the fact that to avoid unduly disturbing export markets, the B S C preferred where possible to maintain its old selling price abroad after devaluation, thus increasing its profits rather than increasing the cut-throat element in international steel markets by reducing its selling prices. B S C estimated in 1968 that capital expenditure would be held down to rather less than £100m. a year during 1968–9 and 1969–70, but that then there would be a sharp jump to about £200m. a year for the next six years, the assumption being that capacity of 35m. tons would be needed by 1975, 15m. tons of it new. With world-surplus capacity amounting to 75m. tons and Japan alone planning an increase to 80m. tons, this is a bold assumption; however, B S C estimated that world demand will grow fast enough to match increased capacity and plans to reduce its production costs by better siting of larger units, by improved productivity and by using much larger ore-carriers.

British exports of iron and steel to the Community slipped in 1965 and 1966 but have since picked up. Even so the trend is for trade in this field between Community and the U K not to rise in the same proportion as total U K trade. Selling to the Community meets with formidable competition not only from Community steel-makers themselves, but from countries like Austria, Spain, the Eastern bloc, and Japan. But some of this trade is by no means profitable. Indeed, some of it is not profitable at all. Governments have been notably reluctant even to attempt to regulate world markets in steel, though they have from time to time attempted to do so for edible commodities.

The standing Council of Association between the U K and the E C S C merely calls for the co-ordination of policies, if and when opportune, and provides a permanent channel of communication on pricing policy, etc. but little more. On the world's markets it is a free-for-all where the major exporters are constantly accused of dumping or something very like it. The U S Congress, for instance, threatened to impose import curbs on Japanese steel in the summer of 1968 if the Japanese did not voluntarily restrict their exports to the U S A. This the Japanese eventually agreed to do – to 5,500,000 tons during the financial year 1968–9 – fearing, not without reason, that once the U S A put restrictions on imported steel it would not readily remove them.

Tariffs are a crumbling barrier against excess imports. The EEC's common external tariff on iron and steel as of 1 July 1968 is 8·4 per cent and by 1972, or 1971, when all the Kennedy Round reductions are completed, it will be as low as 6·5 per cent. The UK duty in 1968 was brought down after the Kennedy Round reduction from 10 to 9 per cent. By 1972 (or 1971 according to whether the final Kennedy Round cuts are accelerated or not) the UK duty will be as low as 8 per cent.

Tariffs (except for some very minor exceptions) were totally abolished between the members of EFTA on 1 January 1967 eighteen months ahead of the EEC. The US tariff has never been a major barrier to UK steel exports to America, which vary widely from year to year according to whether US steel-users wish to stockpile against strikes or fear that some other factors will interfere with long-term supplies. A classic example of extraordinary factors coming into play in the USA was in 1965, when US steel imports from Britain at £31·4m. were double those of 1964.

Since tariffs are no longer an effective barrier against determined exporters anxious to clear unwanted surpluses and governments are understandably unwilling to resort to import quotas which might restrict trade and which would in any case probably violate GATT regulations, some other form of market regulation will have to be worked out, unless chaos is to continue.

The recently formed International Iron and Steel Institute has given some thought to this problem. Its views carry great weight since all the world's top steelmen are members of the Institute, but so far these views have been somewhat vague. The major stumbling block to any sort of international agreement is the rigidity of American anti-trust laws, which prevent American steel companies from joining any sort of international price-fixing agreement which might smack of a cartel, or a fair-trading-practices pact as the old cartels are now euphemistically called. As American anti-trust laws are unlikely to be relaxed merely to allow US steelmen to take part in international price-fixing operations, the American attitude must willy-nilly be very close to the German viewpoint as expressed by Dr Hans-Gunther Sohl, chairman of the board of management of August Thyssen Hütte.

Dr Sohl has called on the highly industrialized nations to end preferences and restrictions on steel imports and to make no distinction between domestic and export prices.

Most steelmen consider this little more than a pious hope. Nearer to the mark is the president of the French Steel Federation (Chambre Syndicale de la Sidérurgie Française), M. Jacques Ferry, who says that the best that can be hoped for at this stage is a minimum co-ordination at international level of large-scale investment plans. This, indeed, would hit at the root of the trouble since it would limit expansion plans and relate them more closely to estimated future requirements. It would slowly eliminate excess world capacity and by the same token the need for dumping. Another solution would be voluntary limitation by the producers themselves of their export prices to an accepted percentage below their domestic prices, otherwise governments would impose a countervailing duty. Both solutions in the last resort require co-operation at government level since steel is nationalized in Britain and all governments on the Continent take a strong hand in determining their countries' steel policies. Compensatory duties are nothing new. The UK resorted to them to keep out galvanized Canadian steel in 1967 and Italian refrigerators in 1968. In the near future they are likely to be the best solution although to some extent restrictive of trade.

A limited remedy to world excess capacity might be found if Britain joined the EEC. The European Community would then become virtually equal with the USA as a producing unit and just ahead of the USSR. It would in theory at least be easier to reach agreed policies on price-fixing and co-ordination of investment, which would eliminate wasteful competition between Community members and give the Community great bargaining power at world level. The voice of the BSC would of necessity carry great weight since it would be producing over 21 per cent of Community production which in turn would represent about 23 per cent of total world production.

Up to now the nationalization of steel has been an embarrassment to the UK Government in its efforts to join the EEC. Nationalized industries are of course allowed under the Treaty of Rome, and there are plenty of them in the EEC, but the very size of the BSC has frightened individual producers in Germany and France, and even the semi-state-owned Finsider in Italy. BSC's modernization and expansion plans, although slow to mature, have had the same effect. By European standards British steel has always been competitive. It will become more so when the industry has been rationalized. Already some steelmaking methods used in Britain are fully competitive with any on the Continent and about 25 per cent of production in the UK is now by the LD, Kaldo, Rotor oxygen-converter method. Like so many inventions in Britain, however, spray steelmaking has got off to a slow start but it could make a significant contribution to efficiency. In its way it is as revolutionary as the Austrian oxygen converter, which knocked £2 a ton off the traditional open-hearth method. It was discovered almost by accident by the British Iron and Steel Research Association (BISRA). If further tests prove that it is economically viable, it could mean a saving of as much as 10s. a ton on production costs. BISRA is also working on a new method of making steel entirely from scrap, known as the FOS system (fuel, oxygen, scrap) which may eventually challenge the more traditional and expensive electric-arc furnace. These new processes have yet to be adopted by the BSC and according to present plans it does not look as if spray-steelmaking will be used extensively by the Corporation until the early 1980s since it does not figure as a major element in its investment plans up to 1975. However, the financial advantages of spray-steelmaking have not been lost on Continental steelmakers since capital costs are lower than on any other plant, working out at about £250,000 for a 400,000 tons per year capacity.

Continuous casting has progressed rapidly in Britain and is now installed on a large scale at the Appleby Frodingham branch of United Steel, and at the Shelton Iron & Steel Works. Here again BISRA has made a significant advance by producing continuously cast shaped beam blanks for section rolling. These beam blanks are known in the trade as dog bones, and are cast instead of conventional ingots. In this way five expensive and time-consuming operations needed to produce material for the universal beam mill are avoided. They were first commercially produced in March 1968 in Canada at the Sault-Sainte-Marie plant of the Algoma Steel Corporation Ltd, the second largest steel company in Canada.

On the technical side, and once reorganization is under way, Britain has little to fear from continental competition. But being by far the largest producer in the EEC (larger than Hoogovens/ Hoesch and August Thyssen put together) its accession to the EEC would raise political issues of the highest order which could only be ironed out once negotiations were under way.

Steel Production (million ingot tons) in the EEC

Country	1964	1965	1966	1967	1968	Growth (%) between 1952 and 1967
West Germany	37·3	36·8	35·3	36·7	41·15	97
France	19·8	19·6	19·6	19·7	20·4	81
Italy	9·8	12·7	13·6	15·9	16·96	337
Belgium	8·7	9·2	9·0	9·7	11·56	89
Luxembourg	4·6	4·6	4·4	4·5	4·83	49
Netherlands	2·6	3·1	3·3	3·4	3·7	389
Total ECSC	82·8	86·0	85·0	89·9	98·62	114

Total Community production in 1969 was provisionally given as 107·1 m. tons – a rise of 8·6 per cent over 1968.

EUROPEAN CHEMICAL INDUSTRIES

The dynamic growth of Europe's chemical industry from 1958–68 has far outstripped the rate of growth of other large-volume industries – overall, the chemical industry has developed about twice as fast as other manufacturing industries. Production, valued in 1968 at $35,000m. a year, accounts for around a third of total world chemical output and the role of the industry in the overall economy of Europe has been dramatically increased.

One of the main reasons for this tremendous upsurge was the formation of EEC (and EFTA). The vastly increased home market to be catered for enabled the chemical industry to switch to the big-plant philosophy so successful in the United States. There was a spectacular increase in the size of plant; in 1960 the largest ethylene crackers were of 50,000 tons, in 1968 ICI opened one of 450,000 tons on Tees-side. Moreover, countries like Holland, which had Royal Dutch/Shell already established with an oil refinery in Rotterdam, were vastly encouraged in their expansion into the petrochemicals industry by the knowledge that the age-old superstructure of import duties, tariffs, and quotas of the vast hinterland was bit by bit to be dismantled. In the first ten years of the EEC intra-Community sales of chemicals increased four times and, within EFTA, sales increased by more than two and a half times – the European growth was higher than that of Japan, the United States, or Canada.

This dynamic growth rate inevitably attracted and was boosted by foreign investment. Foremost was the United States, whose chemical firms have been devoting nearly 10 per cent of their total capital expenditure ($350m. a year) to the EEC. In 1967 their rate of investment was five and a half times as much as they spent in the whole of Europe in 1957. The great names of the American chemical industry, Du Pont, Union Carbide, Dow, Monsanto, and Esso Chemical raced to catch the rising tide of prosperity. Esso (Standard Oil) announced, at the opening of its new £3m. research centre in Brussels in May 1968, further huge investments in Europe and said that the proportion of its turnover from Europe had risen to 30 per cent compared with 40 per cent from the US. Monsanto in the same month announced that a substantial part of several hundred millions of dollars earmarked for expanding its textile division would go into Europe (mainly to Northern Ireland, Britain, and Luxembourg). Investment from all sources in petrochemicals in Europe was estimated for the year 1967 at over $3,000m. – about 25 per cent in Germany, about 20 per cent in the UK, 18 per cent in Italy, and 30 per cent in France and Holland.

The outlook for the industry is one of great changes in structure. Since the organic side of the industry became dependent on oil, not coal, for feedstock, there has existed the constant threat that even the largest independent chemical companies would be taken over by the oil companies, for whom any captive outlet such as petrochemicals which increases the flow of crude oil is a boost to profits. The heavy-inorganic sector, pharmaceuticals and speciality chemicals, do not interest the oil companies but the heavy-organic sector faces a shake-up. Already the oil companies are on the march; this menace together with the threat from U S competitors has brought about great changes.

In France there has been a spate of amalgamations and take-overs – Péchiney and Saint-Gobain have shed their chemical interests and combined them into a separate unit; Ugine and Kuhlmann have merged; S N P A (Société Nationale des Pétroles d'Aquitaine) have taken over Organico.

In Holland K Z K (Koninklijke Zout-ketjen N V) and Zwanenberg-Organon joined forces and are likely to draw other companies into their orbit. In Italy S I R (Società Italiana Resine) and Rumianca have merged. An interesting merger was Agfa/ Gevaert (owned in equal shares by Bayer and Gevaert), where two companies were set up, one in each country, each with the same board of management. Although the E E C set-up demands co-ordinated operations of this kind, such companies cannot yet be incorporated as a single entity. Although a new convention on European companies was signed in 1968 by the Six, much has to be decided. What if one of the partners to such a European company were not a member of the E E C? How can such companies be taxed? Harmonization of company taxation in the Six would surely have to precede this decision.

Besides mergers there have been many take-overs – mainly by large companies wishing to acquire a captive outlet. The German big three, Hoescht, Bayer, and B A S F, are continuing their acquisitive policy not only for outlets but to get as much fat on themselves as possible so that the ever-prowling oil companies will find them too big a mouthful to swallow.

Governments, too, have taken a hand in rationalization and development. In Italy Edison, given enormous government compensation for its nationalized electricity interests, was able to merge with Montecatini, the country's largest chemical producer in 1966 (this involved disbanding Monteshell Petrochimica, the fifty–fifty Montecatini/Shell subsidiary set up only three years previously). Again it was in Italy that the Government handed out huge investment loans and allowances to Società Italiana Resine, who established over forty associate companies, all in Sardinia and all specializing in one or two products within a single petrochemical complex. This policy while excellent for the development of Sardinia and the Mezzogiorno will in the long run prove a hindrance to broad-based international ownership which would appear to be the pattern of the future.

The same nationalist approach has been shown by the Dutch Government, which, while appreciating the need for larger units, does not wish its own highly successful offspring, Dutch State Mines, to join up with the private sector headed by KZO (Koninklijke Zout-Organon NV) and AKU (Algemene Kunst-szijde Unie NV), who for their part have grave doubts about the performance of the featherbedded government organization when faced with stiff competition from the private sector.

Although governments still maintain the strictly nationalist outlook, companies by contrast are seeking compatible partners (manufacturing and marketing) regardless of national boundaries. ICI and the German big three have each set up a large manufacturing complex in another European country – ICI and Hoescht in Holland and Bayer and BASF in Belgium. This has increased their international size and stature and strengthened them against the ever-present threat of a take-over by oil companies. Examples of take-overs by the latter in Europe are the 1966 disappearance of Deutsche Erdol, the German oil refiner with a large chemical interest, into the jaws of Texaco; the buying up of Distillers' chemical interests by BP. Shell, CFP (Compagnie Française des Pétroles), Gulf, ENI (Ente Nazionale Idrocarburi), Continental Philips and Amoco are prowling Europe seeking whom they may devour.

Britain's stake in the EEC chemical scene is small – ICI's annual expenditure on new plants in Europe represents only about 1 per cent of total EEC investment in new chemical plants. But sales abroad of patented inventions and industrial know-how are particularly significant in the chemical field (ICI accounts for about £13m. of the £60m. Britain receives a year from licence fees and royalties – a big contributor was ICI's steam-naphtha reforming process which produces hydrogen in a novel way). BP are working on the production of food from hydro-carbon products at their plant in France. To even out supply and demand, a great international pipeline grid is taking shape, linking the European chemicals giants to their factories. Plastics works as far as seventy-five miles away can receive ethylene through the pipeline (ethylene is now the basic raw material for plastics and a huge range of products from polythene to detergents). The grid is a great step towards an integrated European chemical industry and gives far greater flexibility in the siting of factories, which can be located at any point on the grid.

Small as Britain's investment in the European chemical industry may be relatively, it is very important to her. In 1966 British chemical exports accounted for over 9 per cent of total value of all British exports and they represent 12 per cent of world chemical exports.

The demand for plastics and synthetic fibres and synthetic rubber has lost none of its momentum (demand for polythene alone grows by a steady 15 per cent a year) and with the surge of new ideas, such as the plastic car, the chemical industry has probably only just started on the road. Its growth was inevitable but it undoubtedly gained tremendous impetus from the confidence generated by the EEC idea; the constant stream of discoveries, including new feedstocks, shows no sign of abating; the Kennedy Round tariff cuts should substantially increase trade between the EEC and EFTA and trade between Europe and Japan and Europe and the United States. The future of European chemicals could be spectacular.

MOTOR INDUSTRY

The European market in cars is enormous, rapidly approaching the American market in size. United States production in 1967 was 7,400,000 cars and EEC production 5,700,000. In 1967 the EEC total vehicle fleet exceeded 30 million, of which nearly 26 million were cars – an estimate of about seven persons a car; and in EFTA the fleet was around 17·5 million vehicles, comprising 15 million cars, ownership coming out at about 6·7 persons a car.

Despite some pessimistic estimates of car-saturation, the market has huge potential: when conventional cars have reached their maximum sales point, there will be replacements on grounds of safety, there will be devices which have not yet fully penetrated the European market, such as automatic transmission and over-drive, new materials used, such as plastics, new types such as electric cars, changes of size (already the big American tin cans once valued for prestige reasons are out for parking reasons). It is estimated that car-ownership will more than double throughout Europe by 1980. The rewards open to car manufacturers are glittering indeed.

Running neck-and-neck for the top place in the European league by 1967 were Fiat (Fabbrica Italiana Automobili Torino) and Volkswagen, thanks to Fiat's own phenomenal 17 per cent advance coinciding with a severe setback to its nearest rival, Volkswagen, which in 1966 had topped the table.

List of Largest Automobile Manufacturers in 1967 (by total production of cars and commercial vehicles)		*List of Largest Producers by Country in 1969 for Cars Only (excluding commercial vehicles)*	
1. General Motors	6,489,973	1. U.S.A.	8.8m.
2. Ford	4,145,912	2. West Germany	2.9m.
3. Chrysler	2,328,741	3. Japan	2.1m.
4. Fiat	1,340,884	4. United Kingdom	1.8m.
5. Volkswagen	1,339,823	5. France	1.8m.
6. Renault/Peugeot	1,060,421	6. Italy	1.5m.
7. BMH/Leyland (BLMC)	961,045		
8. Toyota (Japan)	635,451		
9. Citroën/Berliet	520,087		
10. Nissan (Japan)	259,997		
11. Daimler/Benz (Mercedes)	245,293		

From Society of Motor Manufacturers (except for Fiat and Volkswagen figures taken from Fiat and Volkswagen 1967 balance sheets).

The sixty-eight-year-old Fiat company with sales worth nearly £796m. a year is the economic and social backbone of the Turin area, and depends for its prosperity chiefly on its importance in the Italian market, of which it holds an average share of over 72 per cent. Reasons for the giant's successes are its foresight in covering a complete range of cars from Topolinos to the V6 Ferrari-engined Dino; its research and development programme spread over every type of vehicle and not just concentrated on potential best-sellers; its short-term planning (for two years ahead) and its medium-term planning (for five years ahead) covering normal production runs and such projects as gas-turbined commercial vehicles, electrically-powered vehicles, and electronic aids; its willingness to innovate – Fiat is Europe's biggest user of plastic in car design.

The grand strategies of administration are no less well-planned, although the 'old men of Turin', the founders, have handed on their expertise to a new generation. Fiat intends to increase its penetration of the European market but there is no intention of relinquishing any part of the home market. Fiat 'likes to think in terms of a natural zone of influence, the Mediterranean, and in addition of a special relationship with the Communist countries, where the American and West German industries are not able to operate'. (B M C also were well aware of the advantages of such a special relationship, but lost out to Fiat over the Russian contract in 1966.) Besides the Russian agreement, which is expected to put 600,000 Fiats on the road a year, Fiat has assembly or manufacturing plants in Poland, Bulgaria, Yugoslavia, the U A R, Morocco, and Tunisia. It is the most international of European motor companies; global output of Fiat designs is well over two million annually, easily the biggest for any non-American company. Fiat's target is 7 to 8 per cent of total world output by 1972–3; this would give it a hedge against recession at home.

It has been said of Fiat that it is too big for Italy; that it will choke itself with too many models (in an abortive discussion on a merger with V W, it was discovered that Fiat's spare-parts inventory is more than ten times that of V W); that its vertical integration (Fiat or its subsidiaries make many of its components, steel, aluminium castings and paint, heaters, carburettors, and some electrical equipment) could prove its undoing – but Fiat is prepared to modify its policy and to increase its outside buying where necessary; that when other nations catch up with its extremely efficient training programme (Britain was late in starting compulsory industrial training schemes), it will feel the draught.

Profitability is very hard to assess because Italian balance-sheets record only historic costs of assets and historic depreciation provisions but Fiat has always made high depreciation provisions and has been largely self-financing. Fiat sales contribute more towards their own investment plans than do those of

British firms or even of the more profitable American-owned motor companies; the firm is also a sophisticated trader, using whatever policy is available, assembly in foreign markets, agreements under licence, etc. The Fiat–Citroën link, opposed by de Gaulle but which went through in 1968, accords with Agnelli's assessment that in a very few years there will be ten or fewer car manufacturers in Europe (the three Americans, BMC, VW and stable, Renault, Fiat – with perhaps the Japanese and a few small specialist firms).

In October 1969 Fiat was in the grip of ferocious strikes; already loss of production of 172,000 cars had cost the company £150m. – the final cost would be much higher. The huge Rivalta plant was proving something of a white elephant; it took workers an hour and a half to reach it, there was little accommodation nearby and many of the workers were unskilled immigrants from the South. At this moment Fiat took over Lancia (with $3\frac{1}{2}$ per cent of the top end of the home market), paying a lira (about a farthing) for each of the one million shares and also taking over debts owed by Lancia of over £60m. Her performance for 1969 would prove hard to calculate.

Runner-up in 1967 and head of the European league in 1966 was Volkswagen. The seemingly immortal Beetle still leads not only in Germany but in VW's formidable export programme; VW has the lion's share of the American import market and by June 1968 had increased its share for that year by 41 per cent over the previous year. Its subsidiary, Auto Union, which produces the executive Audi, is flourishing and to this stable was added in April 1969 NSU, which shares a joint sales company with Porsche. Future sports cars will be known as VW/Porsche. Clearly a marriage with, say, Mercedes, which would make available a whole range of cars from the prestige 'Merks' down to the Beetle, would put VW in a very strong position indeed. Agnelli thinks VW is the most dangerous rival to Fiat in future years.

Volkswagen survived the 1967 setback in the German motor industry when home demand fell by well over 25 per cent better than the other two of the big three largely because it serves so many world markets; the swings and roundabouts of world demand are sometimes the best insurance of all. Ford (Germany) sales on the German market fell by 18 per cent, VW by 16·4 per cent and Opel (General Motors) by 15·1 per cent. BMW with its 'smaller and better' policy came through the 1967 recession better than any other German firm; by 1970 it will be turning out 700 vehicles a day. BMW are taking advantage of a faulty American appraisal of the market (decisions on models are still imposed from Detroit) and their beautifully engineered and compact cars are capturing a market where the buyers like to buy cars and not acreage of chromium.

The overall picture in Germany as elsewhere in Europe is of mergers taking place or being actively studied to keep the German car industry abreast or ahead of foreign competition, especially American.

In France the car industry is the pacesetter for the economy as a whole, absorbing 25 per cent of French steel production. At the beginning of the automobile year in October 1967 the French motor-car industry was reported to have had a satisfactory year, output registering a slight increase compared with the marked decline of some other European manufacturers, notably the Germans. The good result was attributed partly to the Renault–Peugeot agreement and the merger between Citroën (which had already absorbed Panhard) and Berliet, France's biggest lorry-producer, which gave France two major groups producing complete series of vehicles.

Renault is France's largest car exporter, selling around 45 per cent of its total production abroad and the industry as a whole is estimated to export 40 per cent of production. The EEC provides the best export market for France, and Belgium, which with Luxembourg is traditionally her best customer, takes about one seventh per cent of total exports. Belgium, once without any significant car industry, now manufactures on her own account (164,000 cars in 1967) but is still the biggest assembler of other people's cars and is a fiercely contested market in Europe – recommended retail prices are hardly ever realized as customers can get at least 10 per cent reduction on new models. Other important export markets for France are

Spain and Argentina, where French firms have important assembly lines.

The strike of May–June 1968 cost France a heavy production loss and the consequent very large wage increases conceded (35 per cent for the lowest paid and 13 per cent on average) have put up car prices by an average 5 per cent. Another adverse factor was that when the 1 July 1968 tariff cuts took place, France's last chop to bring her into line with the common external tariff, was 4 per cent compared with only 0·3 per cent for Germany. Only the emergency import quotas imposed prevented a very serious position from developing for the French car industry, which has to compete with attractive-looking and attractively priced German and Italian cars and even with the Mini, which following devaluation was competitively priced.

French company profit margins generally are dangerously thin and nowhere more so than in the car industry but M. Dreyfus, the brilliant president of Renault, points out that in this nationalized industry, where profits after 50 per cent tax are split between government and workers, larger profits are not necessarily the prime consideration. The market share is all important and Renault and Fiat are the only two companies who have consistently increased their share of the European market since 1963. Renault operates on a profit margin of 0·2 per cent compared with VW's 4 per cent. With their profit margins further threatened by wage increases, French companies are finding it harder to obtain the money for capital investment. But the French motor industry is in any case harnessed to the state and must depend for its wellbeing on the prosperity of the state as a whole (in France the state owns roughly a quarter of all industrial plant, along with the railways, public services, and major banks).

The French have always protested vehemently about the threat to their heavy-vehicle industry, should Britain with her competitive and well-organized Leyland group (now part of British Leyland Motor Corporation) be allowed into the Common Market; both Ford and General Motors have concentrated their European lorry-production in Britain. France insisted that lorries should be excluded from GATT tariff reductions. Of the five main lorry-producers in Europe, three are British (British Leyland,

Ford, and Bedford) and the other two are Mercedes and Fiat. The British lorry industry has a home market twice the size of the French and has close links with the Commonwealth and the US. The Citroën–Berliet merger may have improved the French position; Berliet accounted for over half of France's total production and has now taken over the whole production of Citroën vehicles of more than six tons and part of its four- to six-tons production. The long-term picture is that the industry will coalesce around the big five with smaller firms specializing in their own fields.

There was never any doubt in the mind of Lord Stokes, chairman of British Leyland, about entry to the Common Market. At the time of the second application he said, 'If we don't go in, it will be a tragedy, because Europe, and the Common Market countries in particular, offer such an enormous market with growth potential.' Although Britain in the event was left on the table, a big boost to UK penetration of the EEC market was the Kennedy Round of tariff cuts implemented on 1 July 1968, which reduced the external tariff of 22 to 17 per cent, and which coupled with devaluation gave British cars a good price advantage; successive reductions of the tariff over the next five years will bring the hurdle down to 11 per cent. Exports were expected to rise dramatically and did so: sales in the EEC doubled in the first six months of 1968 (in Holland sales went up four times, in Germany three times, and in France they doubled). Overseas sales for the first six months of 1968 hit a new record of £164m. (an increase of 27 per cent over the same period of 1967). Ford (Britain) also reported increased overseas earnings for this period at £106m. and hoped to achieve Target 225 (£225m.) for the whole year.

The new Leyland group, with a capital of £410m., is made up of BMC, Triumph, Jaguar, and Rover cars; Leyland, BMC, Guy, and Land-Rover lorries and vans; Leyland and Guy-Daimler buses. Exports by Leyland, Ford, Guy-Daimler, and Bedford have constituted the bulk of Britain's booming lorry business in Europe against bitter competition from Mercedes-Benz, Saviem, Berliet, DAF, and Fiat, maintaining Britain's place as the world's biggest exporter of commercial vehicles.

The new firm, with nearly 250,000 employees and £900m.-a-year sales, becomes Britain's biggest single exporter (and the motor industry is responsible for one sixth of total British exports). It aims at a streamlined tightly managed enterprise with a management expertise akin to that of the American giants, General Motors and Ford. The tasks of organization are formidable, especially on the dealer franchise and servicing side, and some pruning of the seventy models in production in 1968 will obviously take place. But it is a great advantage for Britain to have a group offering a complete range of vehicles from tractors and earth-moving equipment to cars, vans and heavy commercial vehicles, and buses. Giovanni Agnelli, the Fiat chief, estimates that ferocious competition in Europe may reduce the number of major manufacturers from over twenty to ten by 1980 and only the large diversified firms will be able to stand the pace.

In 1968 British Leyland sales in the EEC rose by nearly 60 per cent and a start was made on a five-fold expansion of its two Belgian assembly plants.

The motor industry of Europe is one of the sectors most infiltrated by American investments; General Motors (Opel) and Ford control over one third of German production; Chrysler (Simca) controls 15 per cent of French production, and in Britain, Ford, General Motors (Vauxhall), and Chrysler (Rootes) control over half of production (Rootes have been told that they will be distributors in England for Simca).

The pattern of the future will inevitably be polarization on the giants. A significant development was the arrangement in 1968 by which Citroën and Fiat will gradually be integrated through a holding company. Despite de Gaulle's opposition, Fiat, though nominally only holding 15 per cent of the shares of the new company, will progressively assume control over research and development, production, distribution, and servicing networks. The joint managing board included three directors from each company. The deal was typical of the complicated lengths to which companies wishing to merge across frontiers are forced to go through lack of any proper provision and legislation on Euro-companies.

7 The Common Transport Policy

A common transport policy was called for under Articles 74 to 84 of the Rome Treaty but a real start was not made until March 1969. Little progress was made in the first ten years, largely owing to the opposition of the Dutch, who up to 1967 had carried around 40 per cent of total road-haulage trade within the EEC and who faced a major upheaval in subscribing to a common policy. The low fuel taxes in the three Benelux countries (roughly half those payable in Germany and France) and the low road tax on heavy lorries (about a quarter of that charged in France) gave them a headstart.

A system of obligatory forked tariffs (i.e. tariffs defined by an upper and a lower limit) proposed by the Commission and aimed at establishing a system of control over freight rates was strongly objected to by the Dutch, who had been free to charge what they could get. Events took a hand. In 1968 the passing of the Leber Plan through the Bonn Parliament changed the attitude of the Dutch.

The German Transport Minister's avowed intention (like that of Mrs Castle in Britain) was to divert more heavy freight from the overcrowded roads on to the uneconomic German railways. To do so, he imposed severe restrictions on long-distance road haulage of heavy goods and was empowered to ban lorries in specific areas (e.g. from the motorways at weekends). He had proposed even harsher restrictions, such as the total prohibition on the carriage by road of a long list of commodities, but this was withdrawn. Only 1,950 permits (against 4,300 permits before the passing of the bill) were issued to specific Dutch firms. A corresponding 1,950 Dutch permits were issued to German haulage companies but, since only one German lorry used Dutch roads for every two Dutch lorries using German roads, this could hardly be described as a reciprocal arrangement. As it worked out, because of the impossibility of having all the permits in use at one and the same time, the number of Dutch lorries in Germany was effectively limited to around 1,200. Lorries, often with perishable loads, queued at the border waiting to take over a licence from some Dutch lorry coming out of Germany. Chaos reigned; bankruptcy faced the smaller firms. Often border control posts closed for the night minutes before the licence-bearing lorry arrived. The idea of the Common Market as a group of countries without barriers became somewhat ridiculous.

A side effect of the Leber plan was to favour the ports of Hamburg and Bremen at the expense of Rotterdam and Amsterdam, as it legislated for a tax-free allowance of 170 kilometres of road transport for incoming goods; this meant that goods coming into Bremen and Hamburg could get free to the Ruhr industrial area but that goods coming into Rotterdam would have used up their 170 km. of free travel by the time they had reached the German border. The Commission told Germany before the passing of the Bill that some of the measures proposed were illegal under the Rome Treaty because they discriminated against member-states but it was obvious that no legal battle between the Commission and Bonn was going to be joined. The Dutch lorry-owners, too, had failed in their appeal to the Hague Court against the agreement forcing them to obtain transit licences from the Germans. It was obvious to the Dutch that whatever the rights of the matter, they were out on a limb and that all in all it would be wiser to subscribe to an overall transport policy within the jurisdiction of the EEC.

So it was that on 19 July 1968 the first big step towards a common transport policy was agreed and a package deal of measures was arranged. One of the principal achievements was the agreement on a bracket system (resembling the obligatory forked tariffs) for road-transport freight rates. Hauliers would not as a rule be allowed to charge more than 23 per cent below maximum Community levels and any special contracts outside this bracket would be subject to a double minimum of a duration of three months and a quantity of 500 tons of goods.

Under the heading of competition it was agreed that pooling arrangements would be permissible between companies that did not have a combined capacity of more than 10,000 tons, provided the biggest partner did not account for more than 10 per cent. The same applied to water transport, the figure of combined capacity being 500,000 metric tons.

The tax-free quota of fuel in a lorry's tank when it crossed a frontier was set at fifty litres, to be increased as taxes on diesel oil in the Six were harmonized. Community licences, allowing international road transport to circulate freely throughout the territory of the Six, would be issued to cover the years 1969–71, the 1,200 to be allocated as follows: France and West Germany, 286 each; the Netherlands, 240; Italy, 194; Belgium, 161; Luxembourg, 33. This made it essential to deal with double taxation, and it was agreed that lorries should be taxed in the countries where they operated rather than in those where they were registered; however, since some lorries would operate in three countries on one day, it proved very difficult to find a workable formula but one was being sought.

Harmonization of social conditions – such as age qualifications of drivers, manning, working hours, and mileage records – was agreed on 29 March, and by 1 October 1969 the limit for all EEC lorry-drivers was forty-eight hours cab-time a week and four hours at a stretch, with a maximum of 450 km. for a driver on his own. This would apply to lorries of non-member countries operating in the EEC by 1 October 1970 and it was hoped to incorporate the provisions in an agreement with the European Committee of Transport Ministers. Some European countries, including Britain, permitted driving hours in excess of this limit. A black box or tachometer to be installed in the driver's cab for the mechanical recording of information on driving time, speed, distance, etc. was proposed for general adoption by 31 December 1969. It will be obligatory for vehicles first commissioned after 1 January 1972 and by 1 January 1974 for all vehicles.

A regulation on state aids was to be drafted as national practices diverge widely on this. It was agreed that fuel and road taxes should more accurately reflect the costs of road building and maintenance. Many other problems remained to be tackled, including the creation of a common accounting system for infra-structure expenditure.

The Rome Treaty was chiefly concerned with transport-market conditions and makes no specific provision for Community action to improve and extend transport infra-structure, but such action is within the spirit of the Rome Treaty and is clearly needed. Road transport in the EEC is hampered by the fact that the road network was originally designed for national needs and so, especially in frontier areas, roads are few in number and small in size, causing constant bottle-necks. Although motorway links spanning frontiers have been built between Germany, the Netherlands, and Belgium, there is no motorway linking Amsterdam with Brussels and Paris; and Paris is not linked with Cologne. Progress is being made on linking the Italian and German motorway networks and on building bridges over the Upper Rhine to facilitate the link-up between France and south-west Germany.

MOTORWAYS

The Alps are a barrier in the system, and although new road tunnels like the St Bernard, the Mont-Blanc, or the Felber-Tauern tunnels have eased the situation, much more will have to be done. Even the Brenner motorway and the road over the St Gotthard will soon be insufficient to cope with the traffic.

First attempts to get action by the Community on road-construction plans failed. The Commission arranged a series of inter-governmental conferences of highway experts but the recommendations they made were not binding on the governments and were largely ignored. But in 1966 the Council instituted a procedure for consultation between the Six on the extension of transport systems which obliges member-governments to consult the other members before putting into effect investment plans of general Community interest – either new communications links or the expansion of existing ones. The technical nature, cost, timetable, and likely economic effects must be disclosed. In January 1967 three motorway projects were notified by the Belgian and French Governments and in April

1967 the Netherlands, Belgium, France, Germany, and Italy all reported projects (mainly frontier-road improvements) which could be discussed, evaluated, and timed for mutual benefit.

The European Investment Bank also makes a positive contribution to Europe's stock of motorways. The Brussels–Paris motorway is being partly financed by a $16m. loan and two loans each of $24m. have been agreed; one towards linking Italy with France through the Val d'Aosta motorway, and the other linking Italy with Austria through the Brenner motorway (the Community recognizes the importance of links between the EEC and non-member countries). Twenty-two million dollars have been granted towards the Messina–Catania motorway in Sicily. In 1966 26 per cent of the loans contracted for with the European Investment Bank were for transport.

Europe is, in fact, now moving fast towards a motorway network comparable to that of the United States; with private cars expected to double by 1980 and commercial vehicles to increase by 60 per cent she must. The 2,250-mile E3 from Stockholm, via Gothenburg, Fredrikshaven, Hamburg, Paris, Bordeaux, and San Sebastian to Lisbon is the most ambitious trans-continental project.

In 1968 there were approximately 7,000 miles of motorway, but by 1980 there should be nearly three times as many – well over 18,000 miles. Germany, with over 1,000 miles of motorway built before 1945, has a detailed programme looking as far ahead as 1985, and Switzerland has settled plans up to 1980. France, whose plans were lagging behind the ambitious target of the Fifth Plan owing to lack of public finance, decided in June 1969 to allow private capital to participate in 280 miles of motorway, and, perhaps a dangerous precedent, to levy its own private tolls as a return on the investment. Both France and Italy operate motorway tolls to subsidize future road developments and therefore encourage long-distance heavy transport to use the motorways, but Germany (like Great Britain) takes the opposite view and discourages lorries by legislation and taxation. Spain's ever-growing tourist industry has spurred the Government on and her rate of motorway growth over the years 1969–80 is expected to be easily the highest in Europe.

By 1980 it is estimated that half of European trade will be carried in containers for which rail or waterways are easily the most economic means of transport over long distances; the share of container traffic then to be carried by road and motorway has been estimated at only 25 per cent of the total.

Europe's Motorways (miles)

	Actual 1968	Planned for completion by 1980
West Germany	2,480	5,000
Italy	1,650	3,230
France	782	1,875
Spain	53	1,875
Holland	443	1,375
United Kingdom	600	1,200
Belgium	220	1,065
Denmark	81	625
Norway	44	500
Switzerland	159	437
Austria	258	312
Finland	62	312
Sweden	225	270
Portugal	44	62
	7,101	18,138

RAILWAYS

The railways of the EEC, like those of Britain, are in the red, and for much the same reason – failure to match rapidly rising costs, especially of labour, with rising revenue. Excluding subsidies, which the French and German railways already get, and which British Railways will get under Mrs Castle's new provisions, British Railways lose around £150m. a year; French Railways, £250m., and German Railways, £300m. Even in Holland, where the limited size of the network is in its favour, the railways lose over £10m. a year.

France has easily the longest track network. In 1966 the figures were France, 24,000 miles; Britain, 14,000 (the Beeching–Marples axe had reduced the figure from 19,000); and Germany, 19,000 (the Leber axe was poised to bring this down to around 16,000). The French Railways, SNCF (Société Nationale des Chemins de Fer Français), were long protected from road transport (freight) and as late as in 1968 a new axle-load tax on heavy lorries was designed to step up this protection. Protection of passenger traffic from airline competition has also been traditional, the domestic air fares being pegged at levels higher than first-class rail; but in 1968 the French Minister of Transport directed that Air Inter should charge the economic fare, related to the working costs of each service. Air competition is growing, especially on the routes which are, or could be, the most remunerative for the SNCF.

Despite the much-publicized Capitole, which reaches 125 m.p.h. on the Paris–Toulouse route, despite the car-sleeper network which attracts tourist money, the *trains de soirée* (evening inter-city services) and the kangaroo freight system, the financial position is deteriorating; orders for electric locomotives under the SNCF Fifth Plan (1967–70) have been cut, since traffic has not measured up to estimates.

In 1969 a Beeching-type plan was announced to withdraw passenger services on one third of the French network by 1974, to reduce employees from 323,000 to 280,000 by 1972 (by natural wastage), and to give SNCF freedom to operate as a normal industry, deciding its own fares and rates and its own investment policy and referring to the government only for subsidy for lines kept open as a social service.

France is a founder member of Intercontainer, the twelve-nation European company set up in Brussels under the chairmanship of a British Rail container expert to pioneer container-train systems in general, including transcontainers (the giant containers used in transatlantic trade). The other eleven members are Belgium, Germany, Italy, Netherlands, Luxembourg, Denmark, Sweden, Switzerland, Spain, Hungary, and Britain – the innovator; Norway, Finland, Yugoslavia, and Greece are associate members. The new company should help recapture some of the railways' freight traffic and rationalize the movement of heavy industrial goods.

German railways were in a worse position than the French

financially when in 1967 the Minister of Transport, Herr Leber, announced cuts in the rail network from 19,000 to around 16,000 miles and in the labour force from 410,000 to 330,000. German railways had been particularly well staffed, using approximately 60,000 more staff to carry a roughly equivalent freight and passenger load to that carried on French railways, which moreover had a track mileage nearly one-fifth bigger than the German system. Herr Leber also imposed severe restrictions on road transport, designed to restore to the railways much of the heavy freight traffic going by road, and announced a government grant for modernization of the railways to be spread over the years 1968–73. German railways, nationalized before the First World War, have a special status approaching that of a civil service department and have not faced up to the stern realities of industrial efficiency and profit-making – track in 1967 was static at roughly the 1960 figure of 19,000 and during this period, while Britain under the Beeching–Marples plans was cutting rolling stock by 40 per cent, Germany's actually increased. Now that the railways are being brought back into the mainstream of economic life and are not looked upon as a special public service (which was not giving the German taxpayer value for his money), the crisis should be surmounted, though it is not expected in Germany that the Leber plan will succeed in rejuvenating the railways. However, Leber showed that he was willing to tackle Germany's transport problem ruthlessly, if need be; the 1968 bill gave him blanket authorization to suspend all lorry movement for limited periods in specific areas. German railways should also benefit from the new twelve-nation container company.

Italian railways have been more successful than those of the other E E C countries in getting a fair share of the growing volume of traffic and have no immediate survival problems.

For many years the Commission made no proposals on the running of the E E C railways, but in 1969 it took a first step towards rationalizing the economic structure of the railways by announcing draft regulations on the standardization of railway accounts and on government help to the railways. Railway accounting systems were to disclose fully all subsidies and in due course, when the exact extent of the problem was clear, some of these subsidies would be progressively eliminated. But the German Government's plans for a $250m. subsidy to transport was held in May 1969 not to contradict the general concept of a Community transport policy. In the longer term it was hoped to eliminate the deficits themselves.

PIPELINES

Pipelines are an invaluable part of the transport system as they relieve the growing strain on road, rail, and inland waterways. They can impinge on other sectors; for instance the offer of a 250-mile Le Havre–Tournai crude-oil pipeline set the Belgian Government the problem of whether to go ahead with enlarging the port of Antwerp or whether to accept the pipeline which would benefit the underprivileged Walloon region of Belgium.

E E C pipelines are naturally shorter than the giants crossing the great Middle East and Russian oilfields but technically they are some of the most advanced in the world. Over 3,500 miles of crude-oil pipeline were laid in Western Europe in 1958–68, most of it in the E E C (not a great deal less than the mileage laid in Eastern Europe joining the great Russian oilfields through the Friendship system to refineries in Eastern Europe). Also, many very short pipelines of around 25 miles link European ports, for example Genoa, with inland refineries.

The total length of oil-products pipeline has lagged behind that of crude-oil pipeline for technical reasons and less than 1,500 miles existed in 1968. But the same amount will have been laid by 1971 as technical advance has made possible and profitable the use of pipeline for the various white products such as motor and aviation gas, naphtha for petrochemicals and town gas, and also diesel fuels. Computers will control the routing of different kinds of petrol products for different companies to different storage points along the route, all through the same pipe; a computer will instruct the master valves when to open and close by remote control.

The companies which use the pipelines are partners in them and it seems probable that they will continue to be largely self-financing. The cost can be enormous, varying from £20,000 a mile to over £50,000 a mile, depending on the terrain and other difficulties encountered. Important joint European achievements were the crossing of the Alps by pipeline from Trieste to Ingolstadt and the pipeline from Rotterdam to the Rhine. Capacity will undoubtedly rise dramatically above the 180m. tons of oil which it was estimated were carried through European pipelines in 1967.

The growing consumption of oil, the establishment of new refineries, the discovery of new oilfields will all contribute to a further dramatic expansion of demand for pipelines. In 1957 pipelines in the EEC were of no importance but in 1967 they conveyed about 30 per cent of imported crude oil from the seaports of the EEC to the hinterland.

Estimated Expansion of Refining Capacity in the EEC

	Capacity mid-1968 (Thousands of metric tons)	Growth in capacity by end-1970 (Thousands of metric tons)	Total (Thousands of metric tons)
German Federal Republic	108,600	18,950	127,550
Belgium	29,970	1,600	31,570
France	90,125	26,600	116,725
Italy	140,615	16,080	156,695
Netherlands	37,300	25,200	62,500
Total	406,610	88,430	495,040

Source of information: Belgian Oil Federation

SEAPORTS IN THE SIXTIES

The Treaty of Rome does not specifically enjoin a policy on ports but under Article 84, paragraph 2 are the much-disputed words:

> The Council of Ministers may unanimously decide whether, to what extent, and by what procedure appropriate provisions shall be made in respect of sea and air transport.

Some interpret this as excluding sea transport and seaports from all the provisions of the Treaty until the Council shall unanimously decide otherwise (most seaport authorities and France take this view). Others point out that since this article is the last of those dealing with transport, the intention was only to exclude sea and air transport from the immediately foregoing Articles, 74 to 83, and not to exclude it from the whole of the provisions of the Treaty. In their view some of these provisions, especially those governing fair competition, should be applied at once.

It is an important area of disagreement, because national policies on seaports and their hinterland vary considerably. Some nations give subsidies and development grants, and locate industry and pipelines to favour a particular seaport. For instance, in 1965 the French allocated increased state subsidies to the six *ports autonomes*, Marseilles, Bordeaux, Nantes St Nazaire, Le Havre, Rouen, and Dunkirk; the first three benefit further because they are also among the eight regional capitals being developed to counterbalance Paris and so qualify for further state favours.

This is a sore point with Rotterdam, up till 1969 left to go it alone using municipal funds to finance development. The French government give French ports 80 per cent of the cost of new basins, approach roads, and locks, 60 per cent of the cost of new quays and all of the cost of making and maintaining (including dredging) all seaward approaches. Belgium has invested £35m. in Antwerp between 1958 and 1968 and plans a further £115m. investment. Germany, too, subsidizes her ports.

It had become obvious that seaport infra-structures involved such huge engineering feats and such enormous investment that finance policy as well as the application of rules of free competition for the Community's seaports would have to be tackled. All the Community's seaports had shared in the dramatic trading upsurge; the E E C economy depends increasingly on the import of overseas raw materials and energy; it exports increasingly large shipments of finished products. Hamburg, Bremen, and Rouen have grown least since the war (Hamburg, because its hinterland is restricted by the iron curtain). Dunkirk, Genoa, and Marseilles have more than doubled cargo (chiefly bulk cargo) handled between 1960 and 1968.

Biggest success story of all was Rotterdam/Europoort, which (largely because of efficient management, freedom from government interference, and its position at the very gateway to the EEC), has become easily the busiest port in the world, handling one third more traffic than New York and more than Antwerp, Bremen, and Hamburg put together – 140m. tons in 1967. It has become a major centre for oil and petrochemical industries and by 1974 seeks to become the 'container capital of the continent' when its new port area near the Hook of Holland, Rijnpoort, will have been completed.

Le Havre is fortunate in being a deep-water harbour able to handle the increasingly large tankers; it was the only one able to take 200,000 tonners in 1968 but Rotterdam was already gouging out the Euro-channel, an eight-mile-long fairway into the North Sea, which would enable 250,000-ton tankers to enter Europoort. Le Havre is determined to keep one jump ahead; believing that the 200,000 tonners will soon be merely coasters, it is considering deepening its harbour to take 500,000 tonners and, looking beyond that stage, hopes to become the megaton harbour of the EEC by constructing an artificial island to take the 1,000,000 tonners; this would be seventeen miles offshore near a natural deep (100 ft below the lowest tide) called the Parfond.

Antwerp, too, has made phenomenal growth, attracting the big oil companies and other industrial giants; it claims to be the best equipped container terminal in Europe (services began in 1966); as terminal of the TERRE, Trans-European Rail Road Express, it is only thirty-six hours from Milan and further trans-European links are planned. Its chief worries are that the Dutch are astride its access routes and that the huge port complex is beginning to run out of land. Its distance, fifty miles, from the sea makes it impossible for the huge new tankers to get up to it and Antwerp, too, is toying with the idea of an artificial island off the Belgian coast, though probably a pipeline from Rotterdam to Antwerp would be a more economic way round the difficulty.

The German Hanseatic League ports, Hamburg, Bremen, and Lübeck, have not fared so well; the fall of the iron curtain in 1945 severed them from their natural hinterland and the birth and growth of the EEC favoured Rotterdam, Amsterdam, and

Antwerp, which were at the bustling centre of the great new market. But their day will come if Britain, and particularly the Scandinavian countries, enter the Common Market. Both Hamburg and Bremen would lie at the intersection of the two economic areas and, if relations with the communist bloc improved, they would stand fair to capture the huge east–west trade.

The great danger to the ports of the EEC is that the enthusiasm of each government for its national ports, and its determination not to be left out of the huge upsurge of seaport development, could result in too many ports being state-subsidized and under-employed. It has been estimated that two or three major container terminals would be enough to carry the whole of the north-European traffic. But each separate nation insists on cherishing its own ports to keep its stake not only in the sea transport business but in the great industrial growth promoted in the hinterland.

Finally on 29 November 1967 the European Parliament spoke. It called for a Community policy for seaports along the following guidelines: port traffic should be allocated solely on economic grounds as indicated by the forces of competition; transport rates for inland traffic to and from harbours should also be based on competition and not subsidized; port authorities should get more autonomy but the state should retain some responsibility for harbours; all major Community seaports should be linked where possible by electrified railway lines, motorways, and inland waterways big enough for 1,350-ton ships. These guidelines were a first tentative step. But decisive action on a Community basis is needed soon. Firm decisions are needed on which ports should be converted to become container ports and on which should handle the jumbo 500,000-ton tankers of the future. The road and rail traffic of such ports would have to be speeded up to unload the great cargoes from the port area. Computers would ease the handling problems; what type and what size? These questions are all the more urgent as the Community's ports are expecting to become increasingly important as world trade is liberalized following the Kennedy Round agreement and as the markets of Eastern Europe are opened up to the rest of the world.

Towards One Europe

INLAND WATERWAYS

Waterways are an integral part of the European transport system. The railways, in particular, wish to restrict their use but this is understandable since in 1965 half as much freight was moved on the waterways (85,000 million ton-kilometres) as on the railways, and the pushers are revolutionizing the speed at which heavy goods can be propelled by water to their destinations.

The canalization of the Moselle has linked up the Lorraine industrial region with the Ruhr and an outstanding instance of canal engineering is the link via the Main between the Rhine and Danube. Charlemagne started work on the link with Fossa Carolin and Napoleon, fascinated with the idea, set his generals to work on the scheme. One fifth of the link has now been built and is in use; completion is expected by 1981, giving ships of 1,500 tons a throughway of 2,000 miles from Rotterdam to the Black Sea.

In July 1968 it was agreed, under the heading of competition, that water transport companies could make pooling arrangements provided the companies concerned do not together have more than a combined capacity of 500,000 metric tons and that the biggest partner does not contribute more than 10 per cent of capacity.

More schemes are projected, e.g. between the Rhine and Seine and between the Rhine and Rhone, and it seems likely that sooner or later the Commission will intervene in these projects, which need huge injections of capital and are plainly of benefit to the EEC economy as a whole.

8 EEC Trading Relations with Non-member Countries

It may well be argued that the whole of the EEC's external trading policy is illegal. It is in direct contravention of GATT (the General Agreement on Tariffs and Trade) since it extends preferential trade arrangements to non-member countries in defiance of the principle of free trade, which GATT exists to uphold.

The EEC has been at pains to disprove that its preferential arrangements with some non-member countries are prejudicial to other non-members with whom it has no such arrangements. A paper was published by the EEC Commission in 1967 to rebut allegations that other developing countries were being adversely affected by the EEC's favourable treatment of the African developing countries who had signed the Yaoundé Convention (see The EEC and Africa, p. 234). But GATT administrators remain unconvinced. The EEC decision (of September 1969) to give citrus-fruit imports from Israel and Spain a 40 per cent tariff reduction was obviously unfair to Brazil, Cyprus, the United States, and other citrus-exporting countries. The EEC asked GATT to waive its requirements that all GATT member-nations should receive the same tariff concessions but it seemed likely that the twenty-six-nation working party studying this request would turn it down. An adverse decision would call in question the legality of many of the EEC's external trading pacts. The GATT argument is that if other trade blocs were to follow the EEC precedent, free trade would become a mockery. The anarchy, already all too plain in agricultural trade, would spread to world trade in general. The EEC's defence was that in some cases these trade arrangements are just one aspect of a rather long-drawn-out prelude to full membership. But the only country for which this would have held true in 1969 was Turkey (Greece, too, if there were a change of régime there).

The EEC is becoming a focal point of the world's trade; trading ties now bind the Community inextricably to many countries. It has preferential commercial relations with over thirty less-developed countries with a total population of 200 million; association and partial-association agreements are constantly under negotiation or renegotiation; trade agreements and trade-and-aid agreements are hammered out; Britain and the EFTA countries have periodically sought admission as full members.

No country can ignore the power of the great European trading bloc, which accounts for something over 19 per cent of all world exports (excluding goods traded internally between the Six members themselves). This is roughly the same proportion as for the USA and much more than for the USSR (6 to 7 per cent). The EEC accounts for around the same proportion of all world imports. Despite its growing self-sufficiency in food, the EEC is still a very large importer of farm produce. The weighting of the Six's external trade is typical of an industrialized group; about 60 per cent of imports are of food, drink, tobacco, oil, and raw materials and only 40 per cent manufactured goods; whereas about 15 per cent of exports and re-exports are of commodities and 85 per cent of manufactured goods.

Yet the EEC's external trade policy has not worked out as envisaged. Under Article 3 of the Rome Treaty a common external policy was to be adopted by 1970; the Six were to agree on the lowering of trade barriers with the rest of the world, on the replacing of bilateral trade agreements between the member-countries and non-member countries by Community agreements (all new trade agreements were to be negotiated at Community level, not by the individual member-countries), and on such matters as anti-dumping and restrictive health regulations. In 1961 the Six did agree not to conclude new bilateral trade agreements with non-member countries without prior consultation between themselves and that any such agreements should not extend beyond 1970 but, apart from this technical gesture, very little progress has been made towards achieving the aims of Article 3. When in 1964 the Commission made definite proposals designed to reach a common policy on trade with Japan (as the prototype of a cheap-manufacture country) and with the COMECON states, implacable opposition was offered by the French Government. The General maintained that external trade policy, especially towards the COMECON countries, is an integral and indivisible part of foreign policy and therefore lies outside the competence of the Commission. Subsequently, de Gaulle's attitude hardened – his intransigent attitude to talks on trade and association with Israel, which happened not to fit in with current Gaullist Middle East foreign policy, caused Holland to threaten to withhold her signature from the partial association pact with Tunisia and Morocco.

In April 1969 the whole issue came to a head when France notified her partners that she was about to negotiate a new five-year trade agreement with the USSR; this, of course, would go far beyond the end of the transitional period (December 1970) and beyond the one-year extension already agreed for certain bilateral agreements, provided they did not conflict with the commercial policy of the Six. It seemed certain that the agreement, allowing USSR increased quotas on the French market, would contravene EEC policy that all quotas must be allocated on a Community basis.

In July 1969 France was granted exemption for the five-year agreement but only on condition that each year she would consult with the other five before settling the exact annual quotas. And in October 1969 the Council of Ministers agreed that for the next three years member-countries would be able to negotiate bilateral agreements, provided the Council was consulted before the talks opened and again before an agreement was finally signed – leaving the Council the power to veto any agreement of which it disapproved. The Council also undertook to lay down guide-lines for such negotiations.

In external trading relations, though some progress has been made towards a common approach, there is no true corporate image. When external trade is debated in the institutions of the Six, we are back in the dark ages of the old diplomacy, with nation bidding against nation, measuring concession with con-cession, answering blackmail with counter-blackmail.

However, the Six do offer a united front in GATT (General Agreement on Tariffs and Trade) negotiations, where the Six are represented by the Commission, holding a mandate from the Council of Ministers, and not by the separate governments. The disadvantages of speaking with a common voice were seen in the Kennedy Round of 1964 when the Commission had to refer back to the Council every time they wished to modify their position and as their brief had been prenegotiated among the Six themselves its contents tended to be known by the opposition or easily deducible. A big advantage was that the Six spoke with more authority than six separate nations and many points which might have been brushed aside if put forward by one small nation were carefully thrashed out.

The very fact that in July 1962 President Kennedy was able to persuade Congress to pass the trade expansion act giving the administration previously unthought-of powers to liberalize trade with the EEC was proof that a united Western Europe could bring about a freeing of world trade (at the time it was thought that Britain would join the EEC, and when her application was seen to have failed the scope of the Kennedy Round had to be restricted). Although the results of the Kennedy Round were less spectacular than was hoped for, many hindrances to trade other than tariffs and quotas were dealt with, such as the USA 'buy-American act', and the American selling price system. Under this system some chemical imports into the USA paid duty not on the basis of their value but on that of comparable American products and this could amount to over 100 per cent ad-valorem tax. The Americans, for their part, pointed to some very high road taxes on top-bracket cars which hindered US sales to Europe. On the industrial side agreement was reached on average tariff reductions of 35 per cent (over the period 1968–73) affecting about a quarter of free-world trade. This could benefit developing countries as more raw materials would be needed as the trade flow improved; but on agriculture agreement was not reached beyond the giving away of 4·5m. tons of grain each year to the developing countries as food-aid (financed mainly by the USA, 42 per cent; EEC, 23 per cent; Canada, 11 per cent; Australia, 5 per cent; and UK, 5 per cent). With this exception, no concerted move was made to deal with aid to developing countries.

Apart from the G A T T negotiations, which sorted out some of the trade and tariff problems, many nations have had to define their trading relationship with the E E C. Most important were the attempts by the United Kingdom and E F T A countries, which twice (1961 and 1967) applied for full membership of the E E C.

THE EEC AND EUROPE – ASSOCIATION

Membership of the E E C is confined to European nations (Article 237) but association is not so limited (Article 238). In practice, associated states in Europe are regarded as potential members whereas associated states outside Europe are not. The eighteen associates of Africa come in a different category, as the Yaoundé Convention is an evolution of Articles 131–6; the Nigerian association was based on the Six's declaration of intent at the time of the signing of the Yaoundé agreement.

Since the signing of the Rome Treaty, six European countries have sought association. Greece and Turkey were successful, negotiations with Austria were prevented when Russia gave notice that any such association would be regarded by her as infringing the State Treaty forbidding Austria to be united with Germany. The dispute with Italy over Alto Adige finally halted the negotiations but it had also become apparent that serious economic difficulties stood in the way, especially Austria's wish to keep a free hand in her trade with the C O M E C O N countries. Spain was thought to have too undemocratic a régime, and with Sweden and Switzerland the stumbling block was that these countries are neutrals. The view of the Six is that a state which, by international treaty (Austria) or by choice (Sweden and Switzerland), takes up a neutral position in international affairs is not a free agent and so is unable to commit itself to the goals of the E E C, especially political unity.

Greece

Greece was the first European country to achieve associate status (1 November 1962). The association agreement gave Greece the benefit of tariff-cuts on intra-Community trade and twelve years in which to remove her tariffs against E E C goods, and in the case of tariffs on industrial products, which comprise about one third of Greek imports, she could take twenty-two years so as to have sufficient time in which to adapt her own industry to competition with the Six. The European Investment Bank would make loans of up to $125m. to assist Greek economic development over the years 1962–7 (though by the end of 1966 the Greeks complained that only $53m. had been lent). The agreement also provided for the harmonization of Greek agricultural, economic, and trade policies with those of the E E C; some headway was made here, although the Greek request for participation in the resources of the European Farm Fund to which she does not contribute was turned down.

Despite such points of difference, association would have been of great help in the long run to Greece which relies heavily on tourism and remittances from migrants to help correct her large and growing adverse visible trade balance.

However, owing to the establishment of the military régime in Greece, the association was suspended in 1967. The Commission decided off their own bat that the association agreement had political as well as economic meaning since it was intended to lead ultimately to Greek membership of the E E C – the actual date, 1984, was mentioned in the treaty. They decided to stop work on the harmonization of agricultural policies and on the negotiation of a new agreement on financial aid (the unused balance from the $125m. originally allocated was $55m.) and the Council acquiesced in this decision. A few minor trade concessions are still being made.

Turkey

The Turkish association agreement took longer to negotiate than the Greek agreement and the date on which Turkey would be deemed eligible for full membership was harder to assess. Although Turkey applied for association at almost the same time as Greece, her agreement came into effect nearly two years after the Greek agreement on 1 December 1964. It envisaged a preparatory period of five years (extendable to nine, though the extension proved not to be needed) aimed at strengthening the Turkish economy chiefly by granting tariff-free quotas of tobacco, dried figs, raisins and hazelnuts, which together account for 40 per cent of Turkey's export earnings, and by granting loans from the European Investment Bank of $175m. for economic development in Turkey. This initial stage was to be followed by a transitional period of up to twelve years during which the Turkish economy would be adjusted to that of the EEC on an agreed timetable; she would then be ready for full membership (1981).

In 1969, when negotiations for stage two were starting, the Turkish Foreign Minister asked for existing preferences on agricultural products to be stepped up and for preferences on a list of new products; besides wishing to increase the financial aid available to Turkey, he wanted to facilitate the movement of Turkish workers into the Common Market. All in all, the Turks were more content with their agreement than were the Greeks; Turkey takes about 30 per cent of her imports from the Six and exports to them rather more than this proportion. A hitch occurred at the start of the negotiations for stage two, when France called in question the propriety of the Commission negotiating for the six 'sovereign states' but a compromise was reached and talks went ahead, with the prospect of increased aid and trade in phase two starting in 1970.

Spain

In April 1967 the Six reluctantly agreed to open negotiations with Spain on a two-stage agreement – the first stage to last six years and the second stage (undefined in scope) to come up then for unanimous approval by the Six. Clearly Franco's undemocratic régime is a stumbling block to association or even partial association; but from his point of view association would be a visible sign that his régime is, if not accepted, at least not totally rejected by the Six. Holland and Belgium frequently expressed doubts on the political implications.

Spain is anxious to reduce her heavy reliance on invisibles (tourism and migrants' remittances) to balance her books; to do this she must expand exports and her ambition is to get inside the tariff wall which is a definite handicap and makes it hard for her goods to be competitive. The Italians, however, have no wish to see Spain, a keen competitor with their own agriculture, brought into the fold. In October 1969 the Council agreed that the Commission should re-open negotiations for a six-year preferential agreement to cover both industrial and agricultural exchanges.

EEC AND THE MIDDLE EAST

No non-European country has yet achieved association status though Tunisia and Morocco were given partial-association status in 1969 and Algeria seemed likely to achieve an equivalent status.

The first country outside Europe to ask for association was Israel, late in 1961. The request came up against the usual difficulty – how could this be reconciled with the need to placate the Arabs? Association was refused, but after talks lasting nearly three years the EEC concluded a trade agreement with Israel in June 1964 by which the EEC lowered tariffs on twenty-one Israeli industrial and agricultural imports, but the agreement was non-discriminatory and the cuts therefore applied to all EEC imports of the goods concerned, though the concessions benefited Israel chiefly. When the agreement ended on 1 July 1967, Israel pointed out that she was exporting to the EEC goods to the value of only threequarters of her imports from the EEC and asked for a broader-based relationship described as 'association entailing the abolition of quotas and tariff disarmament'. The French, however, blocked all attempts at negotiations from 1967 to 1969.

In January 1969 the Dutch Government circulated a memorandum to the other EEC partners pointing out that whereas negotiations with Morocco and Tunisia were making good progress, those with Israel had reached stalemate and that this would mean unfair distortion of trade within the Mediterranean area. While conceding that agricultural difficulties in the Six itself might make it advisable to maintain the status quo for exports of Israeli farm produce, the Dutch called for the removal of all barriers to trade in the industrial sector.

The Dutch attitude was strongly supported by Germany and welcomed by all the other nations except France, who owing to de Gaulle's pro-Arab leanings at the time refused to concede anything at all. In retaliation the Netherlands blocked trade talks with Algeria and threatened to refuse to ratify the agreements for partial association with Morocco and Tunisia which were in the final stages of negotiation. Faced with this threat, France grudgingly agreed to a study of EEC–Israel links, but this is unlikely to lead to the full association which Israel is seeking. Even on tariff cuts there are strong differences of opinion; the Dutch are seeking first-stage cuts on Israeli industrial products of 60 per cent leading to no tariff in the second stage; but the French aim at maximum cuts of 25 per cent and hope to get away with much less.

In June 1969 the Commission reluctantly abandoned hope of negotiating an association agreement between Israel and the Six and started work on a simple commercial agreement proposing cuts in industrial tariffs of around 50 per cent. With the advent of M. Pompidou, a new mandate was agreed giving the Commission powers to negotiate a new five-year preferential agreement covering both industrial and agricultural exports.

The Maghreb

Tunisia and Morocco became partial associates in 1969. At the time of the signing of the Rome Treaty in 1957 Tunisia and Morocco had only recently gained independence; special arrangements governing their trade with France were safeguarded by a protocol to the Treaty. Morocco had particularly favourable treatment; while giving no preferences to French products, 90 per cent of her country's exports to France paid no duty.

At the time when negotiations opened (July 1966) with a view to Tunisia and Morocco becoming partial associates, the position was that the bulk of trade was with France, who would clearly therefore have a decisive voice.

Community Trade with the Maghreb from January to September 1966
($ million)

	EEC	France	Belgium-Luxembourg	Netherlands	Germany	Italy
Morocco						
Exports	271·8	181·9	14·6	10·0	41·6	23·7
Imports	240·0	140·7	11·8	20·6	42·8	23·9
Algeria						
Exports	514·9	412·7	5·4	4·6	63·9	28·3
Imports	339·6	309·5	3·1	3·7	9·4	13·9
Tunisia						
Exports	79·8	40·2	8·1	5·7	6·2	19·7
Imports	99·9	69·4	2·1	2·8	10·4	15·3

Owing to the Ben Barka incident of 1966 and to a good deal of in-fighting over the trading concessions that the EEC was demanding from Morocco, it was not until November 1968 that the EEC and Moroccan negotiating team announced that they had 'in principle' reached a package deal for a partial association. The negotiations with Tunisia were on the same footing as those with Morocco but a stage behind; however, by December 1968 agreement had been reached on most of the points of difficulty and in March 1969 the five-year agreements giving Tunisia and Morocco associate status were signed.

The agreements will be reviewed after three years with a view to moving on to full association, providing financial and technical aid and further trade concessions. The Six undertook to remove all customs duties and quotas on nearly all industrial exports from Morocco and Tunisia (exactly what Israel was asking for); these represented 40 per cent of Moroccan exports to the EEC and 55 per cent of Tunisian exports, and these proportions represented a sizeable portion of total Moroccan and Tunisian exports – in 1967 Morocco sent 61 per cent of total exports to the EEC and Tunisia sent 52 per cent of total exports. As for agriculture, levies will be reduced on olive oil and concessions made on fish products, durum wheat, and citrus fruits coming from Morocco and Tunisia.

In return, Morocco will make 25 per cent tariff reductions on some products and establish or maintain special EEC quotas on others. Tunisia will grant 70 per cent of the preference she gives to French goods on 40 per cent of EEC imports and establish or maintain EEC quotas. Here again, a sizeable portion of total trade is involved: in 1967 Moroccan imports from the EEC were over 50 per cent of total imports; in the case of Tunisia imports from the EEC were over 48 per cent of total imports.

Certain freedom of action was secured to both countries *vis-à-vis* each other and Algeria, with whom they were discussing the organization of a Maghreb customs union or free-trade area.

Algeria

At the time of the signing of the Rome Treaty (1957), Algeria was considered as constitutionally part of France and so an integral part of the Community. In 1962 she became independent, but her position was not greatly changed. Algerian goods, up to July 1966, were generally admitted duty-free into France (though wine paid one eighth of the common external tariff) and fruit and vegetables were subject to minimum price controls. The position with other EEC countries was more complicated; they gave Algeria the benefit of duty-free entry for her major export, crude oil, and extended to her intra-Community tariff cuts up to December 1965 (though for agricultural products Italy and Benelux applied the rules for non-member countries). For their part, the Algerian Government had drawn up in 1963 a complicated system of tariffs with French imports paying one level, other EEC countries a higher level and non-member countries a still higher level. The most-favoured treatment of Algeria by France (who was taking 80 per cent of Algerian exports to the EEC) was obviously unfair to Tunisia and Morocco and the Commission made recommendations.

However, major points of difference between France and Algeria held up any agreement; bilateral trade talks between the two countries broke down in December 1968, with France resisting attempts to persuade her to increase imports of Algerian wine and Algeria accusing France of taking financial advantage of her over the bilateral oil agreements which in 1969 Algeria insisted on revising. She also applied to join OPEC, the Organization of Petroleum-Exporting Countries, and was shifting away from the France–EEC orbit to the Russian-influenced Arab axis.

Malta

Malta became independent in 1964; her special economic relationship with Britain was changing; British defence cuts (1967) were planned to reduce the island to a forward operating base by 1972 and although Britain made strenuous efforts to compensate for her withdrawal by the establishment of factories and hotels, and the granting of loans, the George Cross island (population 320,000) was bent on getting the best of both worlds. When Britain's application was rejected, Malta had kept in her petition for a tailor-made agreement.

In March 1969 the Commission agreed to 'take note of Malta's European vocation' and while not promising eventual full membership of the EEC they agreed to ask the Six governments for a mandate to negotiate association by stages. There would first be an adaptation stage of five years during which Malta would reduce its tariffs on 16m.-dollars' worth of EEC imports by about 35 per cent while the EEC would cut duties on Malta's industrial exports of under $2m. by about 70 per cent. (However, these exports of manufactured goods should increase as Malta wishes to diversify away from tourism and horticulture.) During a second five-year transition period, free access to EEC markets for Malta's agricultural products would be negotiated and Malta would start to apply the EEC common external tariff and the capital and labour movement and right of establishment provisions of the Treaty of Rome.

Iran

A trade agreement with Iran was signed on October 1963 to run for three years and was subsequently renewed. It provided for reductions in the EEC tariffs on carpets, dried grapes, dried apricots, caviare, and raisins. This was a non-discriminatory agreement, though chiefly of benefit to Iran.

Lebanon

A trade-and-technical-assistance agreement was signed in March 1965 by which the EEC and Lebanon accord each other the status of most-favoured nation and the EEC promises technical assistance to the Lebanon, both by sending experts to the country and training Lebanese nationals in the Community. In October 1969 the Commission agreed to talks with the Lebanon and the United Arab Republic to explore ways of balancing Israel–EEC trade.

EEC AND INDIA

Limited trade discussions between India and the EEC opened in Brussels in February 1968 chiefly to discuss India's jute and coconut products and handicrafts. For some years India had been running a trade deficit with the Six; her exports to the EEC had paid for only a third of her imports from the EEC. The memorandum of the Indian Government stressed the poverty of the country (average annual personal income below £30) as compared with the very strong economic position of the Six countries, where 'high tariffs and discriminatory non-tariff barriers continue to afflict products of interest to India in some of the markets of the member-countries'.

The EEC had already waived all duty on tea, worked out a satisfactory arrangement for the import of Indian cotton textiles and were committed (by the Kennedy Round) to lowering its tariffs on India's major tropical products and their derivatives. Here was a case where it would have been of benefit to all parties if the EEC had been enlarged to include Britain and the EFTA countries; in the wider context some form of aid (over and above that already given in the aid to India programme) might have been arranged – this was not possible for the E E C already heavily committed to easing the lot of the less-developed countries of Africa.

THE EEC AND AFRICA

A thorny question arising in the talks leading to the Rome Treaty was what was to happen to the overseas countries and territories which had special relationships with one or other of the member-states. France in particular, besides her largely self-supporting empire in North Africa, was saddled with huge tracts of West and Equatorial Africa where there were few settlers and rudimentary one-crop economies. Belgium and Italy, besides colonial commitments of their own in Africa, administered United Nations' trust territories there. In the Caribbean and New Guinea the Netherlands was still preoccupied with the remnants of her empire.

One of the main difficulties was that Germany and the Netherlands normally bought tropical produce on world markets whereas the three colonial powers, and in particular France, as a *quid pro quo* for supplying the vast majority of their imports, bought most of the exports of their African satellites often at prices well above world levels. A bewildering mesh of bilateral agreements regulated this trade. West Germany and the Netherlands were naturally dubious about any sort of customs union with these African countries; West Germany even insisted on a protocol to the Rome Treaty allowing her to continue to import duty-free quotas of bananas from established sources in Latin America. A straightforward removal of customs duties would also have had the disadvantage of automatically removing the main source of the African governments' revenue (well over half their total revenue is from customs duties) and, if they were impoverished in this way and doomed for ever to be purveyors of raw materials and tropical commodities to industrialized Europe, they would never be able to afford the huge improvements in the infrastructure of their states which are so patently needed.

The formula chosen to reconcile these various interests was

association. Broadly speaking, this laid down that the associated territories would benefit from all tariff reductions which the Six applied among themselves i.e. African products would have free entry into the Six, but the associated states would retain the right to charge duties on their own imports of EEC products, so safeguarding the vital contribution to their budgets and general economic development. Free trade between the associated states themselves was not a condition of the arrangement, although it was not barred. The Six's intent to form the association of overseas countries and territories 'with a view to increasing trade and to pursuing jointly their effort towards economic and social development' was embodied in Article 3K.

When the first association agreement was drawn up in 1958 the eighteen African associates were all colonies or dependencies; it was of their own free will that after independence they decided to stay linked to the Community and a second association convention was signed at Yaoundé (Cameroon) in July 1963, and took effect from 1 June 1964 to run for five years. The signatories were

	Population (m.)
Madagascar	6·4
Ivory Coast	3·8
Congo-Kinshasa (ex Belgian Congo)	13·9
Senegal	3·4
Chad	3·3
Cameroon	4·6
Central African Republic	2·1
Mali	4·4
Burundi (Belgian Trust Territory)	2·2
Niger	3·1
Congo-Brazzaville	0·9
Mauritania	1·0
Somalia	3·0
Dahomey	2·2
Upper Volta	4·9
Rwanda (Belgian Trust Territory)	3·1
Togo	1·6
Gabon	0·4
	64·3

In theory it was hoped to free the associated African states and Madagascar (A A S M) from economic dependence on E E C countries (chiefly France) which bought their produce at above-market prices. The formerly French associated countries would lose part of the special privileges their exports enjoyed on the French market as gradually A A S M prices would be brought down to world price level but they would be compensated for this loss by tariff preferences received from other member-states. In other words, they would no longer be the sole responsibility of France.

In return the A A S M were to open their own markets without discrimination to all Six states; previously, these markets were the exclusive preserve of the exporters of the former mother countries i.e. mainly France. This diversification of trade did not material-ize, at any rate not as fast as might have been expected, and the member-states other than France were only gaining a firm footing in these markets when the Yaoundé Convention came up for re-consideration in 1968 (it expired on 31 May 1969). Moreover, the constant harping on the necessity for the developing countries of adjusting to world market prices has come in for some criticism since the industrialized countries and especially the E E C have contrived to circumvent the discipline of world market prices altogether when it came to protecting their own agriculture. It has even been argued that world market prices do not in fact exist, applying only to the world's leftovers sold at artificial and unrealistic prices. Undoubtedly, the country that has benefited most from association is France, who was able to persuade her European partners to shoulder some of the burden of her huge territorial interests in Africa while retaining for herself many of the advantages.

The Convention also provided for financial and technical assistance through the European Development Fund. The first E D F (1958–63) had totalled $581·25m. but the second E D F (1964–9) had a total of $730m. of which $620m. were available as grants and $46m. as special loans to the eighteen A A S M coun-tries, and another $60m. in grants and $4m. in loans to the re-maining overseas dependencies of France and the Netherlands. These are the French overseas territories of Comores Islands,

French Somali Coast, New Caledonia, French Polynesia, Saint Pierre, and Miquelon; the Dutch overseas territories of the Dutch West Indies and Surinam; and also the French overseas departments (treated as integral parts of France) of Guadeloupe, Guiana, Martinique, and Réunion. In addition to the funds made available from the EDF, the Convention also provided that loans would be available for economic development from the European Investment Bank ($64m. for the eighteen AASM states and $6m. for the overseas territories). The EIB had previously assisted only with development grants in Europe itself.

The Convention also covered the rights of establishment, services, payments, and capital movements and set up common institutions to administer the association – the Association Council, Association Committee, the Parliamentary Conference, and the Arbitration Court. The main difference between the Yaoundé Convention and the earlier association protocol annexed to the Rome Treaty was that after 1969 the Six would no longer guarantee to buy the tropical produce of the eighteen states at preferential prices but at current world prices, and for this reason the second EDF aimed to help the eighteen states to adjust their economies to world markets by giving production and diversification projects first call on the available funds. By contrast, the first EDF was mainly devoted to basic capital projects such as roads, water supplies, schools, medical centres, etc.

The Yaoundé Convention has been criticized on three main scores: first, the Africans have become increasingly dissatisfied as the prices of primary products have not increased at the same rate as the prices charged to them for manufactured goods and services of the industrialized countries (but, as M. Paul Prebisch long ago demonstrated, this is a constant of world trade, the problem of the century; the International Development Association has calculated that all the aid – loans, grants, and commercial credits – given by the rich to the poor countries has not on average been enough to fill the gap). And the trouble is partly of Africa's own making. President Senghor of Senegal, commenting on the 'fragmented economies and mini-markets' of Africa, put his finger on one of the major difficulties – in their obsession with independence the nations have overlooked the need to re-group at regional level so as to be able to establish viable industries; agriculture is too parochial and needs to reorganize into larger-scale production and marketing units. Many of these states have populations no bigger than those of the larger European cities and the need for co-operation is self-evident.

A second criticism is that European protection of tropical products from Africa discriminates against products from South and Central America, the West Indies, etc. Although the Yaoundé-producers have not yet learnt to compete effectively on world markets, the danger is foreseen. In fairness to the Six it must be said that they have made big tariff cuts on some tropical products regardless of origin. In 1963 duties on tea, maté, and tropical hardwoods were suspended, duties on coffee and cocoa were reduced by 40 per cent and on other products such as shellac and some spices by between 15 and 20 per cent. This accusation that the Yaoundé Convention, in favouring African states, has damaged other developing countries can be rebutted by a study of 'Trade of the Developing Countries with the Developed Countries', in particular the EEC 1953–66 (published by the EEC Commission in 1967). It shows that for 1958–66 the EEC's imports from the AASM increased by an average of 4·6 per cent but at a much faster rate for all other groups of developing countries:

Average Rate (%) of Increase of EEC Imports from Developing Countries 1958-66

Latin America	7·6
African countries on the Mediterranean	12·4
African countries (other than AASM)	6·2
Asian countries	6·0
Middle East	6·7
AASM	4·6

There might even be a case here for the AASM to complain. In addition, about 22 per cent of the EEC's imports from developing countries are industrial raw materials which are admitted free. Clearly at the moment the EEC cannot enlarge the Yaoundé

Convention and extend its privileges to all comers; the Six say they are not in a position to increase the considerable financial aid involved and that, if the commercial preferences were offered to an ever-widening circle, they would cease to be significant for the countries already benefiting and would bear most unfairly on any small countries left outside the system.

Many of the concessions made by the EEC to the developing countries concern agricultural products which are an extremely sensitive area within the Six itself; the optimum would be if the EEC were able to discourage the inordinate output from the Six member-countries of products which compete with those of the developing countries, e.g. sugar. Typical of the threat to tropical products is the rise in the EEC's imports from the USA of soya beans, which, being cheaper than groundnuts both as oil and as oilcakes for cattle feed had increased their share from 4 per cent of total EEC imports of all oils and fats in 1954 to over 14 per cent by 1964. Soya beans are America's third largest cash crop; in 1968 she sent 31 per cent of bean exports and 70 per cent of soya-meal exports to the EEC, together making up one third of total US exports to the Six. The EEC is the world's leading importer of oils and fats, producing only 22 per cent of its vegetable oil consumption (only around 7 per cent if olive oil is excluded) and this is a vital market for the AASM, over 90 per cent of whose oil and oilseed exports go to the EEC (oil and oilseeds represent over half of the exports of Dahomey, Mali, Niger, and Senegal). Tropical oils continued to do well on the French market, which was paying more than world prices to producers within the franc-zone, but these guaranteed prices to her ex-territories are being phased out. Soya-bean cake is itself threatened by the huge stocks of skimmed-milk powder which it is proposed to divert to cattle-feed.

In July 1969 the Commission announced that it was preparing for submission to the UN Food and Agriculture Organization a new type of world pact on fats and oils; this would achieve stabilization of prices by a tax on imports with the important proviso that the tax would apply only to imports from indus-trialized countries – the tax would vary from product to product and be at a level agreed among the Six; butter and olive oil would not be included. The revenue thus obtained would finance a stabilizing reserve to help the less prosperous oil-producing countries. This would make unnecessary an earlier Commission proposal to put an internal consumption tax on oilseed and oilseed products to encourage a switch to butter; this proposed consumption tax was causing friction between the EEC and the US.

The third main criticism of the Convention is an internal matter for the Six, who are asking themselves why this market which they have helped to develop through the EDF still looks so much like a French preserve, 75 per cent of its trade still being with France, the best contracts going to France, and Frenchmen still prominent as spokesmen for AASM countries at international conferences. Recently the Dutch and German companies have at last been getting a foot in the door and several African states, e.g. the Cameroon, have begun actively soliciting investment from outside France. Indeed, it was not until the summer of 1967 that some modification of the franc area took place. This area is a monetary union between France and the thirteen members of AASM originally linked with France; it has its own currency, the CFA franc. Until July 1967 France strictly controlled the availability of convertible currencies other than the franc – the African members of the zone receiving only a quota to be approved by France of non-franc foreign exchange each year to cover third-country imports. So, although the African countries were supposedly free to make their own trade pacts, France held the purse strings for the thirteen of the associates who belonged to her franc zone, though it has been argued that even this made for a much-needed unity and prevented still further fragmentation of the area into units which could not possibly have been economically viable. Even after regulations made in July 1967 had freed the CFA franc (making it freely convertible outside the franc area), prior authorization still had to be obtained for direct investment into or outside the area, for trade in foreign stocks or gold, and for borrowing from outside the area. So in effect the African currencies remain tied to the French franc.

Yet despite the defects of this system of association – which has clearly benefited France far more than any other nation of the Six

– the grossly retarded African countries have been given commercial and financial advantages not to be obtained elsewhere. Even among developing countries these were the backward ones from almost every standpoint: income per head, volume of investment, communications, education, health, and housing. The aid they have received from the EDF, besides being neutral, i.e. with no strings attached, has been significant and real, unlike some world aid programmes which tend to stop at the declaration-of-intent stage. Moreover, any member of the Yaoundé Convention can withdraw at any time (as Guinea, under President Sekou Touré, did from the previous association in 1958). The fact that the Yaoundé countries wished to come to the conference table to discuss renewal of the agreement shows that, despite their claims to have been treated poorly, they realize that they have gained something from the deal.

Agreement on a new association to take effect when the original agreement expired on 31 May 1969 was delayed by the failure of the Six to draw up a common position. The French, always opposed to the Commission's political powers, held that the individual member-states should undertake the negotiations, since they were the signatories to the current agreement. But the Commission seemed bent on making a test case of the issue. President Jean Rey announced that if the Council decided in favour of de Gaulle's contention, he would take the matter to the Court of Justice in Luxembourg. He cited Article 228 of the Rome Treaty, which states categorically, 'where this Treaty provides for the conclusion of agreements between the Community and one or more states or an international organization, such agreements shall be negotiated by the Commission'. The Dutch, as ever Community-minded, backed the Commission to the hilt, the Italians and the Germans toyed with complicated compromises. The Commission, already antagonized by the Council calling in question their negotiating role in the second stage of the Turkish association agreement, at first refused to accept a compromise formula but later agreed.

When negotiations finally started, the Africans asked for aid to be stepped up by almost $500m. to $1,200m. over the next five years (the figure for 1964–9 was $730m.). This was to take account of the poverty of their countries, their rising populations, and the unfavourable terms of trade. The European Parliament had recommended on 2 October 1968 that an average of $200m. aid a year should be aimed at, but this was dubbed an extravagant goal by Germany and Italy, who opposed the increase. Finally a figure of $1,000m. was arrived at. France was most active in securing this increase – but with the ulterior motive of keeping alive French influence in Africa; she had the support of Belgium, the other power still involved with ex-colonies in Africa. France, too, had insisted on maintaining the free-trade-area nature of the Yaoundé agreement, an attitude supported by Belgium; but others among the Six, notably the Dutch, resisted this localized viewpoint and wanted to see the eighteen brought into the new system of global preferences for developing countries agreed in principle by the industrialized countries at the UNCTAD Delhi Conference in 1968. They argued that the reverse preferences, i.e. the tariff preferences on industrial imports from the Six granted by the eighteen, might be regarded by the United States, Scandinavia, and other signatories as violating the UNCTAD agreement and so excluding the eighteen from any global system. On the other hand, the eighteen themselves wanted to grant the reverse preferences; they felt that, if these were removed, the Six might re-erect barriers against the eighteen's exports to Europe. Finally the Dutch secured agreement on a protocol to be attached to the new Convention stating that the Treaty does not in any way inhibit the eighteen from co-operating in the UNCTAD world preference scheme. To the same end – that of helping all developing countries rather than those specifically tied to French apron-strings – the Dutch secured some small reductions of the common external tariff on three major tropical products: the duty on raw coffee was reduced from 9·6 to 7 per cent, on cocoa from 5·4 to 4 per cent and on palm oil from 9 to 6 per cent. The new Convention expires on 31 January 1975.

In October 1969 the Six agreed to submit proposals for a new world preferences system for developing countries to UNCTAD. The offer, conditional on other industrialized countries making comparable efforts, would allow duty-free entry into the Six of all manufactured and semi-manufactured industrial goods from developing countries, up to an agreed ceiling (this would be fixed for each product, taking into account the total value of all imports from developing countries, plus 5 per cent of imports from other countries).

While an important side-effect of the AASM had been the degree of cohesion achieved by the eighteen during negotiations, many Europeans and Africans consider that real progress will be achieved much more quickly if Great Britain joins the EEC. Her accession could bring the much more viable English-speaking states into closer relationship with the eighteen and enable Africa's problems to be seen in a better perspective. Although to some states de Gaulle was the 'liberator' and 'father', to others he was an oppressor, using French troops to bolster effete régimes. In 1964 French intervention in Gabon had restored an overthrown president, and in 1968 and 1969 French *légionnaires* were propping up the régimes in the Central African Republic and in Chad, which had become known as 'France's little Vietnam'.

Nigeria

Nigeria's application in November 1963 for an association agreement with the EEC was prompted by the declaration of the Six, when signing the Yaoundé Convention in July 1963, that they would welcome applications from other countries with economic structures comparable to those of the eighteen as additional signatories to the Convention, through a separate association agreement or through a straightforward trade agreement.

The Lagos agreement was signed in Lagos in July 1966. It gave free entry to the EEC to all Nigerian exports except cocoa beans, groundnut oil, palm oil, and plywood for which quotas were fixed; in return Nigeria was to remove customs duties on imports from the Six except where these were a necessary source of revenue or served to protect Nigeria's own infant industries. An important point was that Nigeria undertook not to discriminate between one EEC member-state and another when it came to rights of establishment and to the supply of services, and also agreed not to grant more favourable trading terms to third countries.

This set a precedent in relations between Britain and the Commonwealth because Nigeria was granting more favourable terms to the EEC than to Britain; Nigeria offers very little in the way of Commonwealth preference to Britain though she benefits from British duty cuts on her sales to Britain. To this extent Nigeria was discriminating against Britain in favour of the EEC, with whom she did approximately the same amount of business (in 1965 31 per cent of Nigeria's exports went to the EEC, the same percentage as to Britain: of her imports 20 per cent came from the EEC, 30 per cent from Britain).

The implementation of the agreement (which had not yet been ratified by France and Luxembourg in early 1969) was held up by the civil war in Nigeria, but much useful spadework had been done. No development aid was asked for or given.

The Arusha Convention

When the Arusha Accord expired on 31 May 1969 and the Commission asked for a mandate to renegotiate it, a Gilbertian situation ensued, because the Accord had not yet entered into force. The three East African members of the Commonwealth – Kenya, Uganda, and Tanzania – followed the example of Nigeria and sought an association agreement with the EEC in February 1964. The talks reached a stalemate partly because the three countries were having difficulties in organizing themselves into an East-African common market, but restarted in December 1966.

The Arusha (Tanzania) agreement was signed on 26 July 1968 and, in return for her exports to the EEC ranking equally with those of the Yaoundé-Convention countries (with some restrictions on East African coffee and cloves), the East-African countries agreed to eliminate tariffs on EEC products, thus giving the EEC a tariff bonus of between 2 and 9 per cent on about sixty products.

No aid was involved in the original agreement and in September 1969 a new agreement, almost identical with the unratified version, was signed, known as the Arusha Convention. It expires on 31 January 1975. the same date as the Yaoundé Convention.

In 1968 Zambia, Ethiopia, Somalia, and Burundi started negotiations which could enlarge the three-nation East African Community to create a common market of 70 million; the difficulties are immense, but Zambia will probably go ahead with negotiations for membership of the East African Community. If she were able to make the necessary adjustments to her economy, she might then apply to join the Arusha Convention.

Ghana

Ghana approached the EEC in February 1969 seeking some arrangement on the lines of the Nigerian and Arusha agreements.

EEC AND EASTERN EUROPE

Convinced by Marxist doctrine that the inherent weakness of capitalism would lead to a complete breakdown of the Western nations' economies at any moment, Eastern Europe found difficulty in believing the evidence of its own eyes – the EEC not only did not collapse, it prospered, grew, and acted like a magnet to other countries of the free world.

The first evaluation was that the EEC was one more wicked Western plot against peace in Europe, a NATO organization disguised in economic trappings through which America and Western Germany would pursue their nefarious ends. Later, when this argument seemed less plausible, they seized on the creation of EFTA as an illustration of the 'inner contradictions' of capitalism which could split itself into two trading blocs; in the EEC itself, they saw an 'inner contradiction'; the rich nations, in particular Germany, would quickly gain the upper hand and subvert the poorer nations (although the evidence of their own eyes showed that France from 1963 on was doing the dominating; for them Germany was always waiting in the wings, de Gaulle's understudy); finally, the EEC, being a capitalist organization, would inevitably subjugate the working classes of Western Europe.

When these attitudes were no longer tenable (around 1962),

Krushchev sought to answer the EEC with a revamped COMECON, a super COMECON which would show the world and especially the EEC what planning really was in a vast iron-curtain-countries unit.

All the countries of the Soviet bloc, population 325 million, the USSR, Poland, Czechoslovakia, Romania, East Germany, Hungary, and Bulgaria belong to COMECON, the Committee for Mutual Economic Aid or the Communist common market. COMECON was Stalin's answer to the Marshall Plan and the Organization for European Economic Co-operation at a time, 1947, when the iron-curtain countries were toying with the idea of accepting American aid; Czechoslovakia, who had accepted, was made to change her mind. Stalin was determined that no one should stray from the Communist fold and hit on the idea of COMECON to provide mutual help and to remove bottlenecks in inter-zonal trade.

COMECON was not a success; for one thing, the USSR was so dominant a member that the others scarcely ranked as partners. It has a completely different working structure from that of the EEC; the permanent organization is the Executive Committee made up of delegates of the status of deputy prime minister; besides the co-ordination of development and investment plans, it supervises scientific and technical research and advises on trade and payments to capitalist and under-developed countries. It is handicapped in its dealings with the rest of the world, because the rouble is non-convertible; consequently many deals are arranged on the barter system. The Executive Committee works through permanent committees each dealing with a specific industry or special problem and each with its own secretariat at its headquarters in the capital of the leading country in that particular field, e.g. coal (Warsaw), oil and gas (Bucharest). The Czech Deputy Premier complained bitterly,

We took the idea of decentralization so literally that we now have an army of COMECON civil servants scattered all over the Socialist countries. Some offices which have related purposes and cannot do without each other are in different countries; the COMECON Bank is in Budapest, but the Economic Council is in Prague, and the Chief Accounting House in Moscow.

All attempts to give COMECON a new image and to rationalize production according to the 'socialist division of labour' met with adamant opposition. Romania utterly rejected the suggestion, made in 1963, that she, with Bulgaria, should in the supreme interests of COMECON revert to the mainly food-producing role from which she had been steadily emerging since the war. She flatly refused to be cast as hewer of wood and drawer of water. Another suggestion, put forward at a COMECON Council meeting and backed by the USSR, was scorned on all sides; it was that the consumer industries of Czechoslovakia and East Germany should be transferred to the other two small COMECON countries, Romania and Bulgaria, thus enabling Czechoslovakia and East Germany to concentrate exclusively on heavy industry, which being more concentrated would be more competitive by world standards. Yet another non-starter was the COMECON idea that Poland should get the Czech shoe industry in exchange for leaving the making of cars to the Czechs and East Germans.

Poland all along reserved her position; she had talks in Brussels in April 1965 with the Commission; her farm produce, especially eggs, was suffering under the Six's common agricultural policy. At the time it seemed possible that some trade pact between Poland and the Six might be reached, but nothing concrete emerged. However, in 1968 it was announced that Poland's new ambassador to Belgium had been authorized to keep an 'unofficial watching brief over EEC matters'.

Yugoslavia

Yugoslavia was never happy about the EEC on political grounds; to Tito it seemed a move away from his vision of a world association of non-committed countries and he particularly disliked the influence the EEC would wield in Africa. On economic grounds, too, Yugoslavia had well-founded fears; only an associate member of COMECON, she might easily find herself getting the worst of both worlds.

In December 1964 Tito came out in favour of closer relations with the Community, stating that the EEC was guilty only of minor discriminations, so making relations with it acceptable to Yugoslavia. In May 1965 negotiations on a trading agreement began but were abortive and so were those of 1967 and March 1968. An inspired analysis of the EEC's restrictive influence on exports of Yugoslav farm produce, hinting that it might be necessary to start retaliatory measures, set the ball rolling again. In July 1968 the Council instructed the Commission to open talks. French reservations about the impact of Yugoslav exports of baby-beef held up progress but agreement again seemed feasible when the Pompidou administration was seen to be taking a softer line. Further talks were being considered in October 1969 and if agreement were reached this would be the first trade agreement between the EEC and a Communist country.

EEC AND USA

Right from the start, the USA was in favour of the EEC because it believed a consolidated unit would be more effective in protecting the interests of the Western European nations than any amalgam of treaties or 'spheres of interest'. The USA recognized from the beginning that, in the words of Harold Wilson (House of Commons, 3 August 1961), 'the Common Market is a highly restrictive discriminating trading bloc', but this it was prepared to accept if a united Europe would progressively shoulder more of its own burdens, particularly defence, so relieving the Americans of a responsibility which, though inevitable in the days after the Second World War, could not be shouldered by the Americans in perpetuity.

Clearly a united Western Europe would be in a stronger position to contain the threat of Soviet aggression. However, once the EEC had become a tool of Gaullist diplomacy, the USA modified its attitude. They were less prepared to tolerate the non-tariff barriers to trade such as the operation of the value-added tax, which in their view is used by the EEC to distort the true price of exports and so amounts to a hidden subsidy or border tax to use the American label. Although EEC officials deny the American assessment of value-added tax, the very fact that both Germany and France resorted to VAT adjustments instead of parity changes as between the D-mark and franc after the Bonn crisis of November 1969 confirms the American diagnosis.

When President Nixon's administration took a new look at international trade, the VAT was one of the barriers to international trade that it identified (others were restrictive standards and Japanese quotas). Another was the EEC's agricultural-export subsidy. During the famous poultry war the US, angered by EEC subsidies, had retaliated with subsidies on American poultry – and lard.

If the EEC were prepared to modify these two non-tariff barriers to free trade, the Nixon administration would find it simpler to persuade the very vocal protectionist lobbies (among them steel, textiles and footwear) to ease their demands for curbs on imports from the EEC and for a more inward-looking US policy. The US Steel Corporation are constantly pressing for countervailing duties against most EEC steel imports to offset special tax write-offs which are given to EEC products. If the EEC cannot or will not co-operate, there is a strong chance that the 1962 trade expansion act will be amended to provide for relief to firms and industries claiming damage from imported foreign goods. Such a move could trigger off a chain reaction with the EEC retaliating and a full-scale trade war developing. If, however, the President regains authority to reduce tariffs (withdrawn in July 1967) he could at his discretion compensate countries complaining of US tariff increases or other restrictions and so act as a mediator.

The USA came out strongly against the commercial arrangements or halfway house for Britain which were on offer from the EEC in late 1968 and 1969. Such a link, it declared roundly, would be objectionable because, while not strengthening the EEC as a political entity, it would discriminate against the USA trade-wise. The US also opposes the renegotiation of the highly preferential Yaoundé Convention; some commentators saw in the leisurely approach to the real meat of the negotiations evidence that, thanks to de Gaulle's new-found friendship with America, the General might be paying some heed to American objections and deliberately dragging his feet. If the EEC persisted in granting preferences to Africa, America might be pushed into doing the same for Latin America.

As for the North-Atlantic free-trade area, however desirable it might be in the eyes of certain protagonists in Britain, it had little to commend it, either politically or economically from the US point of view. It was with the EEC, enlarged or not enlarged, that the US had to come to terms.

SOUTH AMERICA

Argentina was the first South American country to seek (in 1969) a trade agreement with the EEC, its most important partner: a similar request from Uruguay was also received in 1969. In 1967 Argentina sent 41·5 per cent of its exports to the EEC and took 23·7 per cent of its imports from the EEC. If these go through, agreements with other South American countries could follow.

Argentina's application is an indication of the limitations of LAFTA, the Latin American Free-Trade Area, which it was hoped might develop into a South American EEC but which has proved little more than a customs union. LAFTA was born of the euphoria which followed the signing of the Treaty of Rome and the successful launching of the EEC; the Treaty of Montevideo was signed in February 1960 by all the countries of South America except Venezuela and Bolivia, who joined later, the tiny countries of British Guiana (now Guyana), Surinam and French Guiana, and Panama. The Central American countries of Costa Rica, Nicaragua, Honduras, El Salvador, and Guatemala in 1960 grouped themselves into a separate Common Market, the Central American Common Market, but Mexico to the north joined LAFTA.

The discrepancy in size and development between the three big fellows, Argentina, Brazil, and Mexico and the relatively less-developed countries, Ecuador and Paraguay, and again between them and the countries with insufficient markets, Chile, Colombia, Peru, and Uruguay, prevented LAFTA being the panacea that the participant countries were seeking. Integration, on any plane, is hard to achieve by countries without money markets, or modern and efficient stock exchanges, where smuggling and currency offences are rife, where inflation on a scale unknown in modern Europe is rampant and where political instability inhibits long-term planning.

South America has constantly criticized the Yaoundé treaty, alleging that Africa is being favoured by duty-free access to the EEC markets, which is not available to other tropical produce sellers, such as themselves.

An urgent appeal was made to the Six by the Commission in July 1969 for a truly European policy towards Latin America; each of the Six had been dealing on strictly national lines with Latin American countries and the Commission wanted them to co-ordinate their policies. Community trade arrangements, such as the ones being negotiated with Argentina and Uruguay on beef, should take the place of fragmented deals; sugar and cereal agreements would, however, best be handled on a world level. Tropical products should not just maintain their level but share in the future growth of the market. It was pointed out that Brazil, Colombia, El Salvador, Ecuador, and Venezuela would benefit from cuts in the common external tariff on coffee and cocoa insisted on by the Dutch at the time of the 1969 Yaoundé negotiations. Co-operation in the technical field should cover export-promotion organizations, collaboration with the Inter-American Development Bank to help regional integration, and also technical education.

JAPAN

Talks to try to eliminate some of the many and irritating obstacles to trade between Japan and the EEC were expected to start in 1970.

9 Defence of the West

After the devastations of the Second World War, the first task of the Western world was to restore the economic health of nations torn by years of strife and to provide for their safety. This was at a time when Soviet intentions were far from clear. Soviet Russia had emerged as the great victor in Europe in the war against Germany. Under Stalin she was determined to reap the fullest reward for her herculean efforts. The break-up of the capitalist system in Europe seemed a distinct possibility. It would provide the best security against a rebirth of pan-Germanism. It would drive the Americans back across the Atlantic and lead to their progressive isolation. Communist parties in Western Europe were regrouping and preparing for battle against discredited régimes which had been responsible for the rape of Czechoslovakia by the Nazis and the defeat of liberty in Spain and indeed for the rebirth of German militarism itself. In France and Italy the Communist parties were potential fifth columns in any assault on the capitalist system. By their own governments they were accused of being little better than Muscovite agents. With Soviet forces still at combat readiness and in full command east and west of the Oder–Neisse line, with lines of communication still open through Hungary to Vienna and a fierce cold war raging against the Yugoslavs, the moment could have been ripe for one grand push right across Europe to the Atlantic. On balance, however, the risks appeared too great and Stalin held his hand under the weight of American atomic power. But the prospect of a Soviet sword of Damocles hanging permanently over non-Communist Europe was intolerable. The Western nations looked to their defences.

The economic health of Western Europe was restored with aid

given under the Marshall Plan, a legacy of which – the Organization for Economic Co-operation and Development – is still operating. The defence of the West was provided for by the North Atlantic Treaty signed in Washington on 4 April 1949 and comprising by 1969 fifteen nations – the United States, Canada, Great Britain, France, West Germany, Italy, Holland, Belgium, Luxembourg, Norway, Denmark, Iceland, Portugal, Greece, and Turkey.

The occasion was historic. For the first time since it gained independence in 1776, the United States had accepted precise military commitments in advance. It marked the end of isolation and confirmed that country as the undisputed leader of the Western world, a role for which it had been irretrievably cast at Pearl Harbour in 1941. The main architects of this momentous reversal of policy were Sir Winston Churchill (Fulton, Missouri speech), President Truman, General Marshall, Mr Dean Acheson, and Senator Vandenberg, whose untiring efforts to obtain the American Senate's acceptance of the Atlantic alliance assured the success of one of the most ambitious international treaties known to history.

The Treaty-Powers made themselves responsible for the security of all their territories in Europe and North America and the Atlantic area from North Cape to the Tropic of Cancer. An attack on one was to be considered an attack on all. The result has been that not one inch of NATO territory has been violated in twenty years. Few treaties in the past can boast such success; though, ironically, before the Soviet invasion of Czechoslovakia in August 1968, the survival of the alliance was uncertain. The emphasis was no longer on a keen vigilance but on seeking a détente with the Russians. After the invasion the Alliance seemed assured of an indefinite future.

Whatever the political motive, the Soviet move created over-night a new tactical situation in central Europe. Under cover of manoeuvres the Soviet Government was able in three days to move seven combat-ready divisions into Czechoslovakia with supporting armour, aircraft, air-borne troops, etc. – in all about 250,000 men, including other Warsaw-Pact forces. The Russians thus found themselves several hundred miles nearer the heart of

NATO territory. So long as they are there, they are able, without any warning beyond what Allied intelligence would be able to glean in the normal way, to strike a lightning blow at Western Germany, the most exposed of all the NATO territories in Western Europe. Highly mobile reinforcements could be on their way within a matter of hours. In fact, the Alliance was caught with its guard down. Fortunately the 'enemy' did not pursue his advantage because the objective was not to launch a full-scale offensive against the West but to quell creeping insubordination by the Czech leaders. Even so, through lack of proper communications, due mainly to installation delays after the transfer of SHAPE (allied headquarters) from Paris to Casteau in 1968, Saceur (Supreme Allied Commander [Europe]) found himself without proper machinery for instant consultation with political leaders on possible emergency action. Not that Allied military intelligence had not accurately assessed the tactical situation in the light of possible Soviet intentions. It had. As far back as April 1968 Soviet military moves pointed to the threat of an invasion of Czechoslovakia and this information duly reached the political branches of NATO. But governments were unprepared for a threat of this sort because there was no agreed interpretation of Soviet policy. The invasion spotlighted the nuclear dilemma very clearly.

There is a danger in Europe that localized aggression with the use of conventional weapons would catch the NATO powers at a grave disadvantage. Their forces are outnumbered on the central front by more than two to one in infantry formations and by nearly three to one in armour. Warsaw-Pact aircraft outnumber NATO's by nearly two to one. The discrepancy is made up by reliance on tactical nuclear weapons. Without recourse to such weapons NATO forces could not withstand a full-scale conventional attack for more than a few days at the most. The danger, therefore, is nuclear escalation. Tactical nuclear weapons have a strategic effect if used in large quantities. Their destructive power can be anything between five and 100 kilotons of TNT. They would confer an immediate advantage on the Allies. It is therefore highly unlikely that the Soviet forces would not use them almost immediately they were used by NATO even though, in the first place, NATO forces had only intended them to be a warning shot across the bows.

Yet, as General Lemnitzer, the former Supreme Allied Commander, has said, unless the allies make it quite plain that they will meet a major conventional onslaught with nuclear weapons, the deterrent power of such weapons vanishes. The problem is to determine at what stage of an enemy attack it is necessary to use nuclear weapons to contain it. The answer has been found in the policy of a flexible response, which means holding out for as long as possible with conventional weapons until it has been shown that the attack is either an accident or a miscalculation, or merely a probing operation, or that it is in fact an all-out offensive against the West. The respite, a few days at the most presumably, would allow diplomacy to play its last card before the holocaust on Churchill's assumption that 'jaw jaw' is better than 'war war'. Any policy that discredits the credibility of the nuclear deterrent is therefore an open invitation to aggression.

The alternative is either to match the Warsaw-Pact forces in manpower and conventional weapons or to rely on a mixture of conventional and nuclear weapons – graduated escalation as it is called. The first solution is technically feasible but politically difficult in the present social climate of the West. Potentially, NATO manpower is superior to that of the Eastern Europeans – about 100 million men of military age of which an estimated 57 million are in Europe, as opposed to 63 million in the Warsaw-Pact countries, of which 46·3 million are supplied by Russia.

With all the scientific, financial, and technical resources at their disposal, the four major powers in Allied Europe – the United Kingdom, West Germany, France and Italy – spend on average between them only 4·7 per cent of their GNP on defence, whereas their counterparts in the Warsaw Pact – the USSR, Poland, East Germany and Czechoslovakia – in 1967 spent, on average, 6·1 per cent (Russia alone devoting 9·6 per cent), a percentage matched only by the USA and then only because of the Vietnam war. The average percentage of regular armed forces to men of military age in the same countries in Allied Europe is 4 per cent; in the same countries in Eastern Europe it is 5·5 per cent and in Russia alone 7 per cent. From these figures it is clear that if the

NATO countries had the political will to match the Warsaw Pact's conventional military forces and weaponry the resources are there. But the will does not exist and there are few countries in the Alliance where governments could go to the people with a plan for massive mobilization of technical, financial, and man-power resources. The exception might be West Germany for reasons which will be dealt with later. On the conventional man-power side, Britain is very low down on the list with 170,000 trained reserves out of 10,700,000 men of military age – 1·6 per cent.

Since there is no intention of catching up with the Soviet–Warsaw-Pact conventional forces, the only alternative is to extract the maximum value and fire-power out of the men and material we are prepared to put into the defence of the West. This can be and is being done by bringing all units up to full strength and improving the quality and quantity of all weapons. The British Chieftain tank, for instance, is a highly sophisticated piece of armour (some say too sophisticated) with tremendous destructive power. The maximum number should be available to all Allied units. Reserves must be brought up to full strength in all countries bearing in mind that in many of them, France and Britain in particular, the emphasis is on cutting down on government expenditure. Indeed, the British Government boasts that it has 'saved' £2,000m. on defence since it came to power in 1964. Research in 1969 was cut by no less than £30m. If more reliance is to be placed on conventional forces in which the alliance is outnumbered, the need is for the utmost efficiency in weaponry – in which case more, and not less, money should be spent on research and development.

Efficiency could be improved in a number of ways. For instance, the rationalization of weapons production and procurement could be developed much further if the political will to do so were there. So far standardization has been achieved mainly by buying American. There could be more day-to-day co-operation in the organization and training of combat forces and in logistics.

Exchanges between Britain and Germany in tank-training have been highly successful in making military co-operation a human reality at company or squadron level. At tactical level an extremely important foundation for multilateral co-operation was laid late in 1968 between Britain and Germany for consultation in hammering out tactical nuclear policy. This was done at meetings of the NATO Nuclear Planning Group in Bonn, from which France was naturally absent.

At a higher level still, one of the largest combined defence projects is under way; the development of a new advanced combat aircraft for the late 1970s by Britain, Germany, Italy and Holland.

At the Ministerial Council meeting of NATO in Brussels in November 1968, when all the implications of the invasion of Czechoslovakia were reviewed, many governments decided to take urgent steps to strengthen NATO forces in ways immediately feasible at the time. The USA decided to speed up the return of certain of its forces to Germany, including two infantry brigades and four air squadrons which arrived well ahead of schedule to take part in manoeuvres early in 1969. Fighter squadrons equipped with F 102 aircraft would have Phantom F 4s as rapidly as possible. Also, and perhaps more important, the US Air Force's Rapid Reaction Force, based in the USA would be earmarked for NATO's European Command. It was also decided to accelerate the expansion of NATO's electronic warfare capability. West Germany's defence effort was also stepped up. Eighty-eight Phantom F 4 fighters were to be bought from the USA and thirty additional artillery batteries were to be provided. This would entail increased budget expenditure of DM. 740m.

The United Kingdom decided to reinforce units already stationed in Europe and the Mediterranean and bring all units up to establishment as soon as possible. Already the decision had been taken, as a matter of long-term defence policy, to concentrate all British forces withdrawn from east of Aden by 1971 in the European theatre. There was every incentive to hasten the process. New forces earmarked for or assigned to NATO before and after the events in Czechoslovakia included: the mobile task force of 20,000 men and three infantry divisions stationed in Britain as part of the strategic reserve; two battalions of the parachute force; the regular Special Air Service (SAS) Regiment; an armoured car squadron (part of ACE mobile force); the RAF 38 Group's close support and short-range transport aircraft, and a squadron of Shackleton long-range maritime reconnaissance aircraft, later to be re-equipped with Nimrods, transferred from the United Kingdom to Malta where the Canberra reconnaissance squadron has remained instead of being brought back to England. Equally, two RN frigates previously due to return to the United Kingdom have remained in the Mediterranean, assigned to Saceur. Also earmarked for the Mediterranean are two helicopter carriers (HMS Bulwark and HMS Albion) both with an embarked commando unit; two assault ships (HMS Fearless and HMS Intrepid) and one helicopter-support ship. Further, from 1970 a guided-missile destroyer will be added to the frigate force in the Mediterranean. From 1970 the UK-based Rapier air-defence units of the RAF, and from 1971 the Phantom fighters previously earmarked for the Persian Gulf and the Far East, will be committed to NATO. All Buccaneer Mark 2s and Phantoms entering service with the RAF over the period 1969–72 will be committed to the Alliance. Another squadron of the new Harrier V/Stol strike aircraft has been assigned to NATO and a further twenty of these remarkably versatile planes were ordered for the RAF.

Another of NATO's weaknesses is that there is no agreed tactical doctrine, and the need for uniform tactics will increase as the years go by because of the more sophisticated conventional weapons which will be brought into service by the mid-1970s. National tactical schools should be replaced by international schools. This would improve military performance and give better value for money. The same is true of common staff colleges which would fit in well with combined NATO staff colleges already in existence at the higher echelons. The school of air warfare might be set up at the RAF at Manby, and Munster Laager, in Germany, seems the obvious choice for siting the School of Armoured Warfare. Another country could take the School of Artillery, etc.

All this points to the need for a European defence community or entity on the lines suggested by the British Defence Minister and other NATO governments. This would have the double advantage of providing a far better integrated European system than exists in NATO today and of meeting American criticism that the European nations are not doing enough in their own defence. But this raises the most delicate political issues connected with the future of Europe and America's role in Europe.

Meanwhile, and for the foreseeable future, Europe's defence is America's defence. America's nuclear arsenal is Europe's nuclear shield, a shield which no European nation alone and no European nations combined could possibly hope to match, if only because of the cost. Only the United States is capable of sustaining a level of defensive power capable of neutralizing Soviet nuclear power.

Mr Robert McNamara, former US Secretary of Defense, has given us a glimpse of this power (*The Essence of Security*): 1,000 Minuteman missile-launchers well out of harm's way; 41 Polaris submarines carrying 656 missile launchers, the majority of which are submerged all the time; and about 600 long-range bombers, about 40 per cent of which are kept in a permanent state of alert. These alert forces alone are equipped with more than 2,200 weapons having enough explosive power (more than one megaton of TNT each) to lay the Soviet Union flat. They are flexible and equipped with devices which ensure that the Soviet anti-ballistic missile screen could be penetrated effectively. Warhead for warhead – assuming accurate delivery – American nuclear offensive power is vastly more destructive than the Soviet Union's.

Saceur (invariably an American) whose headquarters, SHAPE, are at Casteau, near Mons in south-west Belgium, has about forty-five divisions assigned to him and his subordinate land commands in central, northern and southern Europe. Another fourteen divisions could be brought forward if circumstances allowed, together with a considerable number of independent brigades. He also has a mobile force known as ACE, consisting of six reinforced infantry battalions, an armoured reconnaissance squadron with ground-support fighter squadrons supplied by eight countries. This is a powerful force which Saceur may use anywhere between the North Cape and the eastern frontier of Turkey. For air support he can call on some 3,500 tactical aircraft based on approximately 150 standard NATO airfields supplied by a system of jointly financed storage depots, fuel pipelines and signal communications. He is believed to have at least 7,000 tactical nuclear warheads (in American custody), with about 2,250 delivery vehicles (aircraft and missiles).

Ground forces available after mobilization of first-line reserves (excluding French) amount to about another sixty divisions, mostly in brigade strength or brigade equivalent and including armoured, infantry, mechanized, and airborne units. Weapons and aircraft are increased proportionately.

Saceur is not, however, responsible for strategic nuclear planning. This is the task of the American Joint Strategic Planning System at Omaha, Nebraska. This body does, however, plan jointly with NATO and American bomber and missile forces are integrated in NATO nuclear planning. Saceur nevertheless has a small number of American Polaris submarines allocated to him and Britain has committed her medium bomber force and all her Polaris submarines to Saceur's planning control.

There are two other NATO commands – Supreme Allied Commander Atlantic (Saclant), with headquarters at Norfolk, Virginia, with an American admiral in command and Allied Command Channel (Acchan), which covers the Channel and also the defence of the North Sea.

Saclant's responsibility stretches from the North Pole to the Tropic of Cancer and includes Portuguese coastal waters. It is a standby command which in peacetime has no permanent forces assigned to it except for training purposes. In wartime, however, forces (predominantly naval) would be assigned to it from Britain, the United States, Canada, Holland, Denmark, and Portugal. It has various subordinate commands, the most important of which are Striking Fleet Atlantic and Submarine Command.

The nucleus of both is provided by the American Second Fleet with missile-firing submarines and a few attack aircraft carriers. In January 1968, however, it was decided to form a multi-nation naval squadron of escort vessels known as Stanavforlant (Standing Naval Force Atlantic) under the command of Saclant. Normally it consists of four frigate or destroyer-type ships contributed, at various times, by Britain, the United States, Canada, West Germany, the Netherlands, Norway, and Portugal.

In all, Saclant has allotted to it about 500 escort vessels of varying types but mostly designed for anti-submarine warfare and over 150 submarines with similar duties. The Americans contribute by far the largest portion of the 375-odd long-range, land-based naval patrol planes in operation in peacetime. The US Navy also contributes about 800 carrier-borne specialist anti-submarine fixed-wing aircraft and helicopters of which half can be carrier-borne at any one time. Including forces assigned to Channel Command, about 350 such aircraft can be made quickly operational from all carriers on Atlantic sea stations.

Channel Command has its headquarters at Northwood, Middlesex, England, and Sacchan, or Commander-in-Chief, is a British admiral who also acts as a subordinate commander of Saclant in the Eastern Atlantic area. He is assisted by a Channel committee consisting of naval chiefs of staff of the United Kingdom, Belgium, and Holland. Some naval aircraft and most of the smaller warships of the three countries – frigates, minesweepers, and minelayers, etc. – are earmarked for his Command.

Of the twenty-four divisions assigned to the Central European Command (Afcent), eleven are West German, six American, three British and two each from Holland and Belgium. Afcent is again divided into two commands: Northern Army Group (Northag) which under a German general is responsible for the defence of territory north of a line drawn from Gottingen to Liège. In it are the British, Belgian, and Dutch divisions, four West-German divisions and a Canadian brigade. Central Army Group (Centag) includes seven German divisions and the six American divisions. Overall, Afcent has command of tactical air forces amounting to some 2,000 aircraft, of which about 400 are American fighter-bombers. It has surface-to-surface missiles at army and corps level. Rockets and missile-artillery are deployed at divisional level. There is also an integrated early-warning and air-defence system covering Britain, West Germany, Holland, Belgium, Luxembourg, and north-eastern France.

The Southern Europe Command (Afsouth) is centred on Naples and is in the hands of an American admiral who is responsible for the defence of Italy, Greece, and Turkey and for the protection of Mediterranean sea and air communications including Turkish territorial waters of the Black Sea. Fourteen divisions from Turkey, eight from Greece, and seven from Italy have been assigned to him as well as the tactical air forces of all three countries. Naval forces from the United States (Sixth Fleet) and from Italy, Greece, Turkey, and Great Britain also come under his command. In wartime the American Sixth Fleet would become Strike Force South with other Allied naval and air forces.

To keep watch on Soviet warships and movements in the Mediterranean, another NATO command was formed in the autumn of 1968 known as Command Maritime Airforces Mediterranean (Marairmed) with an American rear-admiral in charge at Naples. He reports to the Commander of the Allied Naval Forces, Southern Europe, who in turn reports to the Commander-in-Chief, Afsouth. Marairmed has under its command forces supplied by Britain (a squadron of R A F Shackletons to be replaced by Nimrods), the United States, Greece, Italy, and Turkey. Aircraft and helicopters are supplied from the American, British, and Italian forces. Operations will take place from land bases in Italy, Sicily, and Malta. The French may or may not agree to co-operate.

In January 1969 in Brussels the NATO defence ministers adopted an on-call system for the Allied naval forces in the Mediterranean. Fleets would be assembled twice a year for manoeuvres and goodwill visits to counter Russian political influence in that sea.

In 1966 the US Government recognized the fact that the United States could no longer have a monopoly of nuclear planning within the alliance (as de Gaulle had argued in 1958) and two new bodies were set up: the Nuclear Defence Affairs Committee (NDAC) and the subordinate Nuclear Planning Group. Both were designed to associate non-nuclear members with nuclear planning within the Alliance.

In due course NATO will have its own completely integrated communications system designed to facilitate political consultation in times of crisis – the sort of quick-action network that was singularly lacking before the Soviet invasion of Czechoslovakia.

The weak link, of course, in NATO's dispositions in the field is the future role of French forces, none of which in 1968 was fully integrated with NATO commands. General de Gaulle's decision to withdraw from NATO planning and commands all French forces which would normally be available in time of war resulted in several anomalies. For instance, France is still a member of the North Atlantic Alliance and therefore of the Council but does not, or at least did not in 1968 and 1969, take part in the work of the Defence Planning Committee, because she is not a member of the Military Committee, the top advisory body to the Council, the latter being in permanent session. She shares this distinction with Iceland, but unlike Iceland, she maintains a liaison staff with the Military Committee. The latter is virtually all-powerful in a military sense. All the major NATO commanders are responsible to it although they also have direct access to the NATO Council and to heads of government. Yet France only liaises with it. Again, because of this, France, like Iceland and Luxembourg, is not a member of the Nuclear Defence Affairs Committee (NDAC), nor, therefore, of its subordinate body, the Nuclear Planning Group (NPG). Both are actively concerned with the levels of strategic nuclear forces and the tactical uses of nuclear weapons – clearly one of the most important planning groups in the Alliance. One of their major decisions, taken at the Hague in April 1968, was that it was not – at least at that time – in NATO's interest to set up an anti-ballistic missile system in NATO-Europe, as being too costly and probably ineffective in a crisis because of the collective political decisions required to activate it, by which time it would be too late. The air defence of France has not been integrated with the air defence of the rest of NATO Europe. It has had to be negotiated, with all the complications that that entails, whereas all combat aircraft of Britain's Strike Command are assigned to NATO.

France's Tactical Air Command has been completely withdrawn from Germany and the ground troops which remain (two mechanized divisions and one independent brigade in West Berlin) are there under a status agreement negotiated separately from NATO. Co-operation with the latter has, however, been agreed and France contributes to the improved air-defence and radar system being built by a NATO consortium called NADGE (NATO Air Defence Ground Environment). Nevertheless, all NATO military units and commands, including logistics units, were turned out of France when the decision was taken to continue to enjoy the protection of the Alliance without submitting to its military organization.

This created immediate planning difficulties for Saceur who could never know in advance at what stage the French might or might not co-operate in the use of tactical nuclear weapons to halt an attack. French generals themselves have argued that the two French divisions in Germany are virtually useless unless they have been trained in the use of such weapons, all of which were withdrawn by the Americans when the French left the military structures of NATO.

Again, France no longer has any naval forces in the Mediterranean assigned to NATO but there are certain arrangements for co-operation between French naval forces and allied forces in the Atlantic under Saclant, and occasionally in the Mediterranean.

SOVIET FORCES IN EUROPE

Before the events in Czechoslovakia in the summer of 1968, the USSR had roughly 141 divisions deployed as follows: East Germany 20; Poland 2; Hungary 4; USSR west of the Urals and north of the Caucasus 60; central USSR 10; southern USSR 30; Far East 15. This accounts for about 3,220,000 men in the regular forces plus 250,000 men of the para-military forces, including security and border troops, under command of the Ministry of the Interior, to maintain law and order. There are three degrees of combat readiness and probably not more than half of the 140-odd divisions are normally at, or near, full combat strength. But they could be brought up to strength at short notice, although about a quarter of them are at the lowest degree of readiness and would require major reinforcement.

It is in the Mediterranean, however, that the Russians have recently made a major effort in strengthening their armed forces.

This is a new development of considerable historic and strategic importance. Until the years immediately after the 1939–45 war, the Mediterranean was a Western Allies' preserve. But under Stalin, Russian influence reached progressively further South, to the borders of the Arabian Peninsula, and the passage of Russian warships through the Dardanelles opened a new chapter in the politics of the Middle East. This presence was felt immediately during the 1956 Suez crisis when Russia backed her support for the Egyptians by sending warships to cruise in the waters of the Levant. Today, she has anything between thirty and fifty warships in the Mediterranean armed with surface-to-surface and surface-to-air guided missiles. Their numbers vary according to the political needs of the day. A fleet of auxiliaries can keep the fleet permanently at sea.

At the moment they do not appear to be looking for permanent bases but in return for equipping the Algerian armed forces with Soviet weapons, they may well be given permanent facilities at Mers-el-Kebir, the Algerian naval base, built at great expense by the French and subsequently vacated by them as a result of granting Algeria complete independence. Three of the major Arab countries in the Middle East – Egypt, Syria, and Iraq – have given them facilities, and in some cases what is the equivalent of naval bases (at Port Said and Latakia) and an air base at West Cairo. The facilities are available at Alexandria for the fleet, and at Luxor and Aswan and the old RAF staging-post at Habbaniya in Iraq for Soviet air forces.

Soviet warships have not used the naval facilities extensively, for political reasons, and are content to use the sheltered anchorages near the island of Kithira, off the southern tip of the Peloponnese and in the Gulf of Sollum on the Egyptian–Libyan border, where repairs and maintenance can be carried out comparatively unobserved.

If the Soviet Union's negotiations with Spain for servicing facilities for her merchant and fishing fleets (including, of course, the usual number of 'spy-vessels') lead to final agreement, Russia will, in effect, have penetrated the whole of NATO's southern flank and politically neutralized virtually all the northern shores of Africa which are now denied to NATO forces in time of peace. Russian eyes were already fixed on the Mediterranean at Yalta and, at one stage in the redrawing of the map of Europe, Stalin claimed condominium over Libya.

Russia is obviously moving out of its traditional defensive role based on a substantial number of submarines, and into a more forward, aggressive strategy. In May 1967, at the time of the Israeli–Arab war, she went so far as to demand that the American Sixth Fleet should quit the Mediterranean. She is also starting to form commando units on British lines to increase her mobility overseas. Two aircraft carriers have already been allotted to this task and more are building with the same object in mind. This new forward strategy is justified by the need to protect a fast-increasing fishing fleet and merchant navy. Fishing vessels in distant waters need bases from which to operate. These bases, in turn, need naval forces to protect them, particularly when a number of fishing vessels are also engaged in intelligence work. The bigger the merchant fleets, the more protection they need and by the 1980s, according to present plans, Soviet Russia will have the largest mercantile marine in the world (today it is the sixth largest).

These fleets will sail all oceans and this will be used as a pretext for seeking to establish naval bases in all oceans. In the Indian Ocean, for instance, these bases could be used to threaten western shipping routes using the Suez Canal or making the long journey round the Cape of Good Hope, a route more and more used by the supertankers. The Russians have already been 'lent' a base by the Egyptians at Ras Banas, two thirds of the way up the Red Sea, ostensibly for fishing but which could be used for other purposes. On the Yemeni coast, at Hodeida, they have built a three-berth terminal to take Soviet air supplies to San'a, the capital of the Yemen. They have supplied fighters to the Yemeni Republic and agreed to train crews, and have established a commercial air link between Moscow and San'a. They were quick to recognize the new régime in Aden and are helping the Somalis to build a new port at Berbera 170 miles due south of Aden.

Soviet Russia thus progressively assumes the role of a major sea power – the only one comparable in size to the United States. She is breaking out of a geographical strait-jacket which for centuries has kept her hemmed in on all sides in Europe west of the Urals, with bad sea outlets round the North Cape; with the Swedes, Danes, and Germans in command of the Baltic approaches and the Turks sitting astride the Dardanelles. It is indeed a historical development. In support of this new global strategy, she has 280 non-nuclear-powered non-missile-firing submarines, 178 ocean-going escort vessels, 38 nuclear-powered missile-firing submarines, 50 non-nuclear-powered but missile-firing submarines and 28 large guided-missile destroyers, over and above her vast array of I C B Ms, I R B Ms, and M R B Ms – the latter numbering well over 1,000.

American naval power is greatly superior to Russian at the moment, but the Soviet Union's determination to extend her maritime operations to all corners of the globe has forced the United States to review its global strategy. Both powers appear to be on a long-term collision course.

Ironically, the strategic arms limitation talks (S A L T), which started in Helsinki at the end of 1969 between the U S A and the U S S R (and were due to be continued at Vienna in April 1970), could lead to an intensification of rivalry in the non-nuclear field.

The original – and historic – purpose of the talks was to discuss ways in which the two superpowers could avoid the astronomic expense of setting up ever more powerful comprehensive anti-ballistic missile systems. The folly of escalation in strategic weapons became apparent after President Kennedy and Khruschev faced one another across the nuclear abyss during the Cuba crisis of 1962. But, since deterrence is indivisible, the two great powers found themselves talking of the possible limitation of other weapons in the nuclear armoury, such as missile launching sites, nuclear-firing submarines and even the ordinary long-range bomber.

However, success in the limitation of nuclear weapons would not necessarily lead to the end of rivalry in conventional weapons. On the contrary, the chances are that this would increase and, as Soviet global strategy develops, reliance is likely to be placed more and more on such weapons since they carry less risk of direct nuclear confrontation.

10 The Future of N A T O

The military security of Western Europe is likely to depend for as far as I can foresee on America's commitment to collective defence through N A T O. Anything which weakened that commitment, or even seemed likely to weaken it, would be disastrous.

Mr Denis Healey, British Minister of Defence, after the Czechoslovakia crisis in 1968.

The American commitment to defend Western Europe started during the 1939–45 war and has not wavered since, although from time to time the American administration and people have felt that the Europeans might help more in their own defence. Even so, this commitment has been reaffirmed by all presidents of the United States since the end of the war and was repeated by President Nixon in forthright terms before and after he took power. Despite periodical criticisms of American high-handedness, almost every member of the Alliance has been anxious that the American commitment should remain, since only the Americans have the nuclear forces which can successfully neutralize the power of the Soviet Union.

Only the French have challenged the value of the Alliance, for two main and related reasons. First, the military organization – N A T O – is completely dominated by the 'Anglo-Saxons', which means that Europe's defence is in American hands right down to tactical nuclear level; and secondly, membership of an integrated alliance of this sort leaves no room for the pursuit of independent foreign policies. To be an integrated member of N A T O was to be a protected state moving in the American orbit. For the French, it meant being hosts to N A T O, with all its commands, infrastructure, and considerable bureaucracy permanently installed on French soil.

The decision either to break the American monopoly of

NATO or to withdraw from the military commands while retaining the ultimate protection afforded by the Alliance was taken by General de Gaulle before he came to power. Soon after he assumed command in 1958, he sent the famous memorandum to President Eisenhower asking for equal status with the USA and Britain, since France was by then a nuclear power of sorts: the Alliance, and particularly overall strategy, should be run by a directorate of the three nuclear powers. When the Americans were not even prepared to discuss the matter – and the British were not keen on the idea either – the General found his alibi for leaving the military structure of the Alliance, which he did in April 1966. In fact, he is on record as saying that he put the proposal forward in the certain knowledge that it would be turned down.

Withdrawing from the commands of NATO entailed concluding a bilateral pact with West Germany covering the status of French troops in Germany and agreements renewable each year allowing NATO air forces to use French air-space. It made advance planning that much more difficult for NATO, particularly in view of the political decisions involved in the use of nuclear weapons even at tactical level. Plans had to be drawn up either to include the French or to exclude them. The French argued that there was no need for conventional forces to be integrated in the NATO fashion because the chances of a conventional war being fought in Europe were virtually nil. On the other hand – and this was the strength of de Gaulle's argument in 1958 – they agreed that integration at strategic level was essential in view of the need for joint targeting of nuclear weapons. In other words, joint nuclear strategy should be in the hands of the 'nuclear club', which France unsuccessfully applied to join.

Since the events of 1968 in Czechoslovakia, however, there has been an increasing willingness in France to work more closely with NATO, although still not within it. In the late summer of 1968 the aircraft carrier Foch, which is not normally in the Mediterranean, and several other powerful units of the French Navy took part in combined exercises with NATO forces in that sea. French naval units also take part in the monthly exercises of Marairmed, which keeps a watch on the Soviet fleet.

In fact, not all military leaders in France agreed with the General's contention that integration is not necessary for conventional defence. They argued that the speed and mobility of modern weapons made integration that much more necessary and a high degree of it must be accepted in advance in peacetime for maximum efficiency. They accused the General of having failed to grasp the magnitude of defence problems in an age when there are enough A- and H-bombs to wipe out Western civilization several times over.

They pointed out, as do the NATO commanders, that the activation of a successful conventional defence operation in Central Europe could be a matter, not of hours or minutes, but of split seconds. And, since there is no certainty that conventional warfare will not escalate to nuclear warfare, certain decisions concerning the eventual use of tactical nuclear weapons must be taken in advance and applied instantly in a given set of circumstances. This requires highly integrated advance planning of a kind that cannot possibly be provided by prior consultation under articles of treaties.

So much has been admitted by the Americans, the British, and the Germans, and advance nuclear planning at tactical level takes place between them. But it is necessarily incomplete without the French whose two divisions in West Germany (plus one independent brigade in Berlin) have no nuclear weapons of their own and could be virtually useless without peacetime training in their use.

France's position in the North Atlantic Alliance was thus seen to be ambiguous – a sort of military Nicene creed: of the same substance but not the substance – quite apart from the fact that she is building up a powerful force of ICBMs of her own, whose future role is uncertain. If it is integrated in the NATO nuclear deterrent, it will be on French terms which obviously include France's joining the NATO nuclear club. If it is not so integrated, it is presumably intended to be used independently although in what circumstances it is difficult to see, since, unlike the USA, France does not possess an assured destruction capability, which means that she cannot inflict *unacceptable* damage on an enemy once she herself is attacked either by direct aggression or by retaliatory action. Nor, *a fortiori*, does she possess first-strike capability, which means the ability of the attacker to destroy its victim's retaliatory power.

In the pre-Czechoslovakia days when France's membership of NATO was little more than nominal, General Ailleret, French Chief of Staff at the time (subsequently killed in an air crash), produced under de Gaulle's general guidance a defence concept known as *défense tous azimuths* (defence against all comers). This assumed that in certain extreme circumstances – although examples were never clearly spelt out – France might be called upon to fight a war independently of the other Western powers, in which case her nuclear capability should be stepped up and developed into a nuclear *force de frappe* (strike force) of sufficient destructive power to provide a plausible deterrent. The concept was a military fantasy, since it assumed imaginary nuclear opponents and neglected the real one – Soviet Russia. After the events in Czechoslovakia, it was quietly dropped by General Fourquet and France's defence strategy was again orientated towards the hypothetical threat of a Soviet attack against Western Europe. A *rapprochement* with NATO therefore followed – even before de Gaulle resigned – and in military logic these closer ties should lead to full reintegration. But whether this takes place or not depends on the extent to which the French wish to continue de Gaulle's policy of seeking a political détente with the Soviet Union and Eastern Europe. If they do, then they will wish to retain at least a semblance of independence from NATO.

Meanwhile, the destructive power of France's nuclear *force de frappe* is imposing if taken in isolation and will become more so when ICBMs are added to it. In 1969 it consisted of fifty-odd Mirage IV A medium-range bombers armed with eighty-kiloton A-bombs adapted for low-level penetration. In due course, and despite some drastic defence cuts in the French budget after the May–June 1968 troubles, it will be equipped with H-bombs, the first of which was exploded by the French in August 1968. By 1970–71, a brigade of about 27 IRBMs is expected to be in service and four fleet ballistic-missile submarines (FBMs) are scheduled to become operational by 1970–72. These are Polaris-type submarines firing sixteen plutonium-blended A-bomb rockets each with an explosive power of 500 kilotons.

In a NATO context, of course, all this is overkill, but it does make France a junior nuclear power with Britain. If France's nuclear armoury is to be pooled with anybody's, it can only be with that of the United Kingdom, as part of Europe's own nuclear deterrent. The General was thinking on these lines in 1962 immediately before he vetoed Britain's first application to join the Common Market. But Mr Harold Macmillan, British Premier at the time, was doing the reverse and went off to Nassau, in the Bahamas, to conclude the Polaris missile agreement with President Kennedy.

But clearly, if there is to be a European defence grouping within NATO on the lines suggested by the British Defence Secretary, or a European defence organization as part of a new concert of Europe, Britain and France must sooner or later come together on defence and therefore on the nuclear question.

Either course raises fundamental issues concerning the future of the Alliance. Up to the time President Nixon took over, the Alliance, as de Gaulle was never tired of pointing out, was American-dominated and inspired. The Americans themselves now doubt the wisdom of being the dictators of policy in an alliance of fifteen nations. Under Presidents Truman, Eisenhower, Kennedy, and Johnson, the Alliance moved completely in the American orbit. This was inevitable in the early years when all the power was concentrated in Washington. And even President Kennedy did not find it necessary to consult his European allies on the Cuban missile crisis. They were merely told, after the event, what it was all about. Under President Johnson, equally, the Alliance was an American preserve, although overshadowed by the war in Vietnam.

President Nixon, however, has made a point of associating the European members far more closely with the major decisions, and consultation *before* diplomatic action has been taken by Washington has been on a broader scale than it ever was before. He pointed out to the British, in particular, that the strengthening of Europe's role in the Alliance would not lead to a relaxation of America's own efforts to sustain and promote the Alliance.

There are several factors, however, pointing to a gradual shifting of the centre of gravity in the Alliance away from the American continent and towards Europe. First, there is no guarantee, despite President Nixon's affirmations of a continuing American interest, that the Americans will for ever be automatically committed to the defence of Europe. US governments may feel that this commitment is necessary in the foreseeable future but the American people may have different ideas. There is unmistakably a new form of isolationism growing up in America, arising very largely from disillusionment with Europe's own defensive efforts and with the moral and military support the Americans got in the war in Vietnam – which they were told was in defence of freedom and democracy – both from their allies and from the outposts of Western civilization (Australia, New Zealand, and Hong Kong). This has led to constant demands that American troops should be withdrawn from Europe and these demands have the powerful backing of Senator Mike Mansfield. They have been easily resisted so far by successive US governments, and the events in Czechoslovakia obviously helped the Nixon administration to resist them. But the demands will not diminish with the years. Furthermore, the fact that for some years now the USA has been within full range of Soviet nuclear missiles is bound to make the Pentagon and any American president that much more cautious in deciding on military action in Europe which might unleash a full-scale nuclear attack on the USA. There might be a tendency to play down some localized aggression on the borders of NATO territory in Europe, 5,000 miles away, which, if not resisted, might lead to further encroachments. What may appear alarming to nations with a potential battle-field next door, may appear less so to an observer in the Middle West or on the Pacific Coast of America where there is a tendency, in any case, to let the Europeans, 'with their petty squabbles', stew in their own juice.

Furthermore, neither the French nor the Germans accept, without reservation, the doctrine of flexible response introduced by the Americans (after the USA in 1959 came within full range of the Soviet ICBMs) as a substitute for the massive retaliation of the John Foster Dulles era. They argue, like General Sir John Hackett, former NATO Northern Army Group Commander, that before a decision had been taken on whether the response should be nuclear or not, Soviet troops would be sitting on the banks of the Rhine, with the whole of Western Germany becoming occupied territory overnight and France threatened with instant invasion.

Military experts in both countries challenge the British Defence Secretary's assertion in the House of Commons on 4 March 1969 that the current level of conventional weapons, even improved by the measures taken jointly to increase their capability after the Czech crisis, are 'reasonable' and 'entirely adequate to deter, or suppress, without the use of nuclear weapons, anything short of a deliberate major attack'. On the other hand, they do accept unquestionably Mr Healey's other assertion that 'it is quite impossible to get away from the need for nuclear escalation inside NATO in case of a large-scale attack without having an enormous increase in conventional forces and without this country (Great Britain) reintroducing conscription'.

Opponents of flexible response argue that reliance on nuclear weapons to retrieve a deteriorating conventional battle means getting the worst of both worlds and will inevitably produce the major confrontation which it is the aim of the Alliance to avoid. The answer is either to attempt to match the conventional forces of the enemy in manpower and weaponry (which few governments are prepared to recommend) or to leave the enemy in no doubt whatsoever that any violation of NATO territory on a scale that would get Soviet troops to the Rhine within twenty-four hours would be met with immediate and massive nuclear retaliation. Neither the Germans nor the French want the decision whether or not to resort to nuclear weapons, tactical or otherwise, to be left solely to the Americans. Hence France's decision to develop ICBMs with a thermonuclear warhead just in case Fortress America becomes a reality some time in the future.

Nobody in Europe is asserting, at this stage, that the Americans might one day consider Europe expendable in an emergency. But the suggestion is not as fanciful as it sounds, particularly if the storm clouds gather in Europe at a time when there are no American troops directly involved. Hence the need for the Europeans themselves to shoulder a larger part of their own defence. If Britain, France, and Germany claim the right to direct the course of future battles in Europe, they must be prepared to supply a larger share of the manpower and weapons. This is the key long-term problem because, when the Vietnam war is phased out, the call for American troop reductions in Europe will gather strength, particularly following the unilateral phased reduction of Canadian forces in Europe (about 10,000 men and six squadrons of aircraft) announced in April 1969. If there are American troop withdrawals of any size, they must be replaced, since it is orthodox NATO doctrine that it does not make troop reductions of substance unless they are matched on the other side (the Canadian withdrawal did not come into this category).

If American troops have to be replaced in the foreseeable future, the replacements can only come from Germany. The British and French economies are far too shaky to support increased defence budgets. Indeed, the emphasis in both countries is on pegging or even reducing military expenditure. Only West Germany's economy is in a position to sustain a sizeable increase. On strictly military and economic grounds, this would be welcome to all members of the Alliance since it would have a healthy effect on an over-buoyant economy suffering from persistent trade surpluses and an embarrassing strength of the mark. It would also give the Germans a greater stake in defending their own territory, which is the cockpit of NATO defence in Europe.

But it would raise grave political issues. All former victims of Nazi aggression would be legitimately apprehensive at the sight of West Germany becoming the pacemaker in re-armament beyond the levels already achieved. The search for a détente with the Eastern bloc could not be based on the further re-arming of Germany. Germany has, therefore, become the key problem in a political détente with Russia. The other major problems are the Middle East and the Balkans. In the Middle East the Russians have limited their support of the Arabs to diplomatic action in the United Nations and to the supplying of war material and technical assistance, with the Soviet fleet in the Eastern Mediterranean lending moral support – all of which suggests that a Yalta-type understanding is being preserved with the USA in that area.

In the Balkans, however, a traditional battle-ground for revolt and subversion, the Russians may feel it necessary to intervene, as in Czechoslovakia, to prevent a local conflict from spreading to their own ring of satellites. The situation in the so-called Communist commonwealth in Europe may have stabilized itself temporarily after the Czech affair but discontent and disaffection simmer under the surface in Romania, Bulgaria, Poland, Hungary, Czechoslovakia, and East Germany. Yugoslavia, as a successful challenger of Soviet authority in the days of Stalin, and a constant source of contamination, could one day be on the list for further corrective measures.

Here again the Yalta understanding on spheres of influence seems to have worked in the case of Czechoslovakia, as it did in the case of the Soviet missile bases in Cuba. There was no disposition in Washington to prevent the Kremlin from dealing a sharp blow at a wayward satellite in order to maintain the status quo. Assurances were given by Moscow that no aggression was intended – at least as a follow-up to the events in Czechoslovakia – against either Romania or Yugoslavia. And this was accepted by the State Department, and eventually by London, Paris, and Bonn.

In fact, little progress will be made by way of a détente with Russia if the West harbours thoughts of breaking up the *cordon sanitaire* of buffer states which provide political and territorial, although problematical military, protection against a rebirth of pan-Germanism. These states are to be kept firmly in the Soviet political camp. Marxist–Leninist socialism is official doctrine in all of them. It is held up as the only effective defence against the corruptive influences of capitalism and 'reactionary' régimes which could be the vehicle for the rebirth of German militarism and 'revanchism', the defence against which is almost an obsession in Moscow, after three major onslaughts from the West in just over a century. If the satellites are to have Soviet socialism imposed on them, it is for the good of the Socialist cause. Russia's right to intervene to protect the integrity of the Socialist world was reaffirmed in what has come to be known as the 'Brezhnev doctrine'.

At the Polish Communist Party's Congress in Warsaw in November 1968 Mr Leonid Brezhnev, the Soviet Communist Party Secretary, warned:

When internal and external forces hostile to Socialism try to turn the development of any socialist country in the direction of a restoration of the capitalist order, when a threat arises to the cause of Socialism in that country and a threat to the security of the socialist community as a whole, that becomes not only a problem for the people of the country in question, but also a general problem – the concern of all socialist countries.

This text was produced after the events in Czechoslovakia and, in a sense, to justify them. But it can be used to justify further interventions.

The question of whether, and in what circumstances, NATO should extend its shield to cover countries like Yugoslavia and Romania was studied at length at the Ministerial Council meeting in November 1968. But, understandably, no decisions were reached. The case of Romania is a doubtful one because she is still a member of the Warsaw Pact and one of the buffer states. Yugoslavia is neither. She has asserted often enough that she intends to maintain her independence, come what may. But these are necessary political assertions. It does not follow that she would not accept Western aid to maintain that independence. But, if NATO is to provide aid in an emergency, it must be planned in advance. At some stage of the battle, it might be necessary for NATO forces themselves to be thrown in, with the grave consequences that that would entail.

Advance planning of this sort requires important political decisions concerning the level of regular and reserve forces and increased military expenditure. It is one of the tasks well suited to the Special Planning Group set up to consider 'specifically and continually' the longer-range problems faced by the Alliance. But the longer-range problems are not confined to Europe. However unpredictable Russia's immediate intentions may be in Europe or elsewhere, the long-term objectives emerge clearly from the massive build-up of armed forces to serve a global strategy. Sir Alec Douglas-Home has called it 'creeping expansion round the flanks of the free world'. The Committee on the Armed Forces of the US Congress was even more explicit. In a report it said:

Behind the new Soviet sea-power is an awareness that Communist domination of the globe can only be achieved by supremacy at all major points in the spectrum of conflict. The leadership of the USSR is determined to obtain superiority over the United States and its allies under all combat conditions.

American intelligence reports suggested early in 1969 that Soviet Russia might be aiming at first strike capability by going ahead with the most ambitious programme of ICBMs yet attempted by either of the super-powers with weapons capable of carrying a twenty-five-megaton nuclear warhead or several independently targeted warheads each of several megatons. These reports were used as justification for President Nixon's decision to go ahead with the 'safeguard' anti-ballistic missile defence system.

Whether the Soviet Union's long-term strategy is to outstrip the Western world's defences at all points of the compass may be open to doubt, but there is no doubting that Soviet seapower is being marshalled in support of a forward strategy in northern Europe and in the Mediterranean. The Soviet Baltic fleet increases yearly and is clearly intended to bring pressure to bear on the Scandinavians and particularly the Norwegians and Danes who are members of NATO. The Danes have for years been in two minds about the military protection afforded by the Alliance and the Norwegians have been worried about how effectively they would be defended against Soviet encroachments on their northern frontiers. The Greeks and the Turks are similarly open to pressures of this sort. If American influence within the Alliance tends to diminish because more of the burden of defence in Europe falls on the Europeans, and the French continue to play a lone game, the Alliance could rapidly disintegrate. It could disintegrate, too, if attempts to reach a political settlement between the Western powers and the Soviet bloc in Europe revealed sharply divergent viewpoints in the capitals of the West.

Although the North Atlantic Treaty (Articles 1 and 2) calls for political and economic co-operation between members and between the Alliance and third parties, the organization has never been used as a forum for discussing a political settlement with the Eastern bloc. In fact its political uses have been constantly played down – certainly until the Harmel plan tried to revive them. In the last resort, therefore, the Alliance will survive or collapse if a majority of its members consider on balance that there is or is not a military advantage in keeping it alive.

If the European grouping within NATO gains acceptance it may well involve amending the North Atlantic Treaty or even replacing it by a mutual defence pact between Western Europe and the USA. This would retain the American commitment and at the same time reduce the strong American influence at all echelons of planning and administration which some countries have found overbearing.

But a European defence grouping, which must of necessity be highly integrated, could not be set up except within the framework of a politically united Europe and this in turn presupposes the existence of an organization at the summit which can direct the political and economic future of Europe and its defence policies.

Few now deny the need for unity. The problem is what institutions are best suited to achieving that unity.

11 The Political Organization of Europe

The starting point for any discussion on the political future of Europe is that the Treaty of Rome makes no provision for the political integration of Europe. Integration is implied, since few economic policies are devoid of political content, but nowhere is it mentioned specifically. The founding fathers certainly intended the Community to be the first step towards the political unification of Europe, indeed, towards a federal united states of Europe in the truest sense. But not all countries have interpreted the Treaty in that light. De Gaulle certainly did not and the only party in Britain which has is the Liberal Party.

The Labour Party is in two minds about what it accepts in the Treaty of Rome. Some favour complete European integration along with the Liberals. Others, including Mr Harold Wilson, accept the Community as an *economic* entity but not as a developing *political* entity with supranational characteristics. Answering a question in the House of Commons, the Prime Minister said categorically that the Government did not and 'do not support any federal or supranational structure' for Britain's relations with Europe.

He later repeated this view at a Guildhall banquet in July 1969, emphasizing that Britain accepted only what was in the Treaty of Rome although he was presumably aware that the Treaty itself carries a degree of supranationalism in the shape of majority voting in the Council of Ministers.

During the Hague Congress of European parliamentarians in November 1968, Mr Edward Heath, the Conservative Party Leader, opposed the creation of supranational organizations beyond those already existing in the EEC and by implication accepted de Gaulle's version of the limited powers that could be exercised by the Commission after the period of transition had ended in December 1969. He warned that Europe could not be built without France, just as it could not be built without Britain. Governments together could handle political and defence questions, military procurements, and trading arrangements.

Equally, during the debate in the House of Commons on the first application to join in 1961, Mr Harold Macmillan and Sir Lionel Heald, Attorney-General at that time, fairly expressed Conservative policy when they insisted that Britain was joining for economic reasons only and that no political commitment was intended, or required, since the Treaty of Rome made no mention of political unification. It is ironical that Labour reversed the positions on this point when Mr Harold Wilson asserted that the arguments for joining on economic grounds 'were strong though arguable' but that on political grounds 'they were very strong indeed and unarguable'.

Be that as it may, neither Labour nor the Conservatives foresee the development of the Community on supranational lines. Like the French in the days of de Gaulle, they want to keep political affairs firmly in the hands of sovereign governments. From this it follows that since financial, commercial, and social affairs all have a high political content, they too are proper subjects for treatment at governmental level. Yet well these subjects come, within the jurisdiction of the Community and are referred to specifically in the Treaty of Rome (Titles II and III).

The argument therefore revolves round whether the Community is to develop on the lines originally intended, i.e. towards supranationalism and federalism, or whether it is to be a grouping of independent states co-operating at governmental level. The political battles of the next decade will be fought on this issue.

In Britain there has been much loose thinking on this point. The Britain-in-Europe movement, which has a large following drawn from many walks of life, has campaigned long and hard in favour of the European idea and supranationality. But few of those who support the movement, and indeed few of those who lead it, have explained in precise terms what they mean by supranationality and what fields it is expected to cover.

In its annual report for 1968 the movement stated that foreign affairs, defence, technology, and currency were subjects which fell 'outside the jurisdiction of EEC'. This is not entirely accurate. Technology has been dealt with at length by the Community and in its 1968 report the Commission complained that progress in this field had been held up for a year. Currency is nothing if not a monetary matter, and it is covered specifically in the Treaty of Rome under Title II (economic policy), so much so that a Consultative Monetary Committee was established under Article 105 and given the tasks of keeping under review the 'monetary and financial situation and also the general payments system of member-states'.

Since the Liberal Party is not likely to be in power for some time, it falls to the Conservatives and Labour to take a close look at their own European policies in the light of possible British membership in the early 1970s. And if Britain joins, she may well be followed by Norway, Denmark, and Eire, who applied with her, and one or two others.

What sort of powers will the Community have then? This concerns particularly the Commission since under the Treaty it assumes progressively more importance as the principle of supranationality is more firmly established. In the eyes of the federalists it is to become the virtual government of Europe. If the development of the Community is to be away from federalism and towards a confederation of states – de Gaulle's *Europe des états* – then the growth of the Commission as a supranational organization will be arrested.

In a Community of ten or more power will edge away from the Paris–Bonn axis and towards a quadrumvirate of Britain, France, Germany, and Italy (again a Gaullist concept). The future of the Community will therefore be determined by these four powers. On the evidence, none of them is likely to become committed to a federated united states of Europe on the lines suggested by M. Monnet's Action Committee.

In Italy the major political parties (excluding Communists and right-wing MSI – Movimento Sociale Italiano) have had leanings towards federalism but are not likely to oppose the views of the other three when finally crystallized. In France the idea of federation has made headway among the parties of the Left and Centre, but the Right, and particularly the Gaullist rump, have not in any way committed themselves, nor have the Communists. Only the Benelux countries are firm federalists.

In Germany the two major parties – the Christian Democrats and the Social Democrats – are both committed to European unity through the Community but have kept their options open on the methods by which it is to be achieved. Neither party has been called upon to define in precise terms its views on political unity in a Community context because Gaullist policies made it unnecessary for them to do so.

But in the battles between the General and the Commission on the supranationality issue, the Germans were on the side of the General. They never pushed their opposition to French policies to the point where the net effect would be to strengthen the Commission's position in relation to the Council of Ministers. They were, in fact, quite happy to see the Commission's wings clipped and to allow the General to do the clipping.

This is not to say that the Germans, as a nation, still hanker after power in Europe, but by the nature of things no government in Bonn, or indeed elsewhere, would readily pass up the leadership of Europe if it fell into their lap. The governments of Adenauer, Erhard, and Kiesinger played a skilful waiting game during the years of Gaullist pre-eminence, carefully avoiding driving the General out of the Common Market when he reminded his E E C partners that 'France had lived before without the Common Market and could live without it again'.

They stood by while the balance of power in the Paris–Bonn axis gradually shifted towards the Rhine, ready to don the General's mantle when it was finally cast off. This explains why they were not prepared to break with him over the enlargement issue, since with Britain in the Common Market the Paris–Bonn axis would have become a Paris–Bonn–London triangle with the centre of gravity possibly moving towards London even before the General left the scene.

No government can be blamed for asserting political power through economic strength. Indeed, this is what politics is all about. The Bonn Government of 1961 did not find it necessary to consult its Common Market partners when it unilaterally re-valued the D-mark. Again, in November 1968 and May 1969, internal considerations took clear precedence over international co-operation in the monetary field when the logical step would have been quietly to upvalue the D-mark. Beyond all doubt the currency was undervalued and was acting like a magnet to hot money – poured into Germany in vast quantities by speculators gambling on revaluation – much of which had to be sent back to the country of origin under recycling or swap arrangements, which merely meant that other central banks incurred further short-term debts.

To give the Germans their due, opinion was keenly divided on this issue. Many bankers, economists, and politicians were in favour of revaluation as the best means of curbing inflation at home and of making a minimum contribution to international monetary stability. They included the Economics Minister, Professor Schiller, and the President of the Bundesbank, Dr Blessing.

Both argued that Germany could not go on indefinitely accumulating vast foreign-trade surpluses without causing a fundamental imbalance in world trade and monetary movements. If other nations, fighting hard to redress their own balances, were prevented from doing so by constant German surpluses, the imbalance would become permanent and something would explode.

They were vindicated when the Kiesinger Government indirectly admitted that the D-mark was undervalued by clamping a levy on exports and a rebate on imports. Those who argued against revaluation – at least at that moment in time – did so mainly on political grounds. It would be highly unpopular with the German farmers because under Common Market regulations they would receive less for their produce and this would be disastrous in an election year for any political party which recommended it.

They used a variety of plausible arguments. Why should the Germans, the only people who had managed to run their affairs properly, be punished for other people's mistakes? The medicine was being given to the wrong patient. It was no fault of the Germans if the French, the British, and the Americans were in economic difficulties. The Americans were in trouble largely because of the Vietnam war; the British because they were living beyond their means; and the French because of the 1968 riots and near-collapse of the economy.

This made a lot of sense to a nation haunted with memories of previous inflationary crises – and not without reason if one looks back on the catastrophic financial position of the Weimar Republic immediately after the First World War. When revaluation finally came in October 1969, the German Government stood firm on the question of adequate compensation for German farmers, so minimizing the political repercussions.

The upshot of the monetary crises of 1968–9 was that, come what may, the Germans would defend their own national interests to the hilt even if it meant rocking the international boat to the point where it might sink. There is nothing unusual in this and the world will have to live with this reassertion of power on a world scale. But it does lend weight to the argument that there is little to be lost by the other Western powers maintaining a minimum solidarity between themselves on political and economic issues.

The problem will not resolve itself because the German economy is not likely, within the foreseeable future, to lose its strength in relation to the other economies of the West (although it may well drop behind the American and Japanese economies).

So, whichever way one looks at the future of Europe, Germany becomes the key problem. Her re-emergence as the most powerful state in Western Europe is already giving rise to misgivings about the course she may ultimately pursue. The old fears of hegemony and pan-Germanism are reappearing on the surface here and there, although the Germans themselves may rightly protest their innocence of all attempts at domination.

Europe's institutions must be strong enough to absorb the shocks and strains of Germany's reassertion of power – not perhaps consciously wielded in an aggressive Hitlerian fashion, but underpinning the overall German attitude to European and world affairs. The question, therefore, is whether the Community's framework and institutions are suited, or could be adapted, to this task.

From 1970 on, at the end of the transitional period, the Community's future must in any case be mapped out. The position then will be that the Commission will be more powerful than the Council of Ministers despite the powers of veto – which are in any case limited – enjoyed by the Council under the Treaty of Rome. This is because the Treaty gives the Commission the powers of initiative and effective government, and guarantees its independence. It has the specific task of implementing all Community decisions, of formulating Community policy, and of carrying it out. It is required to work out the remaining common policies for trade and transport and of co-ordinating the policies of individual governments in all economic and financial matters.

In theory all its proposals which are not subject to the veto can be passed by majority voting in the Council and this covers major fields of activity such as agriculture, transport, external-trade policies, and free movement of capital.

The element of supranationality is explicit – and historic. Never before have European nations agreed to a partial merger of sovereignty of this magnitude. But the system has its critics. The wisdom of granting the Commission such vast powers has been challenged. With the transitional period over, the Commission assumes its full stature – that of a governmental overlord of the Six and the government in embryo of a federal united states of Europe. But it is not subject to any effective democratic control and, as we have seen, the Council of Ministers could rapidly become a rubber stamp. The Commission is virtually irremovable. The Council of Ministers cannot remove it and the chances of the Parliament doing so are extremely remote.

The method of appointing its members is discretionary except that their qualifications for the job must satisfy the individual governments. The Treaty requires it to report yearly to the Assembly and to answer questions put to it by members in writing or orally. The Commission itself made a proposal in 1965 to give the European Parliament power to control the use of the revenues accruing from the agricultural levies, which under the Treaty must go into the European Agricultural Guidance and Guarantee Fund. But, as with the majority voting issue, it came up against the firm opposition of the French who were in no mood to agree to the exercise of supranational powers by a body deprived of the normal ability to legislate in the first place.

The functions of the Parliament, even after the transitional period, are purely deliberative and consultative (except for the remote dismissal power mentioned above). Even its composition does not entitle it to speak as a truly representative organ of the people since its members are only indirectly elected and then on an arbitrary basis which varies from country to country and which had until 1968 the effect of debarring any representation of the Communists who are particularly strong in France and Italy. (And yet ironically there was one representative of the small Movimento Sociale Italiano with its neo-Fascist background.)

The Commission, however, did not come out unscathed from its showdown with the French in 1965. On paper none of its powers was impaired and the principle of majority voting by the Council of Ministers was formally retained since to renounce it would have been to deny the Treaty. But in practice, a gentlemen's agreement exists whereby the Council does not insist on resorting to majority voting on proposals which any government considers against its vital national interests. The Commission also agreed that there would be better liaison and prior consultation with governments before it put far-reaching proposals to the Council.

But these adjustments, significant as they are, were agreed in order to get the French back into the day-to-day life of the Community. They still do not alter the fact that the Commission is by any standards one of the most powerful political and economic bodies in the world and that it is not subject to effective control by an elected body of any sort. Its battles are constantly fought with the Council, which acts as a legislature of sorts – in the sense that it sanctions measures submitted to it by the Commission.

Few governments, if any, of an enlarged Community – or even of the Six for that matter – will be prepared to see themselves playing such a junior role in the affairs of Europe when in fact they are responsible to the peoples and parliaments which have put them in office. Nor is the Commission an emanation of a political majority or of a coalition or alliance between parties.

The idealism of the founding fathers gave it these vast powers by design. They were intended to thwart the ambitions of individual nations and to prevent the resurgence of nationalisms which had brought ruin and misery to generations of Europeans. Had they not existed, the Community would not have travelled as far as it has, particularly since de Gaulle came to power just after the EEC's official birth. But what was necessary in birth and childhood may not be necessary afterwards. Indeed, it may be an obstacle to further progress. This progress must be charted from 1970 on, whether the Community is enlarged or not.

There are roughly two courses open: federation or confederation. Both have their attractions and their devotees.

Federation can take many forms as it has done in history. All modern examples of federation – the USA, Australia, South Africa, the old Austro-Hungarian Empire, and the German Reich of 1871–1918 differ in some degree, and even the USSR is a federation of sorts. But all have one feature in common – a general government with overriding powers in certain specified spheres, generally taxation, foreign affairs, and defence – the last two of which may involve treaty-making. If one takes this formula as the point of departure for the unification of Europe the first question which arises is how the general or federal government shall be constituted and what shall be its powers.

Is it to be constituted on American lines with a president and congress elected directly and independently by the people and a supreme court whose powers are even above those of the president and both houses of congress? Suitable political conditions exist in the USA for such a system – two major parties, a common language, and similar cultures.

In Europe few of these conditions exist – at least at present. There is no common language – although English could become one – and certainly no common culture. Indeed, in Belgium language, race, and religion are major obstacles to the unity of a pocket-size country with a population of under 10 millions.

If the federal government is to be elected directly by the people, there must be a federal parliament, preferably with an upper and lower chamber, also elected by the people. The multiplicity of parties, over thirty in Community countries many of which represent sectarian interests, would provide an uncertain foundation for a federal government elected in such conditions. Yet the head of such a government would be in effect the head of the

European state just as the presidents of the USA and France are head of state and head of government. Or the function of head of state could be separated from those of head of government with more or less honorific powers, in which case the head could be elected by the two houses of parliament assuming that parliament is bicameral.

If the European head of state is elected by the federal parliament, why not the federal government? But if the federal government is elected in this way, should its members also belong to the federal parliament? If this is a requirement, an extensive regrouping and reduction of political parties would be needed, otherwise the federal parliament might find itself without the right type of candidate for supreme power.

This would certainly force a new dimension on politics in each country and require a considerable educative effort. In such a system the Council of Ministers of the Communities would become redundant and the Commission would assume the role of a European civil service. The European Parliament, however, could be the starting point for a federal parliament. In working out a federal constitution for Europe much thought would have to be given to the definition and balancing of powers between each institution.

The alternative to federation, but still a step towards greater unity, is confederation. In history the frontiers between the two have often been blurred. But in the accepted sense today each member would retain sovereign power in all fields, and what unity of aims and methods was achieved would be by co-operation at governmental level – a system not far removed from de Gaulle's *Europe des états*, which in the early days was to be endowed, under the Fouchet plan, with a council of heads of state or prime ministers, a European political commission, and a European parliament. This institutionalization of Europe was to be arranged by treaty and all decisions of the council were to be unanimous, although members could abstain without invalidating decisions.

This formula was de Gaulle's answer to the federalists in the Commission and elsewhere. It was designed to restrict the powers of both the EEC Council and the Commission and indeed, in time, to substitute itself for them. Yet it would have been a step forward in the sense that some sovereignty would have been surrendered to a European body, since individual governments would have been subordinate to the new council and national parliaments to the European parliament although the latter's powers would have been deliberative only.

The plan was rejected by the other members of the Six for a variety of reasons, and despite several suggested amendments remained a dead-letter. The federalists opposed it on principle. But it had one undoubted virtue. It allowed for the admission of members other than the Six and, in the circumstances, could have become a suitable framework for an enlarged community. The Benelux countries – and M. Paul-Henri Spaak was one of its bitterest opponents – disliked it because it obviously diminished their own status within a new organization whereas under the majority voting system in the existing institutions created by the Treaty of Rome, they wielded a power far greater than their economic and political status would justify – precisely the situation which the French wished to reverse.

When the Fouchet plan was produced (1961), de Gaulle was at the height of his power and the five considered that the plan would, in fact, have consolidated France's position in Europe. Shortly afterwards, and in part as a consequence, de Gaulle and Adenauer signed the famous Treaty of Co-operation, which to a very large extent also remained a dead-letter.

Nevertheless, a confederation of European states would require appropriate institutions. The existing framework of the Western European Union (WEU) could be used and adapted. WEU was set up in 1955 to replace the old Brussels Treaty of 1948. Its purpose is to co-ordinate the defence policies of the Six and the United Kingdom and to promote the co-operation of these nations in legal, political, cultural, and social affairs. It was dormant for a long time but was used as a meeting place between Britain and the Six during the years before and after de Gaulle's first veto of Britain's application to join EEC. After the second veto the British Government, with some of its sympathizers in EEC, decided to breathe new life into it and to use it as a means of maintaining contact between Britain and the EEC. The intention was to bring the French to discuss, in a non-Community context, what they refused to discuss within the Common Market, i.e., among other things, the broad spectrum of relations between Britain and her European allies.

The move was unsuccessful and the French walked out. But the treaty itself could be used and amended to include any new institutions which might be set up by agreement between the powers.

Alternatively, the Treaty of Rome could be revised and suitable alterations made to the powers and functions of its various institutions. This would have to be done in any case if unification and integration were pursued along federal lines.

But whether WEU or EEC are used as a foundation for the new Europe or whether entirely new institutions are set up, one fact remains clear. The worst solution would be for the Commission through the inertia and complacency of member-states gradually to assume the role of a European government acting under the present voting rules of the EEC which give it such wide powers and authority as a policy-maker and executant not subject to the normal democratic controls.

Its jurisdiction covers such fields as economics, finance, social policy, transport, energy, science, harmonization of laws, etc., all of which have a strong and direct bearing on foreign affairs and defence, neither of which are covered by the Treaty of Rome.

The role of the Commission is therefore central to the future of Europe, whatever the choice of constitutions. Charting a new course for Europe is the supreme test of statesmanship in an age when not only the older generations, some of whom fought two world wars, but youth in most countries are deeply convinced that unity is the only way to survival and prosperity in a world of giants.

This problem could be the occasion for some clarification of thought, not least among the political parties and in Whitehall.

12 The EEC: How it Works

The EEC's institutions are scattered through Europe: the Commission is housed in Brussels, Parliament meets in Strasbourg, and the Court of Justice in Luxembourg. This came about through the ECSC handing down some of its institutions but something was done towards assimilating the various parts when the executives of the Community, the ECSC, and Euratom were merged in July 1967.

The administrative machinery consists of the Commission, the Council, the European Parliament, and the Court of Justice, and one of its greatest weaknesses is that the Commission, the very mainspring, has no adequate independent revenue. The Commission's proposal in 1965 to appropriate for this purpose the levies payable on the import of agricultural products, helped to precipitate the 'empty-chair' crisis. France could not agree to the idea of a financially independent Commission which would be that much less subservient to the will of the Council (i.e. the national overlordship). So the Commission continues to be financed by direct contributions from the members which are in accordance with a fixed scale. France, Germany, and Italy each pay 28 per cent of the annual EEC budget, Belgium and the Netherlands 7·9 per cent each, and Luxembourg 0·2 per cent. Each year the estimates are laid before the Council, and, if approved, they go before the Parliament, which has the right to make amendments; in that case the estimates go back to the Council for reconsideration with the Commission. If no amendments are made, the budget is taken as agreed.

Although the executives of the Commission, the ECSC, and Euratom have been merged, the three Communities themselves have yet to be merged and the drafting of a consolidation treaty should be completed before July 1970. Possibly, this could be the occasion for relieving the individual member-states of the burden of their contributions; the proposal most favoured is that receipts from the common external tariff, from the agricultural import levies, and other Community incomes should be used to make the system as far as possible self-supporting. But there are many objections to these arrangements and, although a solution should be reached by the end of the transitional stage, the whole matter is in the melting-pot. Optimists think that the drawing up of the consolidation treaty could be a convenient opportunity for accession by Britain and other applicants and for amendments to the Treaties which have been found to be desirable.

Originally the ECSC, EEC, and Euratom shared only two of the Community's institutions – the European Parliament and the Court of Justice. The ECSC had its own executive body, the High Authority, and Euratom had the Euratom Committee; both had their own Councils of Ministers. However, a merger of the three executives and councils had become imperative because of the haphazard way in which responsibilities had been split. The worst example was energy, where the ECSC High Authority was responsible for coal, the Euratom Commission for nuclear power, and the EEC Commission for oil and natural gas. Until the merger of the three Communities themselves, the single Commission is implementing the provisions of the three separate treaties, so in the coal and steel sector it retains at the moment the rather broad powers of the former High Authority.

The Commission is the mainspring of the Community. It implements the Treaty of Rome by regulations which are of general application and directly binding on all nationals and by directives which are addressed to the governments of the member-states leaving them free to introduce appropriate legislation at national level to carry them out. Regulations have been used to implement the Treaty provisions in such matters as the free movement of workers, social benefits, competition, and food and drugs. Directives have been used to implement the Treaty provisions for capital movements, transport, the freedom to supply services, and the freedom of establishment (setting up of professional offices). The Commission also issues decisions binding on the parties concerned and recommendations and opinions which are not binding.

The Commission which sits in Brussels consists of fourteen members, three each from Germany, France, and Italy, two from the Netherlands and Belgium, and one from Luxembourg, but, within three years of the July 1967 merger, the number is to be reduced to nine (the number in the E E C Commission before the merger). The members of the Commission, outstanding economists also noted for their managerial abilities, are appointed by agreement among the six member-governments for a four-year renewable spell of office. The president and vice-presidents are appointed from among the members for a two-year renewable term. All the members are, and are expected to be, completely independent; they act as individuals and not as representatives and are specifically forbidden by Article 157 (2) to seek or to take instructions from any government or sectional interest.

The Commission has wide powers of initiation and the Treaty is so drawn that it is impossible for the Council of Ministers to amend the Commission's proposals unless the Council is unanimous in its decision to do so. This strong position has often excited antagonism; de Gaulle once described the Commission as 'an areopagus of technocrats without a country and responsible to no one'. But, contrary to popular belief, the 'faceless Eurocrats' of the Commission working away to determine the fate of the 184m. inhabitants of the E E C are not beyond democratic control since major and final decisions on Community policy have to be taken by the Council of Ministers. Usually when the Commission intends to implement a certain sector of the Treaty provisions, they initiate a dialogue with the Council so that they know in advance if their proposals will be likely to meet with approval and at what rate and in what manner they should go ahead. Furthermore, the Commission can be dismissed *en bloc* by a vote of no confidence from the European Parliament (one of its few real powers).

The Euro-crats numbered in June 1967 6,200 working in the various Community institutions plus some 2,500 research workers and other employees at Euratom's joint research centres. These *fonctionnaires* (civil servants) were allocated as follows:

European Parliament	514
Council of Ministers	537
EEC Commission	2,924
ECSC High Authority	885
Euratom Commission	797
Joint services (statistical, information, etc.)	479
Court of Justice	107
	6,243

Of the 6,200 some 1,700 are in the A grade (comparable to the British civil service administrative class), 1,000 in the B grade (roughly the British executive class), 2,500 in the C (secretarial and clerical), and 350 in D (manual – drivers, porters). About one in ten of all staff are translators and interpreters in the linguistic service (700).

The single Commission has separate tasks relating to the EEC and to the ECSC and Euratom. For the EEC it must complete the establishment of a general common market freed from trade restrictions of all kinds and in which all goods, services, labour, and capital move freely. It must implement common policies for agriculture, transport, and external trade and, with the Council, work towards common economic, monetary, regional, social, and labour policies which will ensure the integration of the economies of the Six.

Another important duty of the Commission is to work out means of harmonizing taxes and the laws, regulations and administrative practices governing economic activity in the Six. It has been said that progress in the EEC is like a man on a bicycle; if he stops he falls off, and experience has shown that as soon as one piece of legislation has been implemented others are automatically called for; e.g. the starting of the transport policy involved decisions on such social matters as the working hours of the drivers which in turn will entail harmonization or agreement on working hours as a whole, at least in industries where public safety is a factor.

For the ECSC the Commission is responsible for supervising the common market in coal and steel, enforcing the Paris Treaty's rules of fair competition, encouraging and co-ordinating investment and research in the coal and steel industries, promoting the redevelopment of declining coal and steel areas, and aiding workers threatened with redundancy. Under the powers inherited from the former High Authority the Commission can take decisions on many matters affecting the coal and steel industries without seeking the consent of the Council of Ministers.

Under the Euratom Treaty the Commission's task is to help create a powerful industry for the peaceful uses of atomic energy. It co-ordinates nuclear research, trains scientific staff, disseminates the results of research, and operates a supply agency for fissile materials. It inspects nuclear installations using these supplies and is responsible for protecting workers and the general public against radiation hazards.

A series of specialized committees composed of national government, Commission, and other experts advise on the initiation and implementation of the various policies. The two most important ones are the Economic and Social Committee consisting of 101 representatives (twenty-four each from France, Germany, and Italy, twelve from Belgium and the Netherlands, and five from Luxembourg) which must be consulted on major proposals in the EEC and Euratom, and the Consultative Committee of fifty-one members which advises the ECSC.

The Economic and Social Committee's members are nominated on the recommendation of the various governments for periods of four years, the present members holding office until 4 May 1970, when they are eligible for re-appointment. The method of appointment is that each state submits to the Commission a list containing twice as many names as the number of candidates to which it is entitled, the names of civic leaders from all walks of life, farmers, industrialists, trade unionists, tradesmen, transport workers, members of the professions, etc. The Commission consider the list and make their choice, but the final say rests with the Council – in this way several French Communists on the original list were excluded, hardly a democratic method of deciding on the members. However, the Economic and Social Committee, which both the Commission and Council are obliged to consult on most important matters before they issue formal decisions, fulfils a vital role in enabling these two bodies to hear the opinions and objections of the public at large. The meetings of the Committee are private and it is always available for consultation.

Specialized committees also advise on less general subjects. The Monetary Committee, consisting of government and central-bank officials and Commission experts, advises the Commission and the Council on monetary matters. The short-term and medium-term Economic Policy Committees help to co-ordinate and plan economic expansion; the first in the immediate future and the second over a five-year period. The Committee of Central Bank Governors discusses credit, the money-market, and exchange matters with a member of the Commission present, and the Budgetary Policy Committee consists of the leading officials responsible for drawing up the member-governments' budgets.

Transport problems can be referred by the Commission to the Transport Committee of national officials and experts and the Administrative Commission for the Social Security of Migrant Workers protects the interests of EEC citizens working in a member-country other than their own. It brings together national officials and representatives of the EEC. The Scientific and Technical Committee advises the Commission on nuclear problems and the Nuclear Research Consultative Committee, made up of government representatives with a chairman and secretariat provided by the Commission, deals with nuclear research.

The Council of Ministers is the only Community institution whose six members directly represent the member-governments. The choice of particular ministers of the national governments sitting in the Council depends on the subject under discussion (for example, economic affairs, agriculture, or transport but for major decisions the foreign ministers are usually present. The Council takes the final policy decisions either on its own initiative or on the basis of proposals put forward by the Commission and can amend such proposals only by unanimous vote.

In the first eight years decisions in many fields had to be unanimous, but weighted majority voting, which is a basic principle of the Rome Treaty (Article 148), became the general rule from January 1966 onwards. For weighted majority decisions France, Germany, and Italy have four votes each, Belgium and the Netherlands two each, and Luxembourg one. On Commission proposals, any twelve out of seventeen votes constitute a majority; in other cases, the twelve votes must include those of at least four countries. The purpose behind the weighted voting system was to protect the Commission against the Council, and the Benelux powers against the big three. Since, when the Council is voting under this system on a proposal submitted by the Commission, any twelve votes are sufficient, this means that any one of the big three acting singly cannot prevent the adoption of the proposal nor can the Benelux countries acting as a bloc. On the other hand, when the Council is acting independently of the Commission but still under the qualified majority rule, the essential twelve votes must include the votes of at least four powers, which means that the big three cannot gang up against the Benelux countries. The entry of Britain and of other EFTA countries would obviously throw the system with its carefully weighted checks and balances completely out of gear. A new voting formula will have to be found to preserve roughly the same equilibrium.

De Gaulle greatly disliked this system of voting which prevented any one member from dominating the others. He could not tolerate a system where a majority of four members with enough votes was sufficient to force through the adoption of policies not wanted by the remaining one or two. Following disagreement in June 1965 on proposals for financing the common agricultural policy and for strengthening the budgetary powers of the European Parliament, the French Government asked for the abandonment of weighted voting on issues which member-governments considered vital to their own interests and for a general revision of the role of the Commission. This precipitated the 'empty-chair' crisis. The other five governments could not accept France's request and so she withdrew from the major Community institutions. However, in January 1966 the Six 'agreed to disagree' on majority voting and to consider some changes in Council–Commission procedures. Full Community working was resumed with the dialogue between the Commission and the Council ensuring that the Commission knew in advance whether the Council was likely to approve its actions or not. In this way further crises could be avoided.

The Council is answerable to no one: unlike the Commission it cannot be dismissed by the European Parliament. Council proceedings are kept secret even from the European Parliament. The communiqués, issued after their deliberations, are couched in terms least likely to reveal what has gone on. European journalists complain that, though they can sometimes get a true story from their own country's minister on what he personally said, the overall picture can only be guessed at. 'The integration of Europe is being conducted under a blanket of mystery,' complained one editor.

The European Parliament has 142 members elected from and by the Parliaments of the member-countries but, ultimately, it is intended that they should be elected directly to Parliament by universal suffrage. The Parliament is the only body which can oust the Commission – on a motion of censure voted by a two-thirds majority. Sessions lasting roughly a week are held in Strasbourg about eight times a year but continuity between sessions is safeguarded by over twelve standing committees which not only prepare the debates of the European Parliament but maintain contact with the Commission and Council. The committee meetings are not open to the public (though the plenary sessions of the European Parliament are) and are usually held in one of the three towns that are the present centres of the Community's activities – Brussels, Luxembourg, and Strasbourg.

The committees are:

1. Political Affairs Committee
2. Economic Affairs Committee
3. Committee for Finance, Administration, and Accounts
4. Committee on Agriculture
5. Committee on Social Affairs and Health Protection
6. Committee on External Trade Relations.

These committees consist of twenty-nine members of the European Parliament; smaller committees consisting of seventeen members of the Parliament are

7. Legal Affairs Committee
8. Committee on Research, Energy and Atomic Problems
9. Transport Committee.

There are also committees appointed to deal specifically with associates such as

10. Committee for the Association with Greece
11. Committee for the Association with Turkey.

The fifteen members of these committees also sit on the EEC–Greece and EEC–Turkey Joint Committees. There is also a Committee on Relations with African States and Madagascar.

All these committees appoint for each problem a *rapporteur* who draws up a report setting out all the relevant considerations and conclusions reached and when the committee have adopted the report (by vote, minority opinion being recorded too) it is submitted to the House for debate and decision by vote in plenary session.

The European Parliament has not yet by any means fulfilled its intended role; the Treaties provided for direct elections, and a twenty-three article draft was adopted in plenary session on 17 May 1960 providing for the number of members to be trebled (making 426) and for their term to be extended to five years; transitional arrangements are proposed during which one third of the members would continue to be appointed by the national parliaments, thus preserving the link with the national parliaments, but ultimately all should be elected by direct vote at elections held simultaneously in all the Community countries at a time when no other elections are being held. However, this abrogation of national sovereignty was too much for de Gaulle to swallow; it definitely whittled away the powers of control of the individual governments; the draft was left on the table; it remains to be seen whether any action will be taken by the EEC now its chief opponent has gone.

Parliament's 142 members are made up from the three major member-states, the two smaller ones, and Luxembourg in the proportion 36:14:6. Each country is entitled to select its delegates in the way it wishes. France chooses twelve from the Senate and twenty-four from the National Assembly by agreement between the Centre parties; this effectively excluded small parties and the Communist deputies (10 per cent of the National Assembly). Germany chooses all thirty-six from the Bundestag by proportional representation. Italy selects eighteen from each chamber by absolute majority vote; this excluded the Communists (20 per cent of seats in the Lower Chamber), but in March 1969 seven Communists were included in the delegation from Italy, who had decided to make it truly representative for the first time. This could lead to a change in the French attitude. The Netherlands chooses four from the Upper House and ten from the lower by proportional voting; Belgium seven from each house by proportional voting; and Luxembourg six from the Lower House, nominated by the Committee for Foreign and Military Affairs.

Once in Strasbourg the members group themselves according to party allegiance; a party may not have less than fourteen members. In 1968 there were four parties in all; the sixty-five Christian Democrats, more than half being German or Italian; the thirty-five Socialists, all members of the various Social Democratic parties; twenty-six Liberals, chiefly belonging to small national parties; and sixteen members of EDU (European Democratic Union) consisting of French Gaullist supporters of the idea of the *Europe des états*, who broke away from the Liberals, and who, opposed as they are to further integration, represent the forces of retrogression. The Socialists, the Christian Democrats, and the Liberals all favour greater integration, though for differing reasons. Voting is usually along party lines, though there are no whips and party discipline varies; it is strict in the Socialist sector, because all belong to basically similar parties in their own countries; it is growing more strict among the Christian Democrats (mostly Catholics); and it is lax among the Liberals, a disparate body but committed and enthusiastic 'Europeans'.

From the viewpoint of the President, the thirty-five Socialists are grouped on the left of the semi-circle, the sixty-five Christian Democrats in the middle, the twenty-six Liberals further to the right, and on the extreme right are the sixteen members of the EDU. The party leader and his advisers sit in front and the other members sit in alphabetical order behind. The president and his eight vice-presidents are elected by secret ballot and so far the principle of fair distribution according to nationality has been kept.

Members of parliament participate in debates and can ask questions in the House and put written questions to the members of the Commission. Since representatives of the Commission and Council attend the meetings, it is possible to clarify points of difficulty on the spot and to keep the Commission on its toes. Voting is, in the first instance, by a show of hands, but if there is no obvious majority, the ayes rise and the noes remain seated. If this is not conclusive, or if demanded by at least ten members, a roll-call is taken.

Parliament's role of influencing decision-making by the Council has been assumed by the Commission. Its powers are, in effect, no more than consultative – more akin to those of a second chamber, say the House of Lords. It has, however, consistently backed up the Commission's efforts to press on with implementing the Treaty of Rome in the face of opposition from the Council where national considerations often predominate.

In any rethinking that is done the question of members of the European Parliament being directly elected will be fundamental. Many Europeans find the present system an offence to democracy. Duly elected members with the weight of the EEC poll behind them would have independence of thought and action; the present nominees have, perforce, a foot in both camps – they must keep a weather eye on those who sent them to the parliament as well as on their own standing in their respective parties at home, while tackling the broader issues of the Community itself. In any case the present system invites inefficiency. The members have far too much to do. Besides attending to their parliamentary duties at home, they have to travel to Strasbourg as many as nine times a year for meetings lasting three or four days; Committee work occupies approximately fifty days a year.

The budgetary powers of the Parliament are at the centre of a long dispute over the exact role of Parliament. In 1965 a Commission proposal that the Parliament should be given powers to control the levies on agricultural goods which accrue to the Farm Fund contributed to the seven-month crisis (from July 1965). The French Government refused to see any increase in the powers of the European Parliament. In October 1969, however, the Commission proposed giving Parliament powers to overrule the Council, if necessary, when the yearly budget is under discussion. Two stages are envisaged; from 1971-3 the Council would, in the last resort, have powers to overrule the combined Commission and Parliament in any dispute over the budget: starting in 1974 the boot would be on the other foot, with Parliament having the last word in any budget dispute with the Council.

The role of the European Community Court of Justice, which meets in Luxembourg, was foreshadowed by the Court of Justice of the ECSC, which was given extensive powers to ensure that the ECSC would not die of over-exposure to the hazards of international diplomacy; if member-states disagreed over the interpretation and application of the rules, the matter was to be submitted to the sovereign ruling of the Court of Justice, which was also given power to pronounce on any apparent infringement by member-states of their Treaty obligations. Not only member-governments but aggrieved private companies had the right to appeal to the Court against any acts of the High Authority which they considered an infringement of the Treaty or of the implementing regulations, or simply *ultra vires*.

The EEC Court of Justice inherited these powers, which were adapted to the Treaty of Rome; briefly, it rules on the application of Community law and decides whether acts of the Commission, the Council of Ministers, the member-governments, and other bodies are compatible with the Treaties. The Commission has brought about twenty cases before the Court charging a member-state with infringement of the Treaty (most concerned with the non-performance of standstill obligations or with the ban on new customs dues). The member-states have found about twelve causes for complaint against the Commission. These low figures show that, thanks to the dialogue between the Commission and the member-states, most problems are settled without recourse to the Court. But, as relations worsened between France and the Commission, both sides constantly felt the need of an umpire. When France called in question the Commission's negotiating role in the 1968-9 Yaoundé-renewal talks, M. Jean Rey, President of the Commission, quoted chapter and verse from the Rome Treaty to prove he was right and said he would ask the Court to confirm this; a compromise was reached. In February 1969 the Commission took France to court for not having abolished by the end of January 1969, as promised, the export aids (a special discount rate for exporters of 3 per cent below the current bank rate of 6 per cent) put on as part of the May–June 1968 crisis measures.

In 1969 the EEC Court of Justice had a busy time. On 20 March the Commission asked it to reopen a case against the Italian Government whose export refunds on engineering products were thought to exceed the taxes actually imposed and, on 27 March, the Commission took the Italian Government before the Court on a charge of having put a higher tax on brandy imported from other EEC countries than on the local product, in violation of Article 95 of the Rome Treaty. The Commission had asked the Italian Government to stop doing this in May 1968, but as no action had been taken it decided to submit the dispute to the Court.

In October 1969 the Commission finally decided to take France to Court over legislation introduced by the French Government in January 1967. This required all foreign companies wishing to invest in France, including EEC companies, to first ask for authorization from the French Finance Ministry. Although this was aimed at preventing back-door investment in France by US companies acting through European subsidiaries and although the French stoutly protested that genuine Community companies would never be refused permission, the Commission saw this as a direct contravention of the Treaty provisions for the free movement of capital and the right of establishment.

In October 1969 it was the turn of Germany to appear before the Court, hastily summoned on a Sunday to rule on the legality of the import taxes imposed on farm products by the German Government while the D.-mark was floating immediately after the German election. The Court found the taxes illegal but expediency forced the Council to agree to their retention pending the revaluation of the D.-mark.

The Court's judgements are directly binding on all parties

whether individuals, firms, national governments or the Community's executive body itself. The Court consists of seven judges, one of each nationality plus one extra to avoid deadlock, and two advocates-general, who are nominated by unanimous decision of the six member-governments for six-year terms of office, so arranged that every three years three or four judges and one advocate-general complete their terms of office (in practice the judges have normally been re-elected). The judges, all barristers, are recruited from a wide field of politics and industry as well as from the bar.

Access to the Court, which is permanently in session, has been made as easy as possible. Litigants plead their cases through an advocate (anyone admitted to the bar in any of the member-countries may appear) and, to avoid excessive travel by litigants, the cases are divided into a written preliminary phase and then an oral phase. At the start of a dispute the plaintiff files a brief of complaint, and the defendant answers. There are replies and rejoinders. The case having been clarified, the parties then go to the Court in Luxembourg for the oral hearing which is often completed in a single day, after which one of the advocates-general gives his conclusions, usually within two or three weeks. The conclusions are a general appreciation of the legal issues of the case, a discussion of the merits of the various points, and a pronouncement in favour of the rejection of the complaint or of its admission as being well founded.

These conclusions do not bind the Court in any way but give the judges the advantage of a well-reasoned view which they take into account in reaching their final decision which is not in the form of individual opinions by the judges but of a judgement by the whole Court (as is usual on the continent, dissenting opinions are not published). The Court attaches very great importance to the investigation of the facts in dispute and contrary to British practice, this investigation (examination of witnesses, documents, experts) is carried out by the Court not by counsel for the parties.

The Court has four main functions: to ensure judicial control of the Community institutions, and in the case of damage by them to third parties to ensure redress; to ensure that the Treaties are correctly implemented by the member-states; to co-operate with the national courts in the enforcement of the Treaties – the national courts may ask the Court for a preliminary ruling on points of interpretation, and if the national court is a 'court of last appeal' it *must* refer to the Court on points of difficulty; to amend the provisions of the Treaty provided the proposed amendments are in conformity with the general principles set out at the beginning of the Treaty.

The Court exercises judicial control by two procedures: the appeal for annulment, which asks for the quashing of illegal decisions; and the appeal to the 'full jurisdiction of the court', which permits the Court to rehear a case since in this kind of appeal it is judging the rights of the parties involved not the lawfulness of an act. In this latter role the Court may not only quash a decision but impose monetary sanctions.

The fact that the provisions of the Treaty were for the most part defined in terms only of a general programme puts upon the Court a task of interpretation that is much wider and more profound than anything the British courts are likely to encounter in the interpretation of statute law. As a result there is growing up a body of Community case law standing as authority alongside the Treaties and affording binding precedent. In one of these cases (COSTA versus ENEL, 15 July 1964) it was held that in the event of conflict between the national law of a member-state and Community law, the Community law must prevail.

Another important case was the Consten–Grundig case (1966), in which Grundig, the German electronics manufacturer, had granted to Consten exclusive rights to import and distribute its radios and tape recorders in France; the Commission had decided that the import monopoly thus created was in breach of the Rome Treaty, Article 85, and that these agreements were prohibited altogether. The Luxembourg Court found that only certain clauses in the agreement were incompatible with the Treaty and, applying the English doctrine of severance, upheld in part an agreement which the Commission had held to be totally invalid. As these exclusive territorial agreements often go hand in hand with price-fixing, a large part of European industry – and consumers – were closely involved.

The Court's main concern is with powers, their derivation, their use and abuse – this rule of law is binding only on the member-states and does not confer rights on their citizens. However, a second class of jurisdiction creates rights and duties for citizens which the national courts are obliged to uphold or enforce – these chiefly concern social security for migrant workers, especially widows' pensions and sickness benefits. But a decision of the Court in June 1966 showed that certain articles of the Treaty may confer rights on individual subjects of member-states, rights which are enforceable, if need be, in the courts of member-states, just as if these rights had originated in the internal laws of these states themselves. The powdered-milk case showed that Article 95 does not apply only to member-states but to individual citizens. The German customs at Saarlouis had imposed on powdered milk imported from Luxembourg, in addition to customs duty, charges equivalent to the turnover tax, which had formerly been imposed in Germany on domestically produced powdered milk. The customs were challenged by A. Lütticke, and the Court ruled that the customs had no right to impose such a charge. However, appeals to the Court by private individuals are kept within strict limits and one proviso is that the decision complained of should be one affecting directly and individually the plaintiff (this rules out appeals by multifarious organizations and associations; e.g. some farmers' co-operatives who wished to challenge the validity of the common agricultural policy were non-suited on this ground).

There has grown up a body of interpretative case law which is supranational and which will continue to grow. On accession Britain would either enact the text of the Treaty as part of British law, or, since the obligations under the Treaty can only be assessed by referring to the implementing regulations, directives, and decisions, she might enact these obligations in statutory form (this is more probable).

On accession Britain would have to accept the principle of lawmaking by Community institutions and so far as future regulations and directives were concerned these would become applicable in Britain without discussion in Parliament, as they do in the Six. Britain would, of course, be contributing directly to this lawmaking as she would be represented on the Council, the Commission, in the European Parliament, and at the Court of Justice. Apart from this, the British legal system would continue untouched; criminal law, police methods, and judicial procedure would not be affected. The existence of the Court of Justice would allow British citizens a freedom at the moment denied to them, although enjoyed by Americans and by most continental Europeans – the right of appeal against an act of parliament to a constitutional court.

The European Investment Bank moved from Brussels to Luxembourg in 1968 to occupy the premises of the former High Authority of the ECSC. The Bank is controlled by a Council consisting of the six ministers of finance, which is responsible for raising the necessary funds and for ratifying the annual budget. The Bank was intended (Articles 129 to 130) to contribute to the 'balanced and smooth development of the EEC' and it does this by contributing to development projects within the EEC and in the associated countries on a non-profit making basis, lending to private borrowers as well as to national enterprises. Its loans are financed partly by capital subscribed by EEC countries and partly by the Bank's own borrowing on the capital markets.

The Council nominates a body of twenty-four administrators who deal with the day-to-day running of the Bank, such as fixing interest terms and granting credits. Under the administrators is a directorate with seven departmental committees responsible for routine work.

Normally the Bank's loans are for terms ranging from five to twenty years and interest payable is at market rates (6 to 7 per cent) although a period of grace is allowed before repayments start and in the case of loans to Africa interest may be reduced (e.g. only 3 per cent is payable on the Ivory-Coast railway loan). Normally the Bank's loans are intended to prime the pump of an approved project and represent somewhere around a quarter of total cost, the rest being raised by the country concerned.

Up to 31 December 1968 the European Investment Bank had approved loans totalling $978·4m. to help finance developments in the EEC, the associated countries – Greece and Turkey and the eighteen associated states in Africa and Madagascar (which also benefit from the European Development Fund).

Industrial projects, especially mining, have been the main beneficiaries, followed by rail and road projects and improvements in agriculture and power supplies. Italy has been a principal beneficiary, taking $524m., over half of the Bank's total lending, chiefly for the development of South Italy; and up to the end of 1967 Turkey had taken $97·6m. Greece has had loans approved of $68·9m. but, since the change of régime in April 1967, no further loans have been sanctioned.

The eighteen Yaoundé-Convention states in Africa have only been able to benefit from the Fund since 1964 when the EIB was authorized to make loans of up to $70m. By the end of 1967 loans totalling $20·9m. had been approved for industrial and agricultural projects in Cameroun, Senegal, the Ivory Coast, and Congo (Brazzaville).

The European Development Fund was established in a convention to the Rome Treaty to enable financial aid to be given to overseas countries, mostly former colonial possessions of some of the member-states. The Fund's total resources under the Yaoundé Convention which expired in May 1969, were $730m., of which $680m. were allocated as non-repayable aid with the remaining 50m. available for special low-interest loans. The first Fund (1958–64) distributed $581m. in development grants – concentrating on improving infra-structures, roads, railways, ports, and bridges – but the second Fund (1964–70), while not neglecting this, is putting more emphasis on production development, improved stock and crop raising, education and training. Up to the end of 1967 $462m. of the second Fund had been allocated involving 223 development schemes of great diversity from asphalting roads in Mali, planting coconuts in Madagascar, building port sheds in Surinam, and buying insecticides for the Central African Republic, to assisting an anti-rodent campaign in Upper Volta. The third Fund was agreed in 1969, after some undignified wrangling, at $1,000m. to be made up of $810m. in outright grants, $90m. in special loans (mostly to commodity price-stabilization funds), and $100m. in loans from the European

Investment Bank. Italy's share was agreed at $140·6m. ($100m. to the previous Fund), Germany and France were each to pay $298·5m. (as against $246·5m.), Belgium and the Netherlands each $80m. ($69m. and $66m. respectively), and Luxembourg $2·4m. ($2m.).

The European Social Fund began operations in 1960. Its function (Article 123) is to promote 'employment facilities and the geographical and occupational mobility of workers'. It provides for the retraining and re-employment within the Community of workers who have become redundant as the result of the running-down of certain industries, of changes of policy, and so on.

Between 1960 and 1968 the Social Fund paid out over $80m. to aid some 950,000 workers in industrial retraining schemes or in removal and reinstallation costs incurred on moving to new areas; this is in addition to the ECSC which provided nearly $94m. in the period 1953–68 to help finance readaptation schemes for about 300,000 EEC coal and steel workers – mostly coal-miners who had become redundant as a result of pit closures; the national governments concerned matched these grants with equal contributions. In addition the ECSC has lent $74m. to establish new industries in defunct mining areas where other-wise there would have been little chance of men finding new jobs. Holland's increasingly successful DAF car is built in factories almost entirely manned by retrained ex-mineworkers.

At the end of the transition period, i.e. 31 December 1969, the Rome Treaty stipulates that, by unanimous vote of the Council, the Social Fund can assume new tasks and the Commission, which has been trying to recast the Fund since January 1965, is absolutely sure what the main task should be – to retrain and resettle millions of workers throughout the Community who are expected to need help by initiating new programmes and anticipat-ing the need for retraining, not as at present by passively handing over retrospective grants to governments who have qualified under the Social Fund's rules.

It is estimated that one in ten workers will change his job over the next ten years as competition accelerates the demise of small outdated firms and forces mergers. The Commission, who have investigated the problem, expect that between 1969 and 1980 two million farmers aged between twenty and fifty-five will have to find jobs in towns and this figure is in line with the Mansholt Farm-plan-1980 estimate. Another hard-hit sector is the textile industry; the report submitted to the Commission in April 1969 forecast that the liberalization of the world's textile trade in the years 1969–75 would put EEC manufacturers under great pressure and cause redundancies between 1966 and 1975 of 310,000 to 330,000 workers (in 1966 1,638,000 were employed in the EEC's textile industry). Over 200,000 men may have to leave the coal industry between 1969 and 1974 but this is the responsibility at present of the ECSC. The run-down of the railways will mean many workers in the rolling-stock industries will be superfluous. Intra-EEC competition will almost certainly lead to the closing of small uneconomic factories making laminates, the less sophisticated household appliances, shoes, gloves, carded wool, electrodes, enamelled tiles, ceramics, and nuts and bolts. Surplus workers are also likely to be found in the leather, lead, zinc, and newsprint trades. While these declining sectors are discharging workers the new technologically based industries will be crying out for workers, but only for properly trained highly skilled ones. The job of the Social Fund will be to fill this need by starting the necessary training before the worker has been put out of a job, not afterwards; the Commission hope in this way to avoid much dislocation and human misery.

Until the end of the transition period (December 1969) the Social Fund was only empowered to refund half the cost of retraining and resettling workers who had already lost their jobs or were under-employed, and the aid was conditional on the worker having stayed in the new job for at least six months. Only member-states could request the aid, which in due course of time went direct to them or to the public authority involved – private undertakings were not eligible for grants.

What is proposed is that this passive role should give way to a dynamic attack on the problem before it develops into a serious threat both to the economies of the countries concerned and to the individual worker caught in the grip of a fast-moving technological revolution. The Commission want private schemes to be eligible for grants and think the scale of contribution by the Social Fund should vary according to the urgency of the project, with a basic minimum of 20 per cent of total cost being charged to the government concerned in all cases.

Up to the end of the transition period the Fund was financed on this scale: France and Germany 32 per cent each; Italy 20 per cent; Belgium 8·8 per cent; the Netherlands 7 per cent, and Luxembourg 0·2 per cent. But the Commission think that the Fund should not in future be dependent on the contributions from individual states but that it should have its own finances – at least $50m. a year to start with, rising quickly to $250m. a year. This would enable the Fund to help between 120,000 and 150,000 workers yearly at a cost of under $2,000 a worker.

The Commission rightly stress the urgency of these proposals, which they would like to see in full operation by 1 July 1970. A reformed Social Fund could prove a crucial weapon in the EEC's armoury as it would attack at one and the same time the huge problems of resettling farm-workers, thus helping to solve the nightmare of the monstrous surpluses which bedevil the common agricultural policy, the regional problems which so far have been merely scratched at, and the problem of providing the EEC's new technological industries with the high-calibre specially trained workers they must have if they are to hold their own with the giants of the USA and USSR.

Apart from this important area of retraining, social services in the EEC are still run at national and not Community level, but although no attempt has been made to impose an overall system, the EEC is working towards a gradual harmonization of the various social services since this will make easier the free movement of labour, the transfer within the EEC of social benefits, travel, and population exchange. At present the migrant workers of the EEC who have special social and welfare problems have a Consultative Committee to look after them – over 600,000 work permits are issued annually; two fifths to EEC citizens, overwhelmingly Italians, and the rest mainly to workers from Spain, Portugal, Yugoslavia, Turkey, Greece, and North Africa.

Many, among them the trade unions, think that progress towards a genuine social policy is too slow. In a note to the Council

European Social Fund's Activities 1960–68

| | Expenditure $m. | | | Receipts $m. |
	Retraining	Resettlement	Total	
Belgium	3·95	0·002	3·95	7·07
France	19·94	0·57	20·51	25·68
Germany	20·19	1·71	21·90	25·68
Italy	23·22	4·00	27·22	16·05
Luxembourg	0·01	—	0·01	0·16
Netherlands	6·65	0·02	6·67	5·62
EEC total	73·96	6·30	80·26	80·26

Number of Workers Helped

	Retraining	Resettlement	Total
Belgium	7,836	13	7,849
France	30,972	78,118	109,090
Germany	57,303	230,101	287,404
Italy	203,310	340,037	543,347
Luxembourg	96	—	96
Netherlands	11,243	229	11,472
EEC total	310,760	648,498	959,258

in 1966 the Commission said 'there is a need for a better sharing out of prosperity and for better conditions of settlement and training to ensure that the word "mobility" loses the painful overtones which it has today'. However, each member-state is now devoting a higher proportion of its national income to this end; in 1958 the percentage of national income spent on social services ranged from 13 to 18 per cent but by 1968 this had risen to a range of 17·6 to 19 per cent. Action in the social field is enjoined on the Six in the preamble to the Treaty of Rome which calls for 'economic and social progress by common action in eliminating the barriers which divide', and Articles 117 to 122 elaborate on social provisions and the fields which they should cover.

There is no blanket social-security system, such as operates in Britain, in any member-country of the Six. The main difference is ideological; Britain has established an all-embracing (cradle to the grave) system covering the entire population, whereas in the

Six misfortune or need are the basic criteria for the receipt of aid. In Britain, where the Ministry of Social Security together with the Ministries of Health and Labour directs the scheme, aid is distributed directly by the state, but on the Continent, trade- or profession-linked societies are usually responsible for the distribution of funds to their members. Funds are provided and paid out on a different basis; in Britain contributions are normally fixed and uniform for all wage- and salary-earners and benefits too are basically fixed, but in the E E C contributions tend to be proportionate to salary or wages earned and the employers' contribution is also graded, and benefits too are highly variable being calculated according to the number of contributions paid, salary or wage normally received, length of service, etc. Britain is now moving towards the Continental systems.

The health services on the Continent, unlike the British, aim at being self-financing, although only the Netherlands has achieved this. Usually health insurance is only compulsory for those earning less than the national average income, though those in upper income brackets can join voluntarily. There is no free consultation service in the E E C except in Germany and Luxembourg; the patient pays in respect of each consultation and asks for reimbursement of the whole or part from his sick fund. Only the Netherlands operates the British capitation-fee method of paying doctors. All E E C countries make prescription charges at around the British level; hospital services are mostly free but are so managed by contributory sick funds that patients have usually qualified by their contributions; in France everyone, except those with no means at all, contributes 20 per cent towards the cost of hospital treatment.

Dental services are free in the Netherlands and Germany, and Germany also runs a basic ophthalmic service, but apart from this in all other countries the patient pays at least part of the cost.

None of these schemes are run by the state; they are either under sick-fund control or run by special corporations or private organizations under national supervision.

Pensions schemes are highly variable in contributions and

benefits, and pensions tend to be well above the rates applicable in Great Britain (where national assistance comes into play to bring the basic pension up to a viable living standard), although the new national pensions scheme announced by the Wilson Government in 1968 should bring Britain into alignment. Industrial-injury schemes, too, for which all contributions are invariably paid by the employer alone, vary from trade to trade, and according to the employee's wages. Unemployment benefit is also highly variable and here the state usually supplements the contributions of employer and employee except in Luxembourg, where the state runs the scheme and guarantees to each of its citizens a minimum living standard in any case. The dole in the EEC tends to be higher than in the UK and better adapted to individual circumstances.

All EEC countries pay family allowances based on employers' contributions according to salary up to a ceiling (but there is no ceiling in Germany, which had no family allowance scheme but introduced one to fall in line with general EEC practice). Only Germany and the UK pay nothing for the first child and these two countries pay considerably less for qualifying children than the other five countries.

It is clear that faster progress on a common social policy is needed in the EEC where the movement of workers needing to take their social-security provisions with them is part and parcel of the industrial scene. Some alignment is taking place and harmonization in related fields such as statistics, and studies on the distribution of pharmaceutical products is being tackled by various specialized EEC sub-organizations.

But this is not enough. Discontent with the social services was part and parcel of the disastrous strikes in Italy in November 1969. Italian employers, like the French, pay a very high proportion of social security costs (60 per cent for Italy, compared with 40 to 45 per cent for Germany and Benelux). Since the contribution rises proportionately with any rise in wages, the employer has every incentive to resist wage increases. The worker, however, gets only, on average, about 60 per cent of the money the employer has paid (cf. over 80 per cent in Germany). So the Italian worker felt he was getting a raw deal, especially as the social services were very inadequate. He felt, with justice, that if the low-cost houses, schools, and hospitals were not forthcoming, he would be better off, fending for himself, with a heavier wage packet. The problem of the mythical social services is going to prove extremely hard to solve in Italy, where corruption is rife in high places. But in an EEC context, the difficulty could be overcome.

If Britain were to join the EEC, there should not be any insuperable difficulties in aligning the various systems as, provided the main risks were covered to an agreed level, the way in which this was achieved would probably still be the concern of each individual state, and Britain does recognize and cover the main risks accepted in the EEC. Britain would, of course, contribute to the European Social Fund and would agree to migrant workers bringing their social-benefit claims with them.

The most persistent critics of the slow evolution of the EEC social policy have been the trade unions. One complication which British trade unions are spared is the division along religious as well as political lines. Trade unions on the Continent split, broadly, into three groups according to the international organization to which they are affiliated; these are the World Federation of Trade Unions (WFTU, headquarters in Prague), to which Communist unions belong; the International Confederation of Free Trade Unions (ICFTU, headquarters in Brussels), to which unions with Social-Democrat leanings belong – the co-ordinating body of the ICFTU unions previously known as the European Community Trade Union Secretariat (ECTUS) changed its name in April 1969 to the European Union of Free Labour Federations; and thirdly, the Confédération Internationale des Syndicats Chrétiens (CISC), which to further its policy of appealing to all workers and not only to those with Christian-Democrat and Catholic leanings changed its name in 1969 to the World Federation of Labour (WCL). All three groups have set up liaison offices in Brussels to co-ordinate their policies towards the EEC and in spite of their ideological divisions, they have very similar attitudes and objectives.

So far, there has been very limited scope for collective action. The employers are not well organized and wages and fringe benefits differ widely from country to country. But, as the EEC develops as a homogeneous economic unit, the trend should be towards standard wages and benefits and the negotiating role of the trade unions could grow in importance. A very small start was made in June 1968, when the first Community-wide collective agreement giving certain workers a five-day forty-five-hour week was signed between Community farmers' organizations and unions affiliated to ICFTU and CISC. Probably the most immediate contribution of the trade unions will be on harmonizing working conditions but in due course they could become responsible for most wage and salary bargainings. An EFTA TUC, comprising Britain, Sweden, Norway, Denmark, and Austria, has been set up in Brussels to keep in close touch with the work of the EEC trade unions.

Three of the objectives of the EEC unions have been achieved – the merger of the three executives, the speeding up of the customs union, and the free movement of labour. This last, finally achieved in July 1968, would not be likely to affect the UK to any great extent as, except in times of unemployment, studies have shown that workers tend to move only to countries with better job opportunities and here Britain has no more to offer than EEC countries and her general standard of living is no higher than in the countries of the Six (with the exception of southern Italy). Commonwealth citizens would not have the right to work in EEC countries unless they were naturalized British subjects, a process which requires five years' residence.

Other main objectives of the trade unions are to further the supranational aspects of the EEC and ultimately to achieve political union, to strengthen the European Parliament, to widen the scope of the Social Fund and give higher priority to social policies, to secure the entry into the EEC of as many democratic European countries as possible, and lastly to secure a more important role for the unions themselves.

At present the trade unions speak chiefly through the Community's Economic and Social Committee (their representatives make up one third of the total membership) and representation is decided by the relative strengths of each member-country's unions. Originally the governments of Italy and France, the only two countries with large Communist-oriented unions, refused to nominate Communists to represent them on the Economic and Social Committee and on various other specialist bodies, but, once Communists were allowed to sit in the European Parliament, this attitude was revised and nominations of Communists went forward for consideration by the Council.

List of Abbreviations

AASM	Associated African States and Madagascar
ACE	Allied Command Europe
Afcent	Allied Forces Central Europe Command
Afsouth	Allied Forces Southern Europe Command
AGIP	Azienda Generale Italiana Petroli
AICMA	Association Internationale des Constructeurs de Matériel Aérospatial
Benelux	Belgium, the Netherlands and Luxembourg as a customs union
BISRA	British Iron and Steel Research Association
BSC	British Steel Corporation
CAP	Common agricultural policy
CBI	Confederation of British Industry
Centag	Central Army Group
CERN	Centre Européen de Recherches Nucléaires
CET	Common external tariff
CETS	European Conference on Satellite Communications
CFA	Community franc area
CISC	Confédération Internationale des Syndicats Chrétiens
CM	Common Market
COMECON	Committee of Mutual Economic Aid (Russia and East European Nations)
ECSC	European Coal and Steel Community
ECTUS	European Community Trade Unions Secretariat
EDC	European Defence Community
EDF	European Development Fund
EDU	European Democratic Union
EEC	European Economic Community
EFTA	European Free Trade Area
EIB	European Investment Bank
ELDO	European Launcher Development Organization
ELDOPAS	ELDO programme for applications satellites
ENEA	European Nuclear Energy Agency

List of Abbreviations

ENI	Ente Nazionale Idrocarburi
ERAP	Entreprise de Recherches et d'activités Pétrolières
ESF	European Social Fund
ESRO	European Space Research Organization
Euratom	European Atomic Energy Community
FAO	United Nations Food and Agriculture Organization
FEOGA	Fonds Européen d'orientation et de Garantie Agricole
FOS	Fuel, oxygen, scrap (in steel)
GATT	General Agreement on Tariffs and Trade
GNP	Gross national product
ICBM	Inter-continental ballistic missile
IMF	International Monetary Fund
IRBM	Intermediate Range Ballistic Missile
IRC	Industrial Reorganization Corporation
IRI	Istituto per la Ricostruzione Industriale
LAFTA	Latin American Free Trade Area
LAS	Large astronomical satellites
LD	Linz-Donawitz
Marairmed	Command, Maritime Air Forces Mediterranean
MRBM	Medium-range ballistic missile
MRCA	Multi-role combat aircraft
MSI	Movimento Sociale Italiano
NADGE	NATO Air Defence Ground Environment
NASA	National Aeronautics and Space Administration
NATO	North Atlantic Treaty Organization
NDAC	Nuclear Defence Affairs Committee
NFU	National Farmers' Union
Northag	Northern Army Group
NPG	Nuclear Planning Group
OECD	Organization for Economic Co-operation and Development
OEEC	Organization for European Economic Co-operation
OPEC	Organization of Petroleum Exporting Countries
Sacchan	Supreme Allied Commander Channel
Saclant	Supreme Allied Commander Atlantic
Saceur	Supreme Allied Commander Europe
SALT	Strategic Arms Limitation Talks
SET	Selective Employment Tax
SHAPE	Supreme Headquarters Allied Powers Europe
SNCF	Société Nationale des Chemins de Fer Français
SNPA	Société Nationale des Pétroles d'Aquitaine
TERRE	Trans-European Rail Road Express

TNT	Trinitrotoluene
UNCTAD	United Nations Conference on Trade and Development
VAT	Value-added tax
VTOL	Vertical take-off and landing
WEU	Western European Union
WFTU	World Federation of Trade Unions

Index

NOTE: *associations, firms and organizations well-known by their initials have been indexed under these and not under their full names: e.g. for* Organization for European Economic Co-operation *see* OEEC

Index

Index

Index

Index

Index

Some other Pelican Books are described
on the following pages.

Politics in France

Pierre Avril

The character of a nation can be read in its food, its clothing, its sports . . . but nowhere more clearly than in its politics. Since the fall of the Bastille in 1789 France has tried fifteen varying constitutions, including two empires, a monarchy, and five distinct republics; since 1871, when the republic was finally established, there have been 140 cabinets. Such government by fits and starts, from crisis to crisis, contrasts curiously with the real stability of French life.

In this new and very comprehensive study of the French style of government, a political commentator examines the uneasy relationships existing between people and state, with or without de Gaulle. Pierre Avril acutely analyses the roles of president, government, civil service, parliament, and parties under the successive republics in an effort to isolate the abiding characteristics of French politics.

With its factual and detailed appendices on many aspects of French history and institutions, *Politics in France* forms an invaluable, up-to-date guide to the complex politics of a people who have usually demonstrated a healthy and impassioned distaste for the whole idea of government.

Reflections on the Revolution in France: 1968

Edited by Charles Posner

According to a nineteenth-century adage, 'when France sneezes, Europe catches cold'. The events of May 1968, when in a ferment of change students and workers broke down the structures of the state and held capitalism to ransom, did not immediately provoke a European revolution. But this is a superficial and short-term judgement. In successfully challenging both the idea and the fact of authority, French radicals have disproved the axiom of Western politics that revolution is impossible in a modern industrial society.

Almost every observer agrees that in May 1968 France was on the threshold of something entirely new. In this 'pre-revolutionary situation' nothing went unquestioned. The western social system was dismantled at the Sorbonne, but the orthodoxies and organizations of the left were similarly scrutinized. Practical experiments in direct democracy, education and the nature of work tested key tenets of Marxist and anarchist thought.

The writers, trade unionists and students who contribute to this volume all believe that our future is foreshadowed in the events of May. And they explain why, after this shock to a regime of seemingly impregnable strength, things can never be the same again.